Zdzisław Najder, one of the world's leading authorities on Joseph Conrad and author of the major biography *Joseph Conrad: A Chronicle* (1983), is widely acclaimed for his particular insights into Conrad's Polish background. The fruits of thirty years of Conrad study appear in this landmark volume of his essays, which explore a wide range of topics: Conrad's national and cultural heritage; his fictions, from the unfinished *Sisters* and *Lord Jim* to *The Secret Agent*; his attitude towards Russia in general and Dostoevsky in particular; his concepts of man and society and the role of the idea of honour in his work. In a series of more general essays Najder goes on to place Conrad's work within a broad European philosophical, political and literary context. *Conrad in Perspective* offers new insights into the life and work of one of the twentieth century's greatest novelists by one of his most perceptive critics.

Conrad in perspective

Conrad in perspective
Essays on art and fidelity

Zdzisław Najder

PUBLISHED BY THE PRESS SYNDICATE OF THE UNIVERSITY OF CAMBRIDGE
The Pitt Building, Trumpington Street, Cambridge CB2 1RP, United Kingdom

CAMBRIDGE UNIVERSITY PRESS
The Edinburgh Building, Cambridge CB2 2RU, United Kingdom
40 West 20th Street, New York, NY 10011-4211, USA
10 Stamford Road, Oakleigh, Melbourne 3166, Australia

© Zdzisław Najder 1997

This book is in copyright. Subject to statutory exception and to the provisions of relevant collective licensing agreements, no reproduction of any part may take place without the written permission of Cambridge University Press.

First published 1997

Printed in the United Kingdom at the University Press, Cambridge

Typeset in Stempel Garamond [SE]

A catalogue record for this book is available from the British Library

Library of Congress cataloguing in publication data applied for

Najder, Zdzisław.
    Conrad in perspective: essays on art and fidelity / Zdisław Najder.
    p. cm.
    Includes index.
    ISBN 0 521 57321 1 (hardback)
    1. Conrad, Joseph, 1857–1924 – Criticisms and interpretation. I. Title.
PR6005.04Z78439   1997
823'.912–dc21   96–37923   CIP

ISBN 0 521 57321 1 hardback

CONTENTS

Acknowledgements viii
Note on the texts ix
List of abbreviations xi

1 Introduction, or confession of a mastodon *1*
2 Conrad's Polish background, or from biography to a study of culture *11*
3 Joseph Conrad's parents *18*
4 Joseph Conrad and Tadeusz Bobrowski *44*
5 *The Sisters*: a grandiose failure *68*
6 *Lord Jim*: a Romantic tragedy of honour *81*
7 *The Mirror of the Sea* *95*
8 *A Personal Record* *102*
9 Joseph Conrad's *The Secret Agent*, or the melodrama of reality *110*
10 Conrad, Russia and Dostoevsky *119*
11 Conrad and Rousseau: concepts of man and society *139*
12 Conrad and the idea of honour *153*
13 Joseph Conrad: a European writer *165*
14 Joseph Conrad after a century *176*
15 Joseph Conrad in his historical perspective *188*
16 Fidelity and art: Joseph Conrad's cultural heritage and literary programme *199*

Notes 213
Index 236

ACKNOWLEDGEMENTS

Earlier versions of nearly all of the papers and essays contained in this volume have been read by one or more of my fellow-Conradologists: John Batchelor, Jacques Berthoud, Addison Bross, Andrzej Busza, Keith Carabine, Hans van Marle and Andrzej Zgorzelski. I am very grateful for their care, patience and numerous valuable suggestions. For the remaining faults, and for my obstinacy, they bear no responsibility. Most of the logistic problems connected with the preparation of the texts have been solved thanks to the generous assistance of Aleksander Kaye.

NOTE ON THE TEXTS

Most of the papers and essays included in this volume have been either published or presented at conferences between 1963 and 1996, in English or in Polish. All texts have been revised, with new documentary material taken into account. However, no sustained attempt has been made to lift the presented ideas and arguments from their original time context. Only exceptionally do I join later debates, although I sometimes refer to analogous thoughts expressed in later publications.

1. 'Introduction, or confession of a mastodon.' Based on a paper, 'Return of a Mastodon', presented in September 1992 at the Geneva Conference of the French Joseph Conrad Society.
2. 'Joseph Conrad's Polish background, or from biography to a study of culture.' Paper presented at the Modern Language Association 1984 convention. *Conradiana* 18 (1986), no. 1.
3. 'Joseph Conrad's parents.' Paper presented in September 1996 at the Joseph Conrad Conference in Lublin, Poland.
4. 'Joseph Conrad and Tadeusz Bobrowski.' Published in Polish in *Przegląd Humanistyczny* (1964), no. 5.
5. '*The Sisters*: a grandiose failure.' Paper presented at the International Conrad Conference in Pisa, September 1983; published in *The Ugo Mursia Memorial Lectures*, ed. Mario Curreli, Milan 1988.
6. '*Lord Jim*: a Romantic tragedy of honour.' *Conradiana* 1 (1968), no. 1.
7. '*The Mirror of the Sea*.' Based on the Introduction to Oxford World Classics edition, 1988.
8. '*A Personal Record*.' As above.
9. 'Joseph Conrad's *The Secret Agent*, or the melodrama of reality.' *New York Literary Forum*, 1980.
10. 'Conrad, Russia and Dostoevsky.' Earlier versions in Polish, *Życie Literackie* (1963), no. 8 and in *Nad Conradem*, Warsaw 1964.
11. 'Conrad and Rousseau: concepts of man and society.' Published in *Joseph Conrad: A Commemoration*, London 1976.
12. 'Conrad and the idea of honour.' In *Joseph Conrad: Theory and*

World Fiction, Proceedings of the Comparative Literature Symposium, Lubbock, Texas, 1974.
13 'Joseph Conrad: a European writer.' *L'Epoque Conradienne*, Limoges 1995.
14 'Joseph Conrad after a century.' A Copernicus Lecture at the University of Michigan. *Cross Currents, A Yearbook of Central European Culture*, Ann Arbor 1988.
15 'Joseph Conrad in his historical perspective.' *English Literature in Transition* 14 (1971).
16 'Fidelity and art: Joseph Conrad's cultural heritage and literary programme.' Paper presented in February 1995 at a Joseph Conrad conference at Kent, Ohio.

ABBREVIATIONS

CL   *The Collected Letters of Joseph Conrad*, eds. Frederick R. Karl
        and Laurence Davies, Cambridge. Vol. I (1861–1897), 1983;
        vol. II (1898–1902), 1986; vol. III (1903–1907), 1988; vol. IV
        (1908–1911), 1990; vol. V (1912–1916), 1996.
CPB   *Conrad's Polish Background, Letters to and from Polish
        Friends*, ed. Zdzisław Najder, transl. by Halina Carroll,
        Oxford 1964.
CUFE   *Conrad Under Familial Eyes*, ed. Zdzisław Najder,
        Cambridge 1983.

All references to Conrad's works are to the Dent Collected edition,
unless otherwise specified.

I

Introduction, or confession of a mastodon

Paraphrasing Conrad, I can say about myself that I have been neither 'revolutionary', nor even post-modernist in my critical efforts. I cannot claim methodological innocence: I lost it nearly half a century ago over Roman Ingarden's theory of the 'literary work of art', and have later exposed myself to structuralism and even to the more florid displays of deconstructivism. Still, my own approach to criticism and scholarship of literature has remained antediluvian.

I believe that poems and novels are there to be read by readers, not to be dissected by scholars. And the point of our reading a sonnet or a tale is that we want to feel, after we have finished, somewhat different than before we began. Perhaps emotionally, perhaps intellectually – whatever colours a given aesthetic experience has, whatever are the artistic components of the given piece of literature.

The critic's sole *raison d'être* is to assist the readers in their enjoyment and understanding. The scholar's primary *raison d'être* is to help the critic to assist the readers, or to communicate directly with the readers, with the same assisting purpose. The theorist's task is to make critics and scholars distinguish between talking sense (of different kinds) and spinning out gibberish. We all, critics, scholars, theoreticians, are middlemen (or better: midwives, performing a noble maieutic function) between the work and the reader; we are the reader's servants.

One trouble is that in the course of acquiring his knowledge and skills the scholar tends to become different from the 'normal' reader; and not only in what she or he knows but also in how he or she thinks about works of literature. To remain useful in their maieutic role scholars have to keep in check their specialist propensities, their professional deviations.

The reader looks to the scholar to help him or her establish the full contents of a given text: the meanings of words used, the sense of images and metaphors and tropes, the significance of dates and names of really existing personalities, the referents of allusions, and so on. Placing the given piece within its historical context and classifying it as 'Romantic' or 'Naturalistic' or 'Symbolic' is equivalent to determining which dictionary of artistic forms we have to use in our interpretation. All these links between signs of various kinds and their meanings are publicly accessible and (in different ways) verifiable. That is, we can check whether 'urgent' could really mean 'severe' in Shakespeare's time; whether in medieval romances the unicorn indeed stood for chastity and invincible virtue; whether when Giorgio Viola mentions the 'accursed Piedmontese race of kings and ministers' he refers to Vittorio Emanuele II and to Cavour; whether Hardy's *Jude the Obscure* links up with the traditions of Zola's naturalism; whether the title of T. S. Eliot's *The Waste Land* is a rendering of St Augustine's 'regio egestatis'; etc. In many of these cases we have to do with the application of a certain convention, that is with the use of a certain more or less precisely defined but identifiable system of signs – a natural language, a traditional set of symbols and so on.

In contrast to this 'public meaning' of a literary piece (or a painting, or sculpture – which artefacts in some ways offer clearer instances of what I am trying to say), one may see in it a plethora of 'private meanings', to be discovered by reference not to some established convention but to the author's biography and/or to various more or less speculative psychological theories.

Of course, for poets or novelists their work may be an expression of internal tensions and urges, or a means of coping with their emotional problems. In parallel, for a psychologist a work of literature may be a document of its author's inner life, or an example of a certain attitude or type of behaviour. (Analogously, a sociologist may look there for evidence of a trend, fashion, etc.) And psychological or sociological criticism may be perfectly legitimate, whatever the degree of their unavoidable speculativeness. Also, the lives of exceptional men and women attract understandable interest; and biographies of writers may be deservedly popular and read as an accompaniment to the reading of their works. They should not, however, be confused with criticism.

Having spent a good chunk of the bookwormish part of my life on research into and writing of a biography of Conrad, I guess I have both the duty and the right to issue a solemn warning against the indulgence in the search for private meanings in works of literature (or painting, or sculpture), an indulgence often fostered by biographers. I think that snooping for biographical allusions is not a particularly desirable form of literary scholarship – and often detracts from research and analysis more proper, that is: more rewarding aesthetically, more informative artistically, more illuminating intellectually. For scholars to spend hundreds of pages on hunts for what I would call private meanings contained in novels and poems is to succumb to intellectual debauchery and to stupefy the readers.

Granted, the distinction between public and private meanings is not a sharp one; the stories of Petrarch's love for Laura or Dante's for Beatrice are so well known that it would be difficult to separate them from what we learn from the text of the *Sonnets* or the *Divina commedia*; one can argue, however, that these are instances of biographies of the authors becoming public myths, and thus elements of the European cultural mythology analogous to the stories of Faust or Don Juan.

The author's 'intention'* is the form of private meaning perhaps most frequently looked for. The speciousness of such a search has been the subject of much argument, of which William C. Wimsatt's and Monroe C. Beardsley's 'The Intentional Fallacy' (1954) is probably the best-known example – although the first and very incisive analysis of the difference between a search for the truth and a search for the intended meaning of an author's words is to be found in St Augustine's *Confessions* (XII, 23–32).

I believe that not only intentions but in general all 'private meanings' of works of literature are of dubious use to literary scholars and either unimportant or even detracting from the text for readers.

To begin with, links between intention and final product are difficult

---

* In the psychological sense of the word; quite different is the concept of 'intention' as used for instance by Erwin Panofsky ('The History of Art as a Humanistic Discipline' [1940], *Meaning in the Visual Arts*, Garden City, NY, 1957, pp. 20–1), or by the phenomenologists.

to describe. We have to install causal connections between mental states (as designs, moods, aspirations, yearnings). If there is no causal connection assumed, then hypotheses about the intended forms or ideas found in a given novel are speculations made not even about that novel but only on the occasion of it. Even if we manage somehow to describe or suggest such links, our hypotheses are impossible to verify. What evidence can one have that the supposed intentions – even, for example, those expressed in a letter – did in fact come to pass? Or lasted long enough to have been implemented? Or were not imposed on the given piece as a hindsight? What Conrad says in his Author's Notes, added to the consecutive volumes of his works when republished in 1919–21, may be interesting as documents of the way he wanted them to be seen by their readers, but does not determine the meaning of the pieces he writes about – and that not only because it is often easy to prove that he dissembles when pointing at his sources or describing the circumstances of writing a given story.

With other kinds of private meanings the situation is similar. Is Thomas Hardy's Jude meant to represent the author, or his late friend Horace Moule? How can we know for sure? And why should it matter for the reader? *The Sun Also Rises* was widely supposed to be a *roman-à-clef*, but even if we manage to reach a near certainty as to 'originals' of Hemingway's protagonists, would not such identification result for the reader in a reduction in the thematic scope of the novel, if taken as a portrait of the 'lost generation'?

A hunter for the private 'Conrad's Secrets in *The Secret Agent*' claims that *The Secret Agent* is 'one of the most caustic and bizarre confessions of its kind in recent literature', and that Conrad was motivated by the feeling of 'having betrayed the revolutionary ideals that martyred his parents'. That Conrad's father had nothing in common with the 'revolutionaries' of the type presented in *The Secret Agent*; that consequently Conrad had no 'revolutionary' ideals to betray; and that his parents were martyred not by any 'ideals' but by the Russian autocracy – all these facts are, as Conrad would have said, 'mighty inconvenient' for the above interpretation. But what is indeed more essential is that, even if true, the cited statements would not add anything interesting to the artistic structure or intellectual content of *The Secret Agent*. Focusing on them distracts both the scholar and the reader from more salient scrutiny: for instance, how Conrad characterizes his types of professional rebels against the existing order. And shouldn't the reader be rather helped to note Conrad's masterful presentation of the police? I often marvel how and where he obtained the knowledge – or intuition? – to describe with such insight his Inspector Heat, his Councillor Mikulin and the historical Joseph Fouché in 'The Duel'.

The search for private meaning is an élitist – if not esoteric – game: only the initiated can play, and for them the more abstruse the alleged hidden signal the better. In practice, this attitude helps to construct a barrier between an ordinary (which does not mean uneducated) reader and the expert, endowed with specialist knowledge, who approaches texts as full of coded (although not in a conventionalized form!) messages about their authors. This makes the discussed novels and poems at once hermetic and self-referential, and turns many readers away. My objections against the search for private meanings are thus based on both methodological and socio-cultural premises. We – scholars and critics – ought to attract the readers to our authors, not to repel them with the gloss of impenetrable superiority.

The life of the author does not form a part of the text of his drama or novel. Biography may only offer pointers in our search for meanings. We read biographies of writers to get acquainted with the authors of books we like, and not the other way around: we do not read *The Magic Mountain* to learn what kind of person Thomas Mann was, nor *The Plague* to get acquainted with Albert Camus. If only for this simple reason, biographical questions have only a secondary importance for literary scholars.

Two examples. The question 'Why did Conrad choose Geneva as the location of the second part of the action of *Under Western Eyes*?' cannot be answered with certainty. Even if 'evidence' were available in the form of an explanatory letter from Conrad, we would have to prove that he was aware of the truth and telling it: an impossible and useless task. What is important for the understanding of the novel is to realize what Geneva stands for, what it represents on the historical, political and moral map of Europe. And was Conrad conscious of the parallel between his novel about St Petersburg and Geneva, and Dickens' *The Tale of Two Cities*? We do not know and do not have to know; nevertheless, the parallel exists, as a fact in the history of the English novel. We are entitled to consider this parallel as an aspect in our interpretation of *Under Western Eyes*.

If the author's biography is not a part of the text, then mixing textual and biographical analysis is a sin (at the least, the sin of conceit in showing off one's privileged information). To conflate hypothetical assumptions about Conrad's attitude towards his father with fragments of his fictional texts may be personally enthralling for the critic but leads to a reduction, not to an enrichment, in his or her interpretation of the content of Conrad's work: ultimately, the given piece is turned into yet another psychological outpouring.

But isn't every interpretation simply another (and equally legitimate) use of the text, as Richard Rorty claims in his discussion with Umberto Eco?* Their fascinating debate has a general philosophical edge to it, a little blunted by the rhetorical skills of the participants – attractive but also conducive to simplifications. I believe Professor Rorty commits an overinterpretation when he adduces Willard Van Orman Quine's 'denial of an interesting philosophical distinction between language and fact, between signs and non-signs' as supportive of his own position of a radical pragmatist who 'makes objects by talking about them'. Apart from the fact that Quine himself considers 'good philosophy' to be 'an exploration of the fundamental traits of reality'† (an 'essentialist's' task, in Rorty's pragmatist eyes), Quine's observation does not deny the fact that the names 'Tower Bridge' and 'Pickwick Papers' refer to different kinds of objects; and so do 'hammer' and 'hypothesis'.

I think the debate whether 'interpretation' differs from 'use' (as Eco claims) or whether there is no difference between them (as Rorty maintains) has been a little misconstrued. The internally non-differentiated concept of 'use', as applied by Rorty, is so all-embracing that it becomes either trivial or empty. I believe that to interpret a text *is* to use it, but in a certain specific way – namely, to use it with respect for its integrity. We are obliged to show such respect notwithstanding whether the text in question is a poem, or a cooking recipe, or a testament; notwithstanding whether we interpret it for aesthetic, legal, or psychological purposes.

---

* See Umberto Eco with Richard Rorty, Jonathan Culler and Christine Brooke-Rose, *Interpretation and Overinterpretation*, ed. Stefan Collini, Cambridge 1992.
† Quine interviewed by Christian Delacampagne, *Le Monde*, 4 July 1994.

This obligation has two grounds. The first lies in professional ethics: the interpreter, to be himself worthy of respect, has to perform his task in such a manner as to allow his statements to be checked and, if proven wrong, overturned; otherwise he becomes a conman. The second is that in principle all users of texts (whom interpreters assist) want to receive a communication from an external source, and not a projection, or secretion, of their own anticipations. Even if, like Anatole France, they want to experience 'adventures among masterpieces', they want to know the masterpieces in question, and not some ahistorical semiotic plasma. There is a conscious and fundamental difference of attitudes between a computer-user interfacing with the contents of anonymous software programmes, and a reader of the equally anonymous but by no means non-personal *Beowulf*.

Interpretation, therefore, seems to be a use with constraints. If somebody says 'horrible' after reading 'My heart leaps up when I behold . . .', or 'very amusing' after having read *King Lear*, would we say that she or he is making a strange use of these texts, or rather simply that she or he failed to understand them? I think that to choose the first possibility would amount to an abuse of our speech.

But where do the constraints come from? I think that under normal conditions most of them come from the text itself. To begin with, we have to determine to what natural language it belongs, with which dictionary in hand one has to read it: it is not for the user to decide whether the text is in Finnish or in English. Or whether it is medieval or contemporary. Or whether it refers to events which are known from other sources to have happened (and thus can be, in this respect, verified), or not. But perhaps to visualize the constraining force of texts – in Rorty's terminology, the fact that the text 'has internal coherence', quite apart from its actual uses – it is best to point to a non-literary example.

The highway code 'exists' in the pragmatists' sense only in the form of drivers following (or not) certain rules; but it has to 'exist' also in another way for us to be able to tell whether drivers follow them or not. In other words: the highway code possesses a coherence independent of the concrete use which is made of it. If I happen to follow other drivers doing 120 km/h on a stretch marked '80' I would be 'using' the code as many others do; but I would be breaking it as well. Literary texts are much more complicated but not fundamentally different.

Yet, they are, by the very nature of the attitudes we adopt when reading them, open-ended semiotic structures. The *Iliad* allows for newer readings, for shoals of fresh associations, for recurrent and changing pangs of identification; but we want to feel that we consort with the same poem, not that we join a free-wheeling line of its 'users', each of whom establishes his or her own pragmatic meaning of the text. The very human need for communication, for breaking through the barriers of loneliness, implies the desire for a common ground, for a language in which we can understand texts with a feeling that we have reached out beyond ourselves.

When we use a literary text by interpreting it, we want to know whether our reading of it is sound *not* in any absolute sense, but within a given system of conventions (language included) and set of criteria. Not excessive imagination but irreverence is the enemy of good interpretation. Even the most radical conventionalism does not justify arbitrariness. Nor is Alfred Tarski's definition of truth as relative to the given language a licence to arbitrariness.

Stefan Collini, the editor of the texts of Eco, Rorty, Cullen and Brooke-Rose, is right in saying that their debate was in fact a debate about values; and not only in the sense that interpretation cannot be separated from evaluation, as Wolfgang Kayser demonstrated a long time ago.[1] He is also right in stressing that the present debate has to be seen as a part of a historical process; half a century ago the great Ernst Robert Curtius, taking the cue from the German philosopher Karl Joël, speculated half-jokingly about the 'binding' (*bindende*) uneven centuries (thirteenth, fifteenth, seventeenth, nineteenth) and the 'loosening' (*lösende*) even ones (fourteenth, sixteenth, eighteenth, twentieth).[2] And when Collini describes the contemporary urge to escape from the 'constraints of history, whether collective or personal', I realize with a pang that such an escape was possible neither for Conrad, nor for most of his European readers, nor for myself. And I believe that even now such an escape is only a debilitating illusion; several of the essays in this volume explain why.

All these pieces are based on a few general assumptions. I think that Conrad wrote his books about the world as he saw and knew it, not about other books. He used other texts as means of communicating not about himself, or about those texts – but about other men and the world they live in.

He was an anachronistic (= out of his proper time) writer. While steeped in tradition, he was not bound by fashions and conventions of his time. On the contrary, he ran straight against some of them, mistrustful of the sovereignty of art for its own sake, suspicious of individualism, unmoved by psychologism. Perhaps this is one reason why many of his works have aged so well and why he has been and still is so widely read by non-specialists.

The fifteen following papers and essays concern various aspects of the work of Joseph Conrad. I suggest that the knowledge of his Polish background allows us to select the proper 'dictionaries', appropriate historical and cultural frameworks of reference in interpreting his stories and novels. The papers about Conrad's parents and his uncle-guardian concentrate on the intellectual and moral legacies bequeathed by them; they are supposed, on the one hand, to help in identifying the traditions and ideas to which Conrad harks back, on the other to put a limit on the more wild speculations concerning his family background. Other essays propose interpretations of a few of his novels and volumes of prose or analyse certain ideas which I consider essential and characteristic for his work, such as the ideas of honour and fidelity; the last two present synthetical glimpses of his writing achievement.

As the distance between Conrad's time and ours keeps growing, our (the scholars' and critics') great problem grows too: that is, how to interpret Conrad in our contemporary terms without simply ascribing to him our contemporary interests, intentions, concepts, terms of reference – but, rather, feeling the tension (aesthetically so fruitful) between his world and ours. My main efforts are concentrated along two lines of analysis: of his ideas and of the forms of his narrative. Not accidentally, as I believe that Conrad's main strength as a writer lies in the innovative combinations and applications of traditional narrative structures, harnessed to a new use in his insistent forcing of the reader to face the fundamental issues of human communal existence.

From the very beginning two factors in Conrad's work have aroused my particular interest: his multifaceted cultural background (which I have been trying to map and describe) and the philosophical and ethical issues he tackled in his novels and stories. Was the latter concern due to my own philosophical professional slant? Rather the contrary. I was attracted by his raising the same problems that had drawn me to study philosophy: the problems of values, evaluations and moral ideals – in other words, the eternal problems of the meaning of life.

In trying to analyse, explain and highlight the intellectual contents of Conrad's works I have joined the company of (in alphabetical and not chronological order) Jacques Berthoud, Andrzej Busza, Edward Crankshaw, Eloise Knapp Hay, Józef Ujejski, Robert Penn Warren, Ian Watt, and many others. I have had the luck to have known most of them, and several have been my friends. It is with great sorrow that I think that Ian Watt will not be able to read this collection; he read some of its ingredients even before their original publication. Let this volume be a humble and inadequate homage to this great scholar and dependable friend.

2

Conrad's Polish background,* or from biography to a study of culture

Every Conrad scholar has heard the hypothesis that the central moral theme of *Lord Jim*, the problem of guilt – or shame – is a reflection of the novelist's own feelings. This idea, developed first by the late Dr Gustav Morf in his pioneering psychoanalytic study of Conrad,[1] has since been

---

* Any discussion of this background requires some basic information about Poland's tangled history. The continuous tradition of an independent kingdom of Poles goes back to the middle of the tenth century. By the sixteenth century, Polish literature flourished and the kingdom had become a multinational commonwealth of Poles, Ruthenians, Belorussians and Lithuanians. The king was elected by a direct vote of the *szlachta* – nobility and gentry together, a group who were endowed with extensive individual liberties (e.g., the *Neminem captivabimus* law, the Polish equivalent to *Habeas corpus*, dating from 1430). Poland was at that time the largest country in continental Europe. However, the Polish *szlachta*'s refusal to extend the promised liberties to Ruthenians led to a bloody rebellion of Bohdan Chmielnicki – who in 1654 in Pereiaslav made the eastern part of the Ukraine subject to Russian rule. In the eighteenth century there followed three consecutive partitions of the Polish Commonwealth, composed of the Kingdom of Poland and the Grand Duchy of Lithuania. In the first, in 1772, Austro-Hungary, Prussia and Russia annexed territories in the southern, north-western and north-eastern parts of the country. Only Prussia and Russia participated in the second, annexing further territories in the western and eastern parts of Poland in 1793: it was hastened by the adoption by the Polish parliament (*sejm*) in 1791 of a new, liberal Constitution of 3 May, in fact the first written constitution in Europe; its acceptance was considered a mortal threat to the autocratic empires of Poland's neighbours. In the third (and final), in 1795, the partitioning powers, in spite of Tadeusz Kościuszko's desperate defence, carved up what remained of the kingdom. Thus by the time Conrad's father Apollo Korzeniowski was born, Poland did not exist as an independent country and Poles lived in three occupied zones: Austrian ('Galicia') in the south, Prussian in the north-west and Russian, by far the largest and most backwards politically and economically. For more details, see Norman Davies, *God's Playground*, Oxford 1981.

reworked many times and in various versions. Generally, it is assumed that Conrad felt guilty of betrayal because he had left his home country and had been writing in a foreign language. This feeling of guilt is supposed to have been awakened, or strengthened, by Eliza Orzeszkowa's acerbic article, published in 1899* – just at the time Conrad was working on the novel.

The consequences of this hypothesis reach far beyond a single Conrad novel and a given period in his life. If accepted, it not only throws a specific light on his creative attitude and gives rise to many analogous hypotheses concerning his other works; it also establishes the categories within which we should look at his childhood and youth. The verification of the hypothesis is clearly a matter of research in Conrad's Polish background. What evidence does this research produce and where does it lead us? I shall briefly recapitulate the results.

The motifs of betrayal, desertion, failing one's duty, and the resulting guilt or shame, occur in Conrad's work from its very beginning. We can see traces of them in *Almayer's Folly*, they emerge more clearly in *An Outcast of the Islands*, to become focal in 'The Lagoon' and 'Karain', and also in *The Rescue*, begun a couple of years before *Lord Jim*. They are present in the early draft of *Tuan Jim*, written by the spring of 1898. Thus if Conrad's feeling of guilt at having abandoned his parents' heritage was a reason for the recurrence in his fiction of the themes of betrayal, escape and neglect of important duty, this reason had existed from the very beginning of his writing activity and had nothing to do with Orzeszkowa's accusations.

But the study of Conrad's family background reveals something else: these motifs are also present in the works of his father, Apollo Korzeniowski. We encounter them in his poems, and also in his dramatic pieces, both finished and unfinished, most notably in a fragment, *Ojciec* (The Father), which contains highly dramatic disputes about fidelity

---

* Eliza Orzeszkowa (1842–1910) was a prominent novelist and essayist, a liberal (she wrote the first important novels about East European Jewry), in Poland one of the most widely recognized moral authorities of her time. In her article 'The Emigration of Talent' (see *CUFE*, pp. 182–92) she sharply criticized Conrad for having left his home country and thus having failed his national duties in favour of following a profitable literary career in a foreign language. She herself, forbidden by the Russian authorities to run her own publishing house, lived most of her life in a small Polish-Belorussian town of Grodno.

and treason, honour and fear, life and death, reputation and shame (see below, Chapter 3). Was there in Apollo Korzeniowski's life an event, a personal crisis, which could have prompted these interests? We do not have any grounds to think so; but, of course, he saw around himself enough acts of fidelity and of betrayal to be concerned with these subjects. And he was far from being original in these motifs. The images of duty abandoned, of betrayal, and above all of desertion, had been common in Polish literature since the early nineteenth century, since the loss of Polish national independence. Adam Mickiewicz, in his *Pan Tadeusz*, wrote: 'Woe to us, who fled at the time of a plague, carrying our timorous heads abroad.'[2] The other national poet-prophet, Juliusz Słowacki, was even more outspoken: 'I have no dignity – I have fled from martyrdom.'[3] And they both had in mind nothing more than a voluntary exile. Thus what at first sight seems to be a peculiar Conradian obsession, apparently grounded in his personal experience, at a closer look turns out to be a literary stereotype, grounded in national history. Or, at least, to be also a literary – and moral – stereotype.

Let me now approach the subject of the study of Conrad's Polish background from a different direction. The most important documents, concerning Conrad's Polish relations, I have collected in two volumes: *Conrad's Polish Background* and *Conrad Under Familial Eyes*. These collections supplement each other, but are far from complete in one sense: very many, and many of the most important, documents which ought to have been included have been destroyed, for example all of Conrad's letters to his uncle and guardian. However, in another sense, in the sense of gathering all the extant and most of the relevant material, both volumes are quite close to completeness. And they are comprehensive in yet another sense: they offer insight into all aspects of Conrad's Polish family connections, relations and interests. When I perused these texts while preparing this chapter I was struck by the proportion of public – as distinct from purely personal and individual – concerns shown by their authors, be they Conrad's mother, or his uncle, or Conrad himself (in his letters), or his Polish friends.

Of course, it is not always simple to distinguish a private from a public – social, national, historical, political – subject. And it would be impossible to say what is the average proportion of subjects private as distinct from public present in various writers' family documents and personal correspondence. But still I believe that any impartial observer would notice that national and political affairs occupy a striking amount of space in the letters written by Conrad's mother and father; that even in the fragments of Conrad's uncle Tadeusz Bobrowski's memoirs, selected because they refer to his nephew Konrad and his parents, and therefore chosen on the grounds of personal criteria, public themes keep cropping up. The 'baptismal song', a poem written by Conrad's father for the day of his son's christening, is perhaps an extreme, but also a powerfully typical, example of these public concerns.

> Baby son, tell yourself
> You are without land, without love,
> without country, without people,
> while Poland – your *Mother* is in her grave.
> For your only *Mother* is dead — and yet
> She is your faith, your palm of martyrdom.
>   Hushaby, my baby son! (*CUFE*, p. 33)

But it is not only that even the most private feelings, like tenderness towards a new-born child, or matrimonial love, were expressed in terms linked to the person's national or social bonds. It is also that these bonds played a very important part in the everyday life of almost all men and women whom we get to know when exploring Conrad's Polish background.

Their spiritual life expressed itself largely in terms of communal obligations, national yearnings, social needs and strivings. The consciousness of belonging, linked to an awareness of concomitant duties, was almost omnipresent. This does not mean that those obligations were always fulfilled and duty always done. What I have in mind is the conceptual framework, which constructed man as a social – and national – being first and foremost. One often hears about Polish individualism and even anarchism. This last expresses itself most typically in disobeying authority, which quite often just happens to have been imposed from the outside. Usually, even the extreme Polish individualists need society, need to feel reflected, applauded, or abhorred. If Poles err, it is rather in the direction of being too dependent on their milieu. They are individualists of the Homeric rather than Bohemian kind, they want to be rather singular than eccentric.

For all these reasons, in exploration of Conrad's Polish background, communal indicators are usually more informative than individual ones. Therefore, the exploration should be conducted on the broadest possible front. We have to investigate not only his family links, or the progress of his learning, but also, and more extensively, the cultural traditions of his environment, its typical moral and political problems, its collective concerns, its whole ethos.

And, what is even more important for Conrad literary scholarship: such a diagnosis of the structural quality of Conrad's Polish background has far-reaching consequences for interpreting Conrad's work, because what may have seemed to be a private code, deciphered only by biographical investigations and pointing to esoteric meaning, turns out to be a cultural language, a public system of signs, which carry meaning independently from the reflections of the novelist's own personality. The motifs of fidelity and solidarity, of obligations, of honour defended or lost, of treason, escape and political double-dealings, of confession, patriotism, sacrifice and exile – all these and some other motifs so typical of Conrad are found in abundance in classical Polish literature; and not only in literature, but also in the repository of moral images and exemplary tales passed by word of mouth.

Therefore, Conrad's Polish biography has to be expanded from individual into collective, and from psychological into cultural. In a word, it has to be transcended and become a study of culture. Perhaps a few examples would help to clarify what I have in mind.

Eliza Orzeszkowa's notorious criticism of Conrad rests on a very simple idea: that of fidelity. Fidelity to one's social and national obligations and to one's principles. Once we recognize that, we can understand better why Conrad felt so deeply hurt by that attack, based as it was on misconstrued evidence. He was castigated in the name of the very principles that he himself extolled. And when we read in Orzeszkowa's article a diatribe against subjecting human activities, including the development of knowledge, to the goal of financial gain, we can easily consider it an amplification of Conrad's own postulates.

A second example: Conrad's father was a poet turned political activist. His political views, for instance about Russia, and their similarity to the opinions experienced by his son, have been noted and described. They can be fully understood only in their historical context; and the same applies to his influence on Conrad, and particularly to

Apollo Korzeniowski's whole way of thinking about political matters. He judged political processes and actions not by their success, but by their conformity, or lack of it, to specific ethical principles. He saw political problems not in terms of power, influence, or wealth – but in terms of liberty, human dignity, tolerance and piety. He was, in a word, the antithesis of a political Darwinist.

A third example: in Tadeusz Bobrowski's memoirs, in Conrad's mother's and father's letters, in nearly all reminiscences of his other family members, one motif keeps cropping up repeatedly. It appears in many forms, but typically in the one of sacrificing personal happiness for the sake either of national ideals or of those who have served these ideals. We may take it as symbolic that the only important pieces of information we have about Conrad's paternal aunt – whose name, Emilia, is a recent discovery – are that she was engaged in a patriotic conspiracy and was later sent into penal political exile. The recurrence of the motif of sacrifice moves it from the plane of individual events onto the plane of a cultural stereotype. Of course, sacrifice implies choice and a conflict of values; instances of this kind abound in Conrad's Polish milieu. And Tom Lingard of *The Rescue* could have easily been one of them.

And finally, a fourth example, the least tangible but perhaps most important. In all family reminiscences, letters and memoirs by and about Conrad's Polish family, we detect traces of some trauma, of an earthquake having been experienced, an earthquake of assaulted and collapsing values, of conflicting civilizations. That trauma cannot be identified simply as the débâcle of the 1863 uprising. It is a pervasive consciousness of a great loss, of a world destroyed, of a cherished order of things smashed to pieces. There is a noticeable streak of morbidity expressed in terms sometimes despairing and nostalgic, sometimes caustic and bitter. It has little, or nothing, to do with the authors' personal attitudes – it is a reflection of a national sentiment.

Evidently, one cannot simply reverse the direction of research and argument, and from the general assertions about Poles, Polish history and the traditional ethos of Polish gentry-nobility deduce that Conrad would, or even had to, think and write in the way he did. Those general statements and observations provide us only with clues and models of interpretation.

But these models are essential. And I believe it may be argued that in Conrad's case there can be detected a natural, inherent propensity of biographical research to lead the scholar away from 'pure' biography towards social and intellectual history, towards ethics and politics, because these explain more, and throw light on many moments and decisions in Conrad's life which would otherwise remain obscure. The same applies, in a higher degree, to his work.

Was it because Joseph Conrad wanted to overcome certain elements of his personality, of his psyche – for example, his depression? Did he perhaps want to construct both his own life and his work over and around a structure of values and ideas, not the structure of psychological inclinations and impulses?

If this was the case, then some accents in the interpretation of even his theoretical statements should be subtly changed. For instance, it should be stressed that his impressionism, as expounded in the Preface to *The Nigger of the 'Narcissus'*, was an impressionism of the medium, not of the sources or the objective of fiction. And also that in Conrad's repeated, albeit variously worded, demand for 'rendering the highest kind of justice to the visible universe', as well as in his exhortation to rescue the ephemeral moments of experience, the stress should be located in the concepts of justice and of rescue. In other words, these appeals should be firmly placed within the correspondence theory of art, of art which reflects, by its own peculiar means, what there is outside the beholder. Such adjustment of accents, resulting from biographical investigations turned into cultural study, lends additional support to Ian Watt's claim that the idea of human solidarity is essential for Conrad's vision of all art.[4]

But perhaps all that I have just tried to describe was not a result of Conrad's private and conscious effort to transcend psychological limitations and reach out to the interpersonal, communal, human. Could it be that it stemmed from his Polish, generally anti-psychological moral and cultural background, a heritage of whose effect he was unconscious, or only partially aware? I do not know, and I suppose we cannot tell.

But I am sure that, at least in the case of Joseph Conrad, the proper study of the biographer is a study of culture.

3
Joseph Conrad's parents

1

While it is certainly true that Joseph Conrad's parents attract special attention today because their son became one of the greatest writers of the last century, it is also true that Conrad's father, Apollo Korzeniowski, was a man of letters and of action who would have been remembered, at least in his native Poland, even if his marriage with a remarkable woman coming from a very remarkable family had remained childless. In fact, very few writers have had a similarly distinguished parentage; in Britain one may think perhaps only of the Mill and Woolf families.

A Conrad specialist who wants to present the portraits of Conrad's mother and father should therefore suspend his awareness that he is writing about the parents of a great man, and try to approach Ewa (née Bobrowska) and Apollo Korzeniowski on their own merits. I believe that most of the numerous misunderstandings and misconceptions concerning these two persons have originated in treating them 'instrumentally', as appendages or even keys to the inner life of their son. How much the boy Conrad – orphaned of his mother at the age of eight and of his father four years later – knew about his parents, and particularly about his father's achievements, will for ever remain a matter of conjecture. But to put conjectures on a firm ground we have first to get the verifiable facts as straight as possible.[1]

2

Apollo Korzeniowski was born on 21 February 1820 in Honoratka, a village near Lipowiec, in the Kiev governship, in a Polish *szlachta** family of modest means, settled in the Ukraine for several generations. His father, Teodor, had been a landowner and soldier who took part in the anti-Russian insurrection of 1830–1 and apparently spent his entire fortune on financing the formation of a regiment of cavalry he commanded.[2] Consequently, Apollo was deprived of his own home when a child and grew up not in his family's hereditary seat, but in estates administered by his father. In other words, while preserving his legal status as a *szlachcic*, he lost the material security of the landowning class.

Apollo attended several provincial schools (where he repeatedly got into trouble because of his unruliness and outspoken patriotism) and later – having been refused a passport to Berlin – studied for six years at St Petersburg University, reading Oriental languages, literature and law. Although we do not know whether or in what he graduated, he was certainly well read, and in several languages: apart from Polish also in Russian, English, French, German, and Latin. All sources testify to his reputation as a sociable, witty and rebellious man. For a few years he helped his father to manage various landed estates. It seems that his heart was not in administration; but whether he was distracted by his literary interests, or rather disgusted with the existent socio-economic relations in the country, or else dispirited by the latent conflict between the predominantly Polish landowners and the Ukrainian-speaking peasantry, we cannot be sure. There is enough documentary evidence to support all three hypotheses, so presumably all three factors played a role. Anyway, Apollo developed a special interest in the situation of the peasantry and acquired some specialist knowledge in agricultural matters – enough to attempt later to publish a periodical for farmers.

---

* There is no equivalent term in English. The word covers both nobility and gentry (even those who were landless), between whom there was in Poland no legal distinction. All members of the *szlachta* addressed each other as *Panie Bracie*, 'Sir Brother'. It formed a very large class, 9–10 per cent of the total population (at the end of the eighteenth century the Polish *szlachta* was about ten times more numerous than the French *noblesse*). When, therefore, Conrad is sometimes described as a 'Polish aristocrat by descent', it is not so much untrue as greatly misleading.

In 1844 he made his literary début: the Polish-language yearbook *Rocznik Literacki*, published in St Petersburg, printed his short religious poem 'Ave Maria'. He continued writing verse intermittently till the end of his life. Most of his known poems are dated between 1849 and 1862; many of them, including some of the most characteristic and interesting, remain unpublished. He had doubts about his poetic talent – 'I do not know if I am really a poet', he confessed in a letter in 1859[3] – and these doubts were not ill-founded. Apollo Korzeniowski's poetic compositions are very often banal in imagery, shaky in their rhythms and derivative in content (Victor Hugo and Zygmunt Krasiński (1812–59), an eminent Polish Romantic writer valued rather as a powerful and prophetic thinker than as a master of poetic form, were the strongest influences). The loftiness of the expressed sentiments, mostly religious and patriotic, coupled with rather monotonous rhetorical clichés, produces tedious effects. Korzeniowski managed to find a firmer and more personal voice only in occasional poems addressed to his wife, to his son, or expressing his immediate reaction to current events.

Typically, his poetic texts raise one of the two following subjects: political – the tragedy of Poland, presented in terms of a Christian historiosophy; or social – the plight of Ruthenian (this was the term used at the time with reference to Ukrainians) peasantry. Both motifs are joined in a forceful, free version of Victor Hugo's 'Paroles d'un conservateur à propos d'un perturbateur' (from his *Les Châtiments*, 1853; the following year Korzeniowski began a translation and paraphrase of parts of the cycle), which ends with words about the man 'who first invented equality: Proletarian–Disturber–Jesus Nazarene!'[4]

The earliest group of verses, titled in the manuscript 'Czyśćowe pieśni' (Songs from Purgatory), dates from 1849 to 1853. 'Słowa z Krzyża' (Words from the Cross), the longest and one of the earliest poems, expresses an idea characteristic of Polish Romanticism:[5] the messianic vision of Poland as the Christ of nations, as a country which by her martyrdom has opened the road to salvation, that is to say liberation, for other oppressed peoples of Europe.

The consoling function of this idea was quite evident. What on the plane of political experience was a psychologically devastating catastrophe – humiliation by the loss of statehood, thousands of soldiers having perished in failed defence, new borders separating families, foreign officials dictating new rules of life – was explained and endowed with a spiritual sense on the plane of religious interpretation, and thus made more bearable. But from the very beginning the idea had also another, mobilizing function: it imposed on Poles a sacred duty to fulfil their mission of redemption and salvation.

In expressing these messianic visions and sentiments Korzeniowski continued the tradition of which the best-known and most influential exemplar was Adam Mickiewicz's stirring *Księgi Narodu i Pielgrzymstwa polskiego* (Books of the Polish nation and of the Polish Pilgrims, 1832). He gave it, however, a certain individual tone by putting a stress on three factors. First, he did not claim that the old Poland had been innocent; on the contrary, he argued that by her martyrdom she was expiating her past sins: egoism and pride of the mighty, the oppression of the poor. Second, he never suggested that God would somehow tip the scales by supporting a particular mission assigned to Poland. Poles, according to him, had a moral duty to fight for their national independence and, by following this call, would both give an example to other oppressed nations and offer support to their causes. In other words, he thought that Polish strivings had a moral and religious meaning, but he did not believe that there existed a transcendental mechanism of deliverance, independent of and separable from practical action. And, third, he saw the future salvation in terms at the same time national and social: the struggle for Poland's independence was to be based on overcoming class divisions and accepting the principles of brotherhood and civic equality.

Thus Korzeniowski's messianism provided a kind of eschatological blueprint for political practice. Nothing illustrates this better than a series of poems written in 1855 in reaction to a peasant rebellion in the Ukrainian district of Skwira.[6] The peasants, stirred by (false) rumours about a decree abolishing serfdom, demanded its implementation. The army quickly put down the mutiny, killing nearly a hundred unarmed men. In ringing verse Korzeniowski castigates the local Polish landowners who fled to the cities and appealed to the Russian military authorities for help, while they should have supported the peasants' demands for emancipation.

Korzeniowski's poetry could circulate only in manuscript copies: it would have been futile (and incriminating) even to attempt to have it published, as Russian censorship was quite stern. He did better as a dramatist. His first play, *Komedia* (A comedy, 1855), although published in a censored version, created a sensation because of its social radicalism.* The main hero, Henryk, is a poet and a 'proletarian' member of the *szlachta*, 'endowed with a soul but not owning souls [=serfs]'. Disgusted with the hypocrisy and opportunism of his own class, he condemns both the exploitation of the serfs by landowners and the speculation of capitalists. His political sympathies are only implied, but he is indubitably a fervent Polish patriot; his social ideals can be described as agrarian: factories and banks are for him inherently suspect. A critic noted later the autobiographical elements of the plot.[8] Like Henryk, Apollo Korzeniowski was a rebel and in love with a girl from a well-to-to landowning family. Unlike Henryk (who rejects marriage, because he does not want to become a serf-owner himself), he married her in the end.

3

Apollo met his future wife, Ewa Bobrowska – twelve years his junior – in or about 1847.† Although they seem to have immediately fallen in love with each other, the girl's family was firmly opposed to the marriage. Not only was the suitor landless and markedly less well-off, but his radical views made him suspect to Ewa's father.

The Bobrowskis were, like the Korzeniowskis, a Polish *szlachta* family, long settled in the Ukraine. However, the political traditions of the families differed: while the Korzeniowskis kept wasting their health and money in anti-Russian insurrections, the Bobrowskis, as in the person of Ewa's father, Józef (1790–1850), concentrated on tending their estates. But the generation of Józef Bobrowski's children became infected

---

* The first half of the play owes much, including fragments of its text, to Alexandr Griboedov's *Gore ot uma* (Woe to the wise, 1824); it seems very likely that Korzeniowski began writing *Komedia* with the intention of paraphrasing the Russian's drama.[7] The entire plot, however, and the last act, which forms the best part of the piece, differ sharply from Griboedov's piece.

† A fuller account of the lives of both Apollo and Ewa Korzeniowski can be found in my *Joseph Conrad: A Chronicle* (Cambridge 1983), pp. 4–27. Here I concentrate on their psychological and intellectual legacies.

with the spirit of Polish irredentism: of all the siblings, only the second eldest, Tadeusz, followed faithfully his father's example of prudence.

In all probability, it was the influence of their mother, Teofila née Pilchowska, which shaped the attitudes and sentiments of Ewa and her brothers Kazimierz and Stefan. Teofila's family had been once quite rich, but both her brothers, Adolf and Seweryn, took part in the November 1830 insurrection and had their estates confiscated. With such definite family traditions of her own, Teofila herself would not, it seems, openly oppose her husband's views, but she managed to imbue the younger children with an ardently patriotic spirit.

Ewa Bobrowska (born in 1832) was a girl known early for her beauty, well educated (at home) and endowed with an independent mind. Her wish to become a teacher must have shocked the whole family: at that time, only destitute women would contemplate such an occupation. Of course, nothing came of this wild idea; and it took seven years to overcome the opposition to another one – namely marriage to Apollo Korzeniowski. The girl's long-lasting depression, which visibly affected her frail health, and the intercession of uncle Adolf Pilchowski finally persuaded Tadeusz Bobrowski (the head of the family after the death of his father) to grant his permission in July 1855. Ten months later Conrad's parents were married.

All known sources indicate that they were a loving, well-matched and happy couple. Apollo wrote in a later, unfinished poem:

> I fear nothing
> Because with me, at my side, my Guardian Angel always stands:
> A Pole, Lover, Lady and Wife.[9]

Tadeusz Bobrowski wrote that his sister adhered to 'most lofty ideals' concerning all aspects of 'individual and collective life', paying no attention to their 'practicability'[10] – which amounts to saying that she did not agree with her 'reasonable' brother. But he admits that 'when she was united with the man she loved, her unusual qualities of intelligence, feeling, mind and heart blossomed out to the full'.[11] Władysław Mickiewicz, the great poet Adam's son, who visited them in 1860, considered Ewa 'a woman of rare distinction, full of devotion'.[12] The memories of her brother Tadeusz and of her husband's closest friend Stefan Buszczyński, support this opinion. I find, indeed, absolutely no evidence to support the thesis of a psychoanalyst critic that she lacked emotional warmth and spontaneity and displayed an attitude of 'cool austerity'.[13]

Her letters give quite a different impression: of a lively spirit, tender and deep at the same time, of wit and facility of expression. Unfortunately, very few of these letters have been preserved – and these only thanks to the fact that they were kept as evidence, incriminating both her and her husband.[14] They prove beyond any doubt that Ewa was a conscious and fully supportive companion of her husband's political activities, both overt and conspiratorial.

Konrad, the only child of Apollo and Ewa, was born when his father was 37 and his mother 25, thus at ages fairly advanced for the custom of the time. All existing accounts indicate that they were thoughtful and devoted parents. There are in Ewa's letters many loving references to the little Konradek, a boy 'with a heart of gold'. She evidently spent much time on his careful upbringing, giving him also religious instruction. Later, when both Korzeniowskis were sentenced to exile, they took care to send their son away as often as possible to spend some time with free members of Ewa's family, at their homes and in much better conditions – against which the boy apparently protested.[15]

Conrad's mother was certainly an exceptional woman. We would wish to know much more about her. But trying to reconstruct her personality we have to rely on our imagination, on what emerges from these letters, preserved thanks to a cruel political paradox.

> Think of me lovingly sometimes ... My dear, please do something for my sake: write less frequently, write less. I correct myself: write a lot but keep it. Some day you will give it to me ... All your letters are obviously being unsealed at the post office ... Konradek is a good boy: it is amazing how God lets him win people's hearts ... I embrace you first on behalf of all those present here, then from Konradek and lastly from myself. Remember to keep this last embrace well secured in your heart until you get another one ... For the last few days people have been saying that some more victims have been deported ... Otherwise mourning is still observed and all is quiet ... As to the peasants – things are far worse here than in Kiev Province ... in the villages belonging to such scoundrels as ... people are slashed to death ... One's heart bleeds to hear what goes on ... No less than you, I am prepared to renounce all

the joys of life so as not to be defiled by *that* which throughout your life you have tried to shun and which until now you have not touched . . . I shall always be happy with you . . . God be with you and with all that you do . . . for God's sake do not return because of personal matters . . . My embraces defy all description. Hope you can feel them . . . what is longing in comparison to the constant danger that, they say, threatens you? . . . today my heart trembles a thousand times more powerfully, my soul yearns for that 'Young Poland' of our dreams, which you will create . . . Millions of kisses – pay them back with interest.[16]

4

After his marriage Korzeniowski did not become a landowner and thus a 'soul-owner' – he never did – but continued his earlier work as an administrator of leased estates. It is easy to notice that his heart was not in this task, and even easier to guess why: he did not wish to be 'defiled', to use his wife's expression, by the condition of owning other human beings.

He wrote less verse and turned more to translation; in 1857 he published his most popular and possibly best-translated piece: Alfred de Vigny's *Chatterton* – a poetic drama, echoes of which can be found in the final chapter of Conrad's *The Nigger of the 'Narcissus'*, in the image of England as 'a great ship . . . A ship mother of fleets and nations!' Two years later Korzeniowski achieved his biggest public succes with his second play, *Dla miłego grosza* (For the love of money, 1859), another bitterly satirical comedy which won the second prize at a competition and has been staged many times to considerable acclaim. Again the edge of his sardonic wit is directed against the wealthy members of his own social class, the *szlachta*. He derides them for their failure to live up to their professed ideals and noble traditions, for crass materialism, snobbery and political opportunism, and he contrasts them with principled representatives of the budding intelligentsia. With both traditional feudalism and nascent capitalism condemned, the implicit positive vision is one of an agrarian community of interests. The protagonist is again Henryk, apparently the same person as the main hero of the *Komedia*. Rather static and rhetorical in the first two acts, the play becomes smoother in the third; the vigour of language and a clear characterization of the heroes constitute its best qualities.

In early 1859 the Korzeniowskis moved to Żytomierz (Zhytomyr)*
in Volhynia, at that time a lively centre of Polish culture. Apollo became
secretary of a newly formed publishing society; apart from that short-
lasting function he devoted himself exclusively to writing and translating, his main source of income. His ambition as a translator was to
raise the professional level of what at that time was usually shabbily
done by amateurs and hacks.[17] And, indeed, several of his renderings of
French playwrights are outstanding: especially, apart from the already
mentioned *Chatterton*, Victor Hugo's *Hernani* and *Marion Delorme*.

In his critical articles, published in various periodicals,
Korzeniowski, as was customary in post-partition Poland, defended the
public and national functions and obligations of literature. This concern
with the social responsibilities of poets and novelists made his pieces
vulnerable to frequent confiscation by political censors; and the periodical nearest to his heart, *Słowo*, was closed after only thirteen issues with
the editor imprisoned on a charge of sedition.[18]

Korzeniowski's utopian agrarianism and his spirited attacks on
industry as a source of materialism, corruption and breakdown of social
cohesion were salient themes of his writings. He planned (but of course
was refused permission for) the publication of a popular weekly for
'agriculturists', a term meant to include both landowners and peasants;
the basic idea was to prevent the massive Russification of the petty
gentry, deprived by Tsarist decrees of their *szlachta* entitlements (to
education, military service as officers, etc.). In one of his articles he
claimed that 'impoverished, landless gentry' are 'our only proletariat' –
thus making explicit one of the underlying ideas of his plays.[19]

Probably about the same time Korzeniowski decided to start his
underground anti-Russian activity, moral as well as political. As we read
in the manuscript of his short poem *Ranek i wieczór* (Morning and
evening, 29 January 1857): 'in the evening, when villainy falls silent –
because silent falls money – quietly, cautiously, secretly rise – Men of the
Future'.[20]

What did these 'Men of the Future' want? As the ultimate goal: a
restoration, if necessary by means of an armed uprising, of a free and
independent, multi-ethnic Poland on her pre-partition territory, and

---

* When mentioning localities in the Ukraine, I give two spellings: Polish – used in
most contemporary sources – and (in parenthesis) Ukrainian – as used today.

legal equality for all her citizens. In the more immediate future they demanded a modicum of civil liberties, including the right to teach Polish and in Polish (not only in Russian) in private schools, local self-government and freedom of travel to the western provinces of the Russian Tsardom, thus also to Warsaw.

One of the most important political problems for Polish activists in central Ukraine was the Ukrainian question itself. The Russian authorities simply denied the existence of a separate Ukrainian language and nationality. Local Polish landowners tended to side with them, for their own economic and national reasons. More liberal-minded Poles, however, often sympathized with Ukrainian national aspirations. Patriotic Polish radicals wanted equality for Ukrainians within a free and democratic Poland. Korzeniowski himself (like his closest political allies) was, as we have seen, ready even to side with Ukrainian peasantry against their Polish landowners. He thought that Russia was the common enemy of both oppressed nations and dreamt about a reconstructed Polish Commonwealth, where Poles and Ukrainians would enjoy the same civil liberties.[21]

This is one reason why calling him a 'nationalist' may be misleading.* An anonymous poem, preserved in Kiev police archives and ascribed (I believe wrongly, but revealingly) to Korzeniowski, written in the form of a prayer, expresses the idea of brotherhood even between Russians and Poles – a brotherhood in joint aspirations to freedom.[22] (We know less about his attitude towards Jews, who constituted a large part of the urban population in eastern Poland and western and central Ukraine. We can be certain that he was not an anti-Semite; in 1862 he strongly protested when Catholic nuns in Warsaw had surreptitiously baptized a Jewish girl.)[23]

In April 1861 a peaceful patriotic demonstration in Warsaw was fired on by Russian troops, with more than a hundred killed. The massacre caused among Poles a great wave of emotion, expressed mainly in

---

* Orwell's differentiation between a 'patriot' – who is devoted to a 'particular way of life' which he believes 'to be the best in the world but has no wish to force upon other people' – and a 'nationalist' – who places his nation 'beyond good and evil' and considers his supreme duty to advance its interest even at the expense of other nations – seems here particularly apposite. George Orwell, 'Notes on Nationalism' [May 1945], *The Collected Essays*, Harmondsworth 1970, vol. III, p. 411.

the form of commemorative religious services, and black clothing worn by women and children. It also greatly strengthened underground irredentist movements. Korzeniowski (who was now steadily watched by local political police), in compact with his friends in Żytomierz and Kiev, decided to move to Warsaw – the centre of Polish political action.

5

Apollo Korzeniowski's political and social opinions are sometimes presented as not only quixotic but also incoherent, as his own peculiar concoction of romantic nationalism and social radicalism infused with a strong dose of religiosity. Such opinions stem from a combination of cultural prejudice and insufficient information.

Korzeniowski saw political activity in moral categories: not as a means to win and keep power, but as an instrument to implement general ethical principles. And, as is the case with most political moralists, in practical terms it is often easier to define what he was against than what he was for. We must not, however, forget that conspiracies and underground leaders do not normally leave behind a full documentation of their concrete goals and means; moreover, most Polish private collections and family archives were destroyed in the wars and revolutions of the twentieth century. Korzeniowski's political role has to be reconstructed painstakingly from bits and pieces of documentary evidence.

Korzeniowski was outstanding but not atypical. He continued quite faithfully the tradition of Polish Romantic political thought. If his political ideas may seem incongruous to some of us, his contemporaries did not perceive them as such. Nor was the combination of these ideas of his own making. He belonged, in fact, to the mainstream of a political movement called the 'szlachta revolutionaries'. This movement originated immediately after the partitions of Poland, and developed fully during and after the November 1830 insurrection.[24] The 'szlachta revolutionaries' combined the demands of national sovereignty with a programme of radical social reform: they postulated the reconstruction of an independent Poland in which all citizens would acquire the same political entitlements as those given to the szlachta. Thus they combined traditionalism, in the form of harking back to the time when Poland was an independent country, with radicalism in the form of linking the demands of national liberty with those of political equality. A strong component of religious inspiration made Korzeniowski close also to the 'Christian social radicals', a group of Polish thinkers and activists who interpreted the goals of national liberation, social justice and brotherhood in the spirit of the Gospels.[25]

The ostensible purpose of Korzeniowski's move to Warsaw in 1861 was to start a new periodical, a fortnightly modelled on the Paris *Revue des Deux Mondes*. He was energetic and successful in securing regular contributions from a large group of journalists and writers. But his main field of activity lay underground. He quickly managed to become the most influential member of the radical ('Red') wing of the Polish irredentists in Warsaw. The fact that he was by far the eldest among their leaders (most others were between ten and twenty years younger) might have helped him to establish his authority – but he was an outsider, coming from far away, and he does not seem to have either flattered the youth or played up to them by flashy radicalism. On the contrary: as far as we know, while being unflinchingly principled as far as the ultimate goals were concerned, he at the same time tried to exert a moderating influence with regard to the tactics applied. Thus he must have been a persuasive, perhaps even charismatic, leader and a skilful organizer. Within a few months he laid the foundations for a national centre of the underground movement of the 'Reds', who formed the most enterprising (if not always realistic) faction among politically active Poles. The 'Reds' linked the struggle for national independence with a programme of broad social reforms, beginning with the liberation of the peasantry. For the time being Korzeniowski wanted to concentrate on expanding organizational links and mobilizing public opinion for demands of local self-government, freedom of assembly, and generally a degree of national autonomy.[26]

Ewa and the little Konradek remained for a while in the Ukraine, sending letters by various 'occasions' (correspondence sent by mail was carefully inspected, and sometimes stopped, by the police). They joined Apollo in early October 1861. About a fortnight later, and three days after a sudden proclamation of martial law in the Polish provinces of the Russian Empire, on 17 October, at a meeting of about a score of activists in the Korzeniowskis' flat in the centre of Warsaw, the National Committee of the Movement was formed. Apollo Korzeniowski – its initiator – was elected one of the three members. The Committee became the kernel of the future (1863) National Government, which was to acquire an authority of mythic proportions.

Meanwhile, Korzeniowski's political activity had come to the attention of the local Russian police and military authorities, which had in any case been warned by their Kiev counterparts. He was arrested in the night of 20/21 October and incarcerated in the notorious Pavilion X (for important political prisoners) of the Warsaw Citadel.

'[I]n the courtyard of this Citadel – characteristically for our nation – my childhood memories begin', wrote Joseph Conrad thirty-five years later.[27]

6

Conrad apparently went to the citadel with his mother. Ewa Korzeniowska would carry supplies for her imprisoned husband, who suffered from rheumatism and scurvy.[28] She herself was also charged with unspecified crimes and repeatedly interrogated, but not arrested.

Apollo must have covered his tracks quite well, as the charges brought against him by the special Military Tribunal were vague and often off the mark, and the incriminating evidence consisted mainly of Ewa's letters to him – suggestive of defiance but containing no concrete details of any subversive activities.

On 9 May 1862 the Military Tribunal sentenced both Korzeniowskis 'to exile, under strict police supervision';[29] General Alexandr Lüders, the viceroy of the 'Polish Kingdom', added in a handwritten note: 'Mind that they do not stop on the way.'[30]

Two weeks before the official verdict, the same Lüders informed another general, Illarion Vasilchikov, governor-general of Kiev

> 'Korzeniowski, while interrogated, brazenly and obstinately refused to admit the truth, and his wife denied even her own handwriting when she was shown, as circumstantial evidence, her letters written to her husband, full of suggestive expressions; however, considering that the letters from his wife and other documents and manuscripts of rebellious content found at his place show that he was one of the most zealous anti-authority activists, and that his wife most likely participated in all his actions, while he himself had had, according to the report of a gendarmes' officer of the Kiev Governship, as a writer a considerable influence on the society and behaved very cautiously – I have deemed

it necessary to order that both he and his wife are sent in exile to the city of Perm, under strict police supervision.³¹

During the last weeks of his incarceration (some of which he spent in the prison hospital) Korzeniowski was allowed pen and paper; he translated Hugo's *Le Roi s'amuse* and wrote a few poems. They express a grim tenacity in the face of persecution and bitter criticism of the appeasing gestures of church authorities, which decided to stop special services commemorating the victims: 'Virtue downtrodden. Treason rewarded.'³²

7

The governor of Perm, a university friend of Apollo Korzeniowski, asked that the condemned be sent somewhere else; after a tiring journey, during which the Korzeniowskis' son fell gravely ill, they were finally directed to Vologda in northern Russia – a traditional destination for exiles, and known for its unhealthy climate.

Apollo wrote to his cousins in Poland:

Apart from us there are men from 1830 [November insurrection], 1846 [Szymon Konarski's conspiracy] and 1848 ['Spring of the Nations' movement]... For them our arrival was like a few drops of water fallen on quick-lime. They recall their language, customs, religion... Anyway we do not regard exile as a punishment but as a new way of serving our country. There can be no punishment for us since we are innocent... Our serene faces, proud bearing and defiant eye cause great wonder here... So do not pity us and do not think of us as martyrs.³³

Acording to the memoirs of contemporary Russian and Ukrainian exiles in Vologda, the Korzeniowskis' wooden cottage quickly became a gathering-place. On Apollo's initiative a special code of honourable behaviour was drawn up. Poles were expected to offer a moral example to other exiles and to show them 'how to strive for constitutional freedom'.³⁴

The climate, however, rapidly affected Ewa's and Apollo's health. Thanks to the friendly intervention of Vologda's governor, the Korzeniowskis were given permission to be transferred south, to Chernikhiv in the north-eastern Ukraine; they moved there in January 1863. A few weeks later, on 22 January, an insurrection – provoked by the Russian authorities, which ordered a massive compulsory conscription

– broke out in Poland. It was the worst season of the year to begin guerrilla warfare, and the first months of the uprising were disastrous. Poorly armed and insufficiently prepared insurgents were, for all their enthusiasm and bravery, outnumbered and outgunned by Russian troops.

'[A]ll life within us has come to an end, we are stunned by despair', wrote Korzeniowski to his cousins.[35] He realized that the call to arms issued by the clandestine National Government was tragically premature, although perhaps unavoidable. He probably shared at least some of the illusions of the Polish radicals. They overestimated the number of prospective insurgents, the general readiness of Poles for sacrifice, the support of the peasantry (which was emancipated by a proclamation of the National Government, but by and large remained passively mistrustful) and, especially, the expected support of the 'democratic forces' in Europe. And they underestimated the ruthless determination of the Russian authorities, the scale of infiltration by spies and the cruelty of repression.

From Chernikhiv, Korzeniowski managed to send abroad the manuscript of his long essay 'Poland and Muscovy', begun in Vologda. It is a combination of personal memoirs of imprisonment, interrogations and exile with historiosophical musings about Russia and her relations with the rest of Europe. The text was published anonymously by a Polish émigré periodical.

The author attacks everything Russian with vehemence. According to him, Muscovites do not constitute a nation: they are kept together by the machinery of 'hosudarstwo',* their state system. (This denial of Russian nationhood was for Korzeniowski a headlong escape from the dilemma of how to reconcile his hatred of the Russian regime and its policies with his belief in the dignity and historical legitimacy of all nations.)

Tsarist Russia is an embodiment of political evil, an antithesis of the spirit of liberty.

> But then, the whole of Muscovy is a prison ... The aim of Muscovy's development is to bring to a standstill all progress of humankind ...
> Meanwhile, to keep in training, Muscovy chews living Poland as if she

---

* I.e., *gosudarstvo*, government; for some reason Korzeniowski uses the Ukrainian version of the word.

were dead. Poland has been swallowed but not digested.* The process of digestion has just begun. When it ends, the turn of other nations will come. A slavery most hideous, because inflicted by a vile hand, hangs over Europe.[36]

Korzeniowski castigates the countries of Western Europe – Austria, Prussia, England and France – for their vacillation and cowardice in succumbing to Russian pressures, demands and blackmail. Their weakness allows Russia to expand her evil empire. He warns: 'Whoever in his relations with Muscovy just for one moment trusts her tsars, if only fleetingly, considers Muscovites a people capable of freedom – he will be outwitted and thus defeated.'[37] While the rhetoric of condemnation sounds extremist, we have to note that very similar thoughts had been expressed in France by Marquis Astolphe de Custine in his *La Russie en 1839*, in Poland by Zygmunt Krasiński, in Germany by Karl Marx, and in Russia itself by Pyotr Chaadaev.

During his exile in the 1860s Korzeniowski began several other dramatic pieces, most of which he never finished. He planned to continue the story of Henryk (the protagonist of *Komedia* and one of the main characters in *Dla miłego grosza*), and to raise in his dramas some fundamental problems of Polish history and public morality. Only *Akt pierwszy* (Act one, 1869) has been published, with the author's preface.[38] It is worth noticing that, evidently hurt by the charges of plagiarism, this time Korzeniowski signalled in the subtitle that the play was not 'original' – although he could not remember the source of his idea.[39]

Among the incomplete fragments *Ojciec* (The Father), the second part of a planned trilogy, begun in the early sixties and probably continued later, is the most interesting and best written.[40] A young Son leaves home against his Mother's wishes to do what he considers his patriotic duty. Next we see him in prison, sentenced to death. But his Fiancée's father, a traitor, has secured his reprieve – on the condition that he divulges the names of his fellow-conspirators. Most of the ensuing dialogue concerns the choice between death and betrayal. The Mother wants her Son to live, appeals for his pity and ridicules the argument

---

* Probably an allusion to Jean-Jacques Rousseau's famous advice to Poles: 'If you cannot prevent [your Russian neighbours] from swallowing you, at least you can try to prevent them from digesting you.' (*Considérations sur le gouvernement de Pologne*, Geneva 1782, ch. III).

that treason would bring him disgrace: what is reputation in comparison to death? The Fiancée revels in visions of their potential happiness, but wants her beloved to do his duty. The Son wavers, swayed by the fear of death and his Mother's supplications. Half-delirious, he exclaims that he will tell the names. At this moment the Father intervenes, appealing to the Son's honour, whose guardian he remains; and here the fragment ends. *Ojciec* spells out all the basic questions posed by the ideal of fidelity. Fear collides with shame, love of life with personal dignity, compassion with honour. There were many cases of identical conflicts, differently resolved, among Korzeniowski's fellow-conspirators.*

Although the climate in Chernikhiv was much better than in northern Russia, Ewa Korzeniowska's health continued to deteriorate. She died of tuberculosis on 18 April 1865. Apollo was himself afflicted with the same disease; after the loss of his wife he suffered severe bouts of despair and depression. 'I am here so very much alone: no other company but this silent grave, bewitched in silence, deaf to prayers, unresponsive to tears... When She is not here, when all I dream about is to see her again... doubts overwhelm me and call out: and if my faith is but deluded imagination?'[42]

Outbursts of despair and sometimes even despondency in Korzeniowski's letters to his closest friends written after the death of Ewa should not obscure the fact that the years which he spent in exile were for him a time of very hard work. This gravely ill man lived with his wife and son, and then only with his son, on the verge of poverty, in primitive cottages or rooms sometimes without any service. He watched his wife die. And during these years he wrote several articles and essays (including a very interesting one about Shakespeare's dramaturgy), a handful of poems and dramatic pieces, and translated a few thousand pages, in verse and prose, from English and French: notably Shakespeare's *The Comedy of Errors* and *Much Ado About Nothing*,

---

* Korzeniowski may well have known the story of Roman Rogiński, his fellow-conspirator in Warsaw. A successful commander of a detachment of insurgents, this young (21-year-old) man was captured in March 1863 and, possibly influenced by his mother's pleas, gave the interrogating authorities many names of other conspirators and details of underground structures. He was sentenced to death and then reprieved.[41]

Dickens' *Hard Times*, and Victor Hugo's *La Légende des siècles*, *Les Travailleurs de la mer*, *Marion Delorme*, and some other dramas, the texts of which have been lost.

He also wrote many letters, of which only about forty survive. He discussed in them his writing and translating projects, works of other writers, his own and his friends' family lives, including his worry about his son's future, the problems with his books and his furniture left in storage in Warsaw. These letters are the most convincing evidence against the opinion that Apollo Korzeniowski was 'death-oriented' or, in Frederick R. Karl's words, 'caught up by martyrdom'[43] – whatever this precisely means. He never expressed a wish to die, but only moods of weariness and grief, which were quite understandable, given his experiences, situation and state of health. He repeatedly rejected the label of a 'martyr'; remarkably there is little self-pity in his letters. In the face of a string of personal and national disasters he often adopted an attitude of boisterous irony.

Apollo also conscientiously supervised his son's education; having himself learned English from a Robertson manual, he successfully worked out, along the same lines, a manual of French for the little Konradek.[44] While it is true that the money he received for his writings and translations was not quite sufficient to cover all his current expenses and that to a certain extent he had to rely on the assistance of his wife's relatives, we have to say that he valiantly strove to meet his family responsibilities.

8

In January 1868 Korzeniowski finally received permission to leave his exile and go abroad. Algiers and Madeira were mentioned as the destination, for health reasons; but the mortally sick man had neither money nor strength for a long journey. Instead, at the end of February, he went with his son to Lwów (Lviv), in the Austrian part of Poland, which at that time enjoyed a considerable degree of civil liberties and self-government.

This move had on Korzeniowski the effect of decompression. It quickly transpired that his idealistic dreams of a future free and democratic Poland were easier to uphold against the stony, frozen structures of

Russian autocracy than within the shifting, motley, chaotic scenery of Austro-Hungarian semi-democracy. He underestimated the achievements of Poles in Galicia, who had had to struggle for their semi-autonomy. He was furious at their daily compromises with the Viennese imperial authorities and their internal squabblings. He was alarmed by the influence of German on their language and in their schools. His letters are full of acerbic complaints.

Increasingly weak, aware of the progress of his illness, he continued working and making plans. He was to become a member of the editorial board of *Kraj*, a new liberal weekly to be published in Cracow, to be responsible for commentaries about international events, notably about developments in England: his interest in that country was not limited to translation of its classics. In December 1868 he finished his last known work: a preface to his drama *Akt pierwszy*. There he summed up his views on the national obligations of literature:

> We behold an entire generation of writers and poets who hold the quill like a sword ... It is difficult to lay the blame for such everlasting weapons upon men who have nothing and ought to regain everything. Before the tasks of life sometimes the demands of Art have to step aside ... No author invoking the slogan of 'Art for art's sake' would agree with this principle. May God be with them. We, like many others, claim no right to be called writers but have been using our pens for a long time.[45]

He died on 23 May 1869, shortly after a move from Lwów to Cracow. His funeral three days later – the funeral of a person hardly known in that city but symbolic – turned into a massive patriotic demonstration. On his gravestone we read the words: 'Victim of Muscovy's tyranny'.

> By the innate power of his spirit and will man often masters, if only momentarily, the events – and then he notices how they become even more sluggish and stubborn on the road by which he has compelled them to move. And in this struggle, finally, when his life is smashed to pieces, man perishes – but with that quality, with which God has endowed him for all time in the act of creation, *intact*.[46]

These words from Korzeniowski's essay on Shakespeare have the ring of an auto-epitaph.

9

There exist today two Apollo Korzeniowskis: one known to historians of nineteenth-century Poland and to a few Polish literary scholars – and the other known to the Conrad specialists. The latter have relied, understandably, mainly on his portrait as drawn by Tadeusz Bobrowski, his brother-in-law and Conrad's guardian, benefactor and correspondent. Unluckily for the real Apollo Korzeniowski, his brother-in-law did not approve of him – neither politically (Bobrowski was an appeaser and opponent of all insurrections), nor socially (he was for enfranchisement of the peasantry, but not for giving them legal equality), nor psychologically (he prided himself on being a cool, calculating rationalist, in contrast to Korzeniowski, an emotional visionary, as befits a poet).

Bobrowski noted his brother-in-law's reputation for sarcasm – and acknowledged, with slight puzzlement and perhaps a pinch of jealousy, his personal popularity. He charged Korzeniowski with 'impracticality' and with applying 'two sets of measures: one for the weak and ignorant, the other for the mighty of this world'.[47] Neither charge is easy to verify. Korzeniowski was indeed not very successful in doing things he was not interested in or did not approve of (as, for instance, using serf labour). To what extent his compassion for the underprivileged was likely to take the form of naive idealization of all the weak, poor and simple, we are unable to tell.

The difference of their political options evidently coloured not only Bobrowski's evaluation of Korzeniowski's behaviour, but also his presentation of facts in question. To give a small but telling example of this bias: the formal petition made in 1858 to the Kiev provincial censorship office for permission to publish a weekly for 'agriculturists', was signed by Apollo Korzeniowski together with Tadeusz Bobrowski[48] – but the latter not only never mentioned it, but claimed that the interest Conrad's father took in the plight of peasantry was only an expression of the sentimental snobbery of a poet. Bobrowski claimed even that Korzeniowski hesitated on the issue of the enfranchisement, wanting to leave the initiative to the landowners.[49] Many other instances of such biased information (or misinformation), sometimes perhaps unconscious, could be adduced.

Roman Taborski, author of the most comprehensive study of Korzeniowski's poetry, says curtly that he 'lacked fictional imagination'⁵⁰ – and this is a verdict with which Korzeniowski himself would have probably agreed. Why did he persist in writing, then? There were, I believe, two reasons.

The first was brutally simple: that was the best (and, later, the only) way to earn money he knew. For landless *szlachta* members those were increasingly difficult times: it was rapidly becoming harder and harder to live on leasing or administering estates. Official and better clerical positions were practically reserved for Russians. This was why so many Poles were emigrating at that time.

The other reason was that he saw in writing the best way of doing what he considered his duty; and duty was his obsession.

> I *must* write, because at the present time I cannot do anything else. I *must* close myself within a most narrow circle of the unanimous, because the motley crowd, common here, does not fit my ideas and my self-dignity . . . Therefore you see that there is no merit to my life, as everything is determined by *must*. There is nothing in me to admire, because I only do my duty and nothing more.

Thus he wrote in a letter sent abroad (and therefore knowing that it would be read by political police) to a man whom he considered his moral and ideological authority.⁵¹

As early as his mid-twenties Korzeniowski was, according to all evidence, passionately interested in politics. The conditions of his time and place limited the possibilities of political activity to conspiracy. And in the Ukraine there was precious little scope for conspiracies in the 1840s and 1850s. Apollo – with his dreams of an independent Poland and his awareness of the plight of the Ukrainian peasantry – impatiently wanted change. But the scope for practical social and educational action was limited. The prevailing custom of the time pointed to literature in general and poetry in particular as the best means of influencing other people's behaviour.

This does not amount to saying that Korzeniowski treated literature purely as a means: far from that, he regretted being didactic. He was endowed with keen taste and knew how to enjoy Shakespeare's comedies as pure poetry. He realized that his own talent for writing and versifying was limited, that he lacked original imagery and a facility for story-telling. As his letters to friends and his 'memoirs' 'Poland and

Muscovy' indicate, if not restrained by political censorship he would probably have stopped writing poetry and drama and have turned to straightforward description.

Thus what made Korzeniowski become a professional writer were also his non-literary interests, obligations and ambitions. He was not a poet *manqué* who, missing literary success, turned to political activity – but, on the contrary, rather a man of social and political action, stymied by the circumstances, who sought in literature the means to foster his moral and ideological goals.

10

What Conrad felt and thought about his parents may be deduced from what he said about them, both in *A Personal Record* and in his private letters.

He did not say much. To Edward Garnett Conrad wrote in 1900 that his mother 'certainly was no ordinary woman'. Almost four years later he confessed to Kazimierz Waliszewski: 'I can hardly remember her, but judging by what I heard about her and by the letters to her brothers – which I read later – she must have been a woman with uncommon qualities of mind and spirit.' These letters, not only to her brother but also to his own father, which were for him 'a revelation', he apparently destroyed himself in 1890, according to his letter to Garnett. Why, he did not explain.

In his 'Author's Note' (1919) to *A Personal Record* Conrad dates his earliest memory of his mother to autumn 1861, the time of his father's imprisonment in Warsaw, when he was less than four: 'my mother [was] dressed in the black of the national mourning ... I have also preserved from that particular time the awe of her mysterious gravity which, indeed, was by no means smileless. Perhaps for me she could always find a smile.' There is only one other reminiscence, of the summer of 1863 (misdated in the text as 1864), when he was five and a half years old. Conrad identifies this as 'the year in which I first begin to remember my mother with more distinctness than a mere loving, wide-browed, silent, protecting presence, whose eyes had a sort of commanding sweetness'. He describes in some detail the day of their return from a stay with Ewa's relatives in Nowochwastów to exile in Chernikhiv. But he never says anything about the following two years, spent with his parents in

Chernikhiv. Why? We may only guess the reasons for his discretion. These were the years of his mother's terminal illness; his experience must have been traumatic – all the more since death by tuberculosis in that era was a very ugly business.

We may receive an intimation of his painful feelings from 'Poland Revisited', an essay written in 1915. Conrad gives there, briefly but movingly, his sombre memories of the winter of 1868 spent with his dying father in Cracow. (In fact, they both moved there only in February 1869, three months before Apollo's death.) These final memories seem to expand and throw an impenetrable shadow on the entire last three years of his father's life – much of which time they spent together.

In general, Conrad says much more about his father than about his mother, but what he says is mostly information about Apollo Korzeniowski's literary and other activities. Personal reminiscences are few, and not always reliable. To Garnett he writes:

> A man of great sensibilities; of exalted and dreamy temperament; with a terrible gift of irony and of gloomy disposition; withal a strong religious feeling degenerating after the loss of his wife into mysticism touched with despair. His aspect was distinguished; his conversation very fascinating; his face in repose sombre, lighted all over when he smiled. I remember him well.

However, in *A Personal Record* there are only two remembered scenes. One of 1866, when Apollo found his son immersed in the reading of his translation of *Two Gentlemen of Verona*. The other (in the 'Author's Note') of early May 1869, when Apollo ordered

> the burning of his manuscripts a fortnight or so before his death . . .
> I happened to go into his room a little earlier than usual . . . My father sat in a deep arm-chair propped up with pillows. This is the last time I saw him out of bed. His aspect was to me not so much that of a man desperately ill, as mortally weary – a vanquished man. That act of destruction affected me profoundly by its air of surrender.

But in truth Korzeniowski's manuscripts were not destroyed; he bequeathed them to his closest friend, Stefan Buszczyński. Moreover, in his letter to Garnett Conrad had given a different version: 'There were piles of MSS, dramas, verse, prose, burnt after his [Apollo's] death according to his last will.' Here he does not say anything about himself witnessing the scene. Could it be that some other documents were burnt in his presence? Again, we may only guess why Conrad wanted to believe that all his father's works had perished. In his note to *A Personal Record* he confesses: 'For many years I believed that every scrap of his writing had been burnt, but in July of 1914 the Librarian of the University of Cracow ... mentioned the existence of a few manuscripts of my father and especially of a series of letters written before and during the exile to his most intimate friend.' This is a little misleading: there were not 'a few' but two large volumes of Apollo Korzeniowski's manuscripts in this library; 'the most intimate friend' was Kazimierz Kaszewski. In his 'First News', an article written in 1918, Conrad writes that he had a look at his father's letters to Kaszewski (where, as the librarian correctly informed him, he himself is often referred to) but does not mention anything about seeing his manuscripts.

Conrad confesses in the 'Author's Note' to *A Personal Record* that by 1914 he had imagined his father

> to be completely forgotten forty-five years after his death. But this was not the case. Some young men of letters had discovered him, mostly as a remarkable translator ... The political side of his life was being recalled too; for some men of his time had been in their old age publishing their memoirs, where the part he played was for the first time publicly disclosed to the world. I learned then of things in his life I never knew before [. . .] from a volume of posthumous memoirs dealing with those bitter years I learned the fact that the first inception of the secret National Committee intended primarily to organize moral resistance to the augmented pressure of Russianism arose on my father's initiative, and that its first meetings were held in our Warsaw house.[52]

There is a strong element of dissembling here: virtually all the information mentioned above Conrad could have garnered from Stefan Buszczyński's pamphlet *Mało znany poeta* (A little-known poet), published in 1870, which he himself had mentioned in his letters to Garnett and Waliszewski.

What rings true in his 'Author's Note' is Conrad's surprise in 1914 at the fact that his father was still remembered in Poland, and remembered well. The fiftieth anniversary of the January 1863 insurrection brought indeed a spate of reminiscences, in which Korzeniowski figured prominently. Conrad's new friends in Poland brought that fact to his attention; and he apparently read (or re-read?) Buszczyński's pamphlet.

Thus we come to the question: how much did Conrad know, or

remember, about his father? This, I am afraid, will for ever remain a matter of guesswork and conjecture. The contrast between the real Apollo Korzeniowski and the image of him, impressed upon Conrad by his uncle and guardian, was substantial. To add one more example: there is, in Korzeniowski's late letters and other writings, little if any evidence of 'mysticism touched with despair', mentioned by Conrad in his letter to Garnett; and it is doubtful that a boy of eleven could have reached such a diagnosis – it was most probably suggested by Tadeusz Bobrowski. It seems that Conrad himself did not, at least till 1914, make an effort to learn more about his father and better understand his motives.

Still, he defended him spiritedly, in the 'Author's Note' to *A Personal Record*, against the classification as a 'revolutionist'. 'No epithet could be more inapplicable to a man with such a strong sense of responsibility in the region of ideas and action and so indifferent to the prompting of personal ambitions as my father.' When we remember what Conrad said earlier, in 'A Familiar Preface' (1911) to *A Personal Record*, about the 'revolutionary spirit' which is 'mighty convenient in this, that it frees one from all scruples as regards ideas', we have to agree that Apollo Korzeniowski did not fit Conrad's own definition of 'revolutionary'. And when we remember his general contempt of revolutions, expressed in his letters and fiction, we shall understand his aversion to having his own father called a 'revolutionist', especially in the wake of the horrors of October 1917 in Russia.

However, the factual question remains: was Conrad right in claiming (in the same 'Author's Note') that his father 'was no more revolutionary than the others, in the sense of working for subversion of any social or political scheme of existence'? And here the answer cannot be simple. Korzeniowski and the other Polish 'Reds' wanted not only to liberate the peasants but also to give every citizen of a reborn Poland equal civic liberties. That would have certainly amounted to a change of 'social [*and*] political scheme of existence'. But this momentous change was supposed to be achieved, if possible, by non-violent means, and inspired by the ideas of a common human dignity and brotherhood rather than class warfare; such a brotherhood was not of proletarians without history and nationality, but grounded in the traditional ideals of patriotism, piety, fidelity and honour. Thus Conrad's father *was* a revolutionary, but certainly not in the sense given to this term by the great French and Bolshevik revolutions.

11

Joseph Conrad's attitude to the memory of his parents was evidently a very complex one. And, given the spiritual force of their heritage and the psychological tensions caused by Conrad's unusual life and career, this complexity, and even ambivalence, is understandable. It will always remain an object of analysis and speculation.

It is often said that Conrad felt guilty of failing his personal and national duties, as bequeathed to him by his parents. This hypothesis certainly helps to explain many of his statements and actions. For example, Apollo Korzeniowski did not die a 'vanquished' and 'surrendering' man; but if Conrad believed that he did, his own feeling of guilt would have been greatly lessened.

Still, I believe that this is much more a case of 'shame' than of 'guilt'. One feels guilty of having consciously taken a wrong decision, of having broken a moral law. But in the case of a glaring contrast between a certain vision of man's social and national duties, and an accumulated effect of many half-conscious choices and only partly controlled turns of events, one is more likely to experience a feeling of shame. Conrad seems never to have made a considered decision to leave Poland for ever, or to renounce his national allegiance, or to become an English and not a Polish writer; thus he did not directly challenge the inherent demands of his heritage and therefore could not feel guilty of breaking them. But when he compared his own life with that of his parents, he must have been aware of a stark contrast between their altruism and his own egocentricity. A feeling of shame was a natural reaction of one who grew up in what was, according to a well-known classification, a 'culture of shame' – as cultures cherishing the chivalric code and the ideal of honour are.[53]

Even more than a feeling of guilt, a feeling of shame is likely to produce self-defensive reactions in the form of resentment against the person or thing or idea which is the cause of that feeling. I think that Conrad's at times ambivalent attitude towards the memory of his father and towards Poland in general can be best explained in these terms.

4
Joseph Conrad and Tadeusz Bobrowski

1

> I cannot write about Tadeusz Bobrowski, my Uncle, guardian and benefactor, without emotion. Even now, after ten years, I still feel his loss. He was a man of great character and unusual qualities of mind. Although he did not understand my desire to join the mercantile marine, on principle, he never objected to it. I saw him four times during the thirty [!] years of my wanderings (from 1874–1893) but even so I attribute to his devotion, care, and influence, whatever good qualities I may possess.

So wrote Conrad in 1903 to Kazimierz Waliszewski.[1] He paid homage to his uncle and guardian not only in his private letters. He dedicated his first book, *Almayer's Folly*, 'To the memory of T.B.'; and in *A Personal Record* wrote: '[My uncle] had been for a quarter of a century the wisest, the firmest, the most indulgent of guardians, extending over me a paternal care and affection, a moral support which I seemed to feel always near me in the most distant parts of the earth.'[2]

Even if Conrad were less effusive in his statements about Bobrowski, the latter would have to attract the attention of Conrad's biographers and critics for purely factual reasons. For over twenty years, most of Conrad's money came from Bobrowski's purse, and during all these years Bobrowski was also Conrad's main link with his home country and his faithful (if grumbling) adviser. Bobrowski's influence on his nephew is undeniable. His letters constitute the most important source of our knowledge about Conrad's life between 1869 and 1893; and still more: Bobrowski's *Memoirs*, published in 1900, is the only book from which Conrad consciously and openly grafted whole fragments into his own work.*

2

Tadeusz Wilhelm Jerzy (George) Bobrowski was born on 31 March 1829, the second of eight children of Józef Bobrowski (1790–1850) and Teofila née Biberstejn-Pilchowska, in Volhynia, a south-eastern area annexed by Russia in the second partition of Poland in 1793. He owed his three given names to the memory of Tadeusz Kościuszko, Poland's famous freedom fighter and George Washington's companion in the War of Independence, Wilhelm Tell and Washington himself. Despite the invocation of such rebellious traditions, his own father, a moderately well-off landowner, steered clear of risky political engagements and did not participate in the Polish insurrection of November 1830 nor in any other irredentist movement of his time.

Tadeusz Bobrowski must have been well aware of ideological tensions within his own family: his two maternal uncles, Adolf and Seweryn Pilchowski, had their estates confiscated for taking part in the 1830 insurrection; and among his siblings he was – apart from his elder brother Stanisław, who died young as an officer in the Tsar's Guards – the only one not directly engaged in anti-Russian conspiracies.

A sickly child, he was educated at home till the age of ten. Then he spent three years at school in Żytomierz, followed by two in Kiev. He began to study law at Kiev University when he was only fifteen; in autumn 1846 he moved to the most prestigious university of Russia, that of St Petersburg. There he soon demonstrated considerable intellectual abilities and ambitions. He kept away from politics and preserved a cautious distance from his more volatile and less reasonable colleagues, whose idealistic engagements he describes in his memoirs with ironic condescension. In February 1848, when the heads of many other students were inflamed with the ideas of the Spring of the Nations, bringing

---

* The instances of Conrad's borrowings from Anatole France, Maupassant and other French writers, as presented in Yves Hervouet's study,[3] are different: intentionally or not, they are seamlessly woven into his own text as integral elements, distinguishable only to a specialist eye. In the case of Bobrowski's *Memoirs*, Conrad himself is signalling that he is, in a given fragment, paraphrasing a story which had been told by someone else.

hopes of liberty and international brotherhood, Bobrowski obtained a silver medal for his dissertation 'On Buying out Family Estates'. When we read in Bobrowski's memoirs the pages devoted to the time he spent at St Petersburg, it is impossible not to think about an analogy with another student of the same university – Kirylo Razumov of Conrad's *Under Western Eyes* – who also worked on an 'essay' for which he hoped to obtain a silver medal. What Razumov thinks about his irresponsible and garrulous conspiring comrades seems to echo Bobrowski's opinion about other Poles at St Petersburg University. And what Razumov says about Victor Haldin, a revolutionary, sounds similar to what Bobrowski writes about Zygmunt Sierakowski, later one of the leaders of the 1863 insurrection. There is even in Bobrowski's memoirs a story of an unexpected visit of a colleague 'who never before nor after came to my quarters', who asked what he intended to do 'in the face of the developments'. To which Bobrowski retorted: 'I intend to pass my final exam.'[4]

He passed his master's exam – international law and public law in Europe – on 14 December 1849, and shortly afterwards received the prestigious offer of the chair of international law at Kazan University. His father, however, objected to its acceptance: he wanted his son to pursue not an academic, but a diplomatic or administrative career in the capital itself. Bobrowski evidently considered his chances good, in spite of the fact that he was, as a Pole and a Catholic, refused the position of a councillor in the censorship office (!) at the Ministry of Education. But all his plans fell through when his father died suddenly on 1 November 1850.

Tadeusz Bobrowski was barely twenty-one, but the remainder of his life was to pass in the shade of that event. His elder brother, Stanisław, was by that time an officer of the Tsar's Guards, esteemed by superiors and much liked by his companions; important future promotions seemed well assured. His sisters and his brother Kazimierz were in their teens, the youngest brother Stefan was ten. Tadeusz Bobrowski, much to his chagrin, had to assume his duties as the head of the family.

He returned to the Ukraine and took over the running of the modest estate (Oratów) – left by his father in a fairly poor shape, with outstanding debts of 34.000 roubles (at that time about £5,000–6,000) and a pressing need to augment the number of oxen, used for ploughing. Tadeusz Bobrowski knew little about agriculture and was not much interested in it; he kept the administrator employed by his father and concentrated on financial management. Very quickly he earned the reputation of an excellent legal adviser, honest, scrupulously fair and independent. He served as executor of many testaments, arbitrator of conflicting estate claims, and the legal guardian of numerous wards – widows and orphans.

In June 1857 Bobrowski married Józefa Lubowidzka, the well-endowed daughter of a landowning family. Their marital happiness lasted only ten months: his wife died giving birth to a girl, also Józefa, who turned out to be a very sickly child, needing constant care. She died in 1871. Bobrowski never remarried. His parents-in-law proposed that he keep for life the estate of his late wife, but he declined this magnanimous offer and withdrew to the much smaller Kazimierówka, his own family's property. There he spent the rest of his life. He died suddenly on 10 February 1894, shortly before his sixty-fifth birthday.

3
'Sitting quietly in the country – "procul negotiis" – I do not have anything better to do than read and scribble. Therefore I compose my notes about affairs and men of my time – which some time, to somebody, may become useful for a picture of the affairs and men in our province.'[5] So wrote Bobrowski in 1880, shortly after beginning work on his memoirs. Thus he wrote no longer as an active participant but as an outsider, looking at those 'men and affairs' from a distance and with a critical, disillusioned, often jaundiced eye. He worked diligently – amassing an enormous amount of impressively detailed information – but unhastily, by 1892 bringing his story only up to 1863, as if he did not have anything really important to add. The memoirs, nearly one thousand pages in two volumes, were published posthumously in 1900 and created an angry uproar; not so much because of the author's controversial political and social opinions, as because of the incredible amount of gossip, mainly concerning illicit love affairs (some resulting in plebeian or Jewish blood in well-known families), financial misdeeds of all kinds, stupidity and alcoholism. The descendants concerned were understandably upset, and many copies of the book were apparently destroyed.[6] Bobrowski must have expended a lot of time on accumulating all these trivial and unsavoury stories. My guess is that behind it lay a gnawing conviction,

of which he may not have been entirely conscious, that his life had passed among people much below his own intellectual standards.

As a piece of literature, the memoirs are not remarkable. Bobrowski wrote without much care for style and grace of phrase; he aimed at precision and tended to achieve it by pedantry rather than clarity; he was exhaustive rather than expressive. He does not seem to have possessed any feeling for the aesthetic. There is nothing in his book about the charms of the Ukrainian landscape – so much a feature, to this day, of Polish literature; nothing about either the appearance of villages and manors, or local architecture and painting, although there was no lack of outstanding works of art in the vicinity and in the residences which Bobrowski visited. Again, we learn nothing about everyday life, local customs, or social relations, about food, dress, or games played. Unlike other memoirists of the region – and there were many, from Teodor Tomasz Jeż to the two Augusts Iwańskis (father and son) – Bobrowski evidently did not write to give a general picture of what he had seen and experienced, but only to note what was of interest to him. And his main interests were distinctly those of someone specializing in civil law.

It is mainly thanks to the wealth of incidents and anecdotes reported by the author that one may read the book with interest. Bobrowski's portrayals of innumerable personalities, known and unknown, are valuable thanks to his discriminating eye and impressive memory for detail. For a social historian of the time his book is a veritable mine of raw material, particularly concerning estates and financial deals, often grotesquely intricate. With precision and gusto he shows the role played by money in the life of the Polish landed nobility. Interestingly, he dwells rather on the ways money was lost than on the ways it was made; he looks at rural economy from the point of view of an accountant rather than of a manager. Perhaps we should not wonder; he himself was a country squire only by necessity.

The general impression of the Polish landowning class in the Ukraine one receives from Bobrowski's memoirs is quite unappealing. He accuses it of having narrow horizons, little education, social snobbery, laziness mixed or alternating with greed, etc. Was it really as bad as that? An attentive reading of the *Memoirs* reveals that the whole is judged to have been worse than the sum of its elements would indicate. Even from these pages it transpires that, in spite of the debilitating political atmosphere and stifling social conditions, the Polish community in the Ukraine produced a rich crop of outstanding men in all fields of activity, from science to industrial management to literature; but, as Bobrowski himself notices, the best of them perished in consecutive rebellions against the Russian rule or had to emigrate.

A reader of the *Memoirs* may never realize that its author almost completely ignored the existence of about 90 per cent of the population of the country he wrote about. Bobrowski lived most of his life (with the exception of a few years spent in St Petersburg) in the Ukraine; however, Ukrainians crop up only occasionally and on the margins of his horizon. Jews, with whom he must have had many contacts (they formed up to 50 per cent of the urban population – as in his county town, Lipowiec – and about 12 per cent of the total), are sometimes mentioned, but only as individuals. The peasants, on the contrary, exist only as a nameless mass, never singled out as persons.

In the *Memoirs* Ukrainians are denied a separate nationality and treated as Russians of a lesser breed: usually, Bobrowski does not even apply to them the name of 'Ruthenians', generally used at that time in Polish, but calls them 'Little Russians', in distinction from 'Great Russians', that is Russians proper.[7] In this he follows the Russian authorities and Russian nationalists in general, who even today refuse to recognize a distinct Ukrainian identity. He even confesses his own general repugnance to the 'Little Russians' (in the copy of the *Memoirs* once owned by Conrad, this fragment is marked in the margin).[8] Thus Bobrowski seems completely indifferent to the question which was fundamental to most politically active Poles and Ukrainians of his time: whether and how these two nationalities should co-operate in the face of Russian oppression. (On this issue men like the greatest Ukrainian national poet, Taras Shevchenko, and Conrad's father, Apollo Korzeniowski, were close allies.)

4

How reliable are Bobrowski's *Memoirs* as a documentary source? The answer cannot be simple, since in the case of many persons and events his evidence is unique. However, in matters which can be checked against other documents Bobrowski is quite often wrong, sometimes surprisingly so. Although ostensibly pedantic, he is not always reliable in his dating. For instance, it is hard to guess why he claims that his brother Stefan was born on 22 April 1841 and not on 17 January 1840. He gives two different dates for the marriage of his sister (26 and 28 April 1856) – both wrong, as she was married on 22 April (Julian calendar, i.e. 4 May Gregorian calendar). Michał Grabowski, a well-known conservative writer, did not drop his mission to St Petersburg (for which Bobrowski blames him) and go to Warsaw in 1861, but went there only two years later.[9] Often his errors seem to be a matter of an unconscious slip, as when he says that in April 1839 he was nine (and not ten).[10] Sometimes he pronounces on events and persons he knew too little about; e.g. he blames Ludwik Bernstein, 'a Jew from Warsaw', for betraying the location of a clandestine printing press in Kiev – while in fact the traitor was Leon Estreicher, a young officer of the Hussars.[11] And so on.

But it was impossible for Bobrowski not to have known that his sister, Conrad's mother, was also sentenced to exile. His claim that she accompanied her husband of her own free will makes nonsense of his own story of her compulsory return to Chernikhiv (retold by Conrad in *A Personal Record*).[12] Furthermore, writing about his wife's grandfather, General Stefan Lubowidzki, he denies the fact of the general's treason, although he must have known that for his going over to the Russian side Lubowidzki received from Catherine the Great not only the Cross of Alexander Nevsky, but also an award of 20,000 ducats.[13] Such skewed accounts betray his political bias; and there are many other instances of its presence. For example, Tadeusz Bobrowski knew little about his brother Stefan's beliefs and his position within the 'Red' movement of anti-Russian Polish patriots, none the less he denied, contrary to facts, his radicalism. What he wrote about the political circumstances of his brother's staged duel, in which Stefan was shot – in effect, being a very short-sighted person, murdered – by a representative of the 'Whites', is also incorrect in many important details.[14] (In Chapter 3, above, I point out several distortions of facts which resulted from Bobrowski's lack of sympathy for Apollo Korzeniowski.)

5

What were Tadeusz Bobrowski's own political convictions? It is not at all easy to sum them up. A closer look at his self-professed cool rationalism reveals awkward contradictions, and what he considered reasonable often transpires to be based largely on his own wishful thinking.

Both in his memoirs and in his letters Bobrowski repeatedly declares his deep attachment to Polish culture and tradition, and we have no reason to doubt his sincerity. However, this attachment seems to have been only a passive one. We find no evidence of his doing anything – outside his family circle – to oppose the officially enforced Russification or to help the people who, like his nephew Stanisław, imprisoned in 1892 for teaching workers, were trying to educate those who did not even have access to schools. As to whether he read contemporary Polish literature – we simply do not know, as he does not mention the names even of the best-known writers, such as Orzeszkowa, Prus and Sienkiewicz.

Bobrowski's attitude towards Russians was a mixture of spite, fear and resignation. He considered them culturally inferior to Poles. He describes in detail their practice of confiscating the estates of Polish landowners, either in reprisal for participation in uprisings and other patriotic involvements, or under some legal pretext. He was aware of the scale of repressions after each surge of Polish irredentist movements (e.g., a 10 per cent tax levied for five years on all Poles after the 1863 Rising). Even if he did not know Tsar Nicholas' stark question, posed in 1831 in a letter to his brother Grand Duke Constantine, then the Viceroy of Poland – 'Which one of the two nations has to die – as it seems that one should die – Russia or Poland?'[15] – still it is difficult to surmise on what ground this self-professed realist believed in the possibility of a 'peaceful and lawful development of the [Polish] nationality even if under Russian rule'.[16]

To make his own wishful thinking plausible, Bobrowski pronounced the Polish victims of the persecution guilty, because they had provoked their oppressors.[17] He gleefully stressed that aristocratic representatives of the Tsar's power often preferred, on social occasions like the governor-general's dancing parties, the company of the Polish nobility to that of their own bureaucracy; but he somehow missed the real meaning of these displays of class solidarity, which bound wealthy Poles with Russian autocracy.

Thus Bobrowski managed to combine nationalism with appeasement, the belief in Polish superiority with resignation from national self-defence. Shunning involvement in active opposition, he put his trust in the workings of history: 'we ... have to preserve our individuality and our own standpoint, till the time comes when Nemesis, as a result of our own efforts, spins out some situation which will give us the right to have a real national existence – and possibly something more'.[18] What

'Nemesis' stood for here – Laws of History? Divine Justice? – and how those 'efforts', limited to passive self-preservation, were supposed to influence her 'spinnings' were questions Bobrowski never answered. In his view, history was supposed to provide the motion; he himself did not have to intervene.

This basically quietist attitude found fuller expression in another of his letters to Conrad. He polemizes here with his nephew's pessimism:

> Thus my assertion is: that although this world is not the best that one could imagine, it is nevertheless the only one we know and is tolerable to the extent that we neither know any other nor are we able to create one; ... that [society] is open to improvement provided that individuals try to improve themselves, – which in turn is bound to take place provided that with the idea of duty ... they will combine not the idea of compulsion and necessity ... but the thought and conviction of the satisfaction arising from fulfilling altruistic duties.[19]

Bobrowski's musings are not quite consistent: a few sentences earlier he declares that 'you will never change the roads along which humanity goes' and advocates 'thinking of [one]self as a modest tiny ant which by its insignificant toil in fulfilling its modest duty secures the life and existence of the whole nest!' He is suspicious of all 'geniuses' and rails against 'visionaries', whom he characterizes as men shunning all practical work; it is clear that he disliked all leaders. His 'duty' comes therefore disturbingly close to unquestioning obedience; it seems to be a sort of a Hegelian submission to what has been preordained.

Anyway, what Bobrowski preaches here is not only an ethics of duty – which Conrad, as we know, embraced, although not in such a passive and individualistic version – but also a philosophy of optimistic determinism ('improvement ... is bound to take place'), which Conrad never accepted. His idea of morality is not only individualistic, but even reclusive: duty seems to be detached from all institutions, from any concrete community. It is a vision of morality characteristic of a loner who has made his loneliness a standard.

Tadeusz Bobrowski is often described as a progressive, enlightened liberal. Nineteenth-century European liberals, and their Polish equivalents commonly called the 'Positivists', were activists: they saw the material world as pliable, as a challenge and an opportunity, and were eager to instigate social reform, technological innovation and economic reform. If Bobrowski sympathized with them, he did it with full discretion. His reputation as a progressive is based on his participation (1858–9) in the local committees of landowners which prepared, for the central government, proposals of laws emancipating the peasantry. The obsolescence of the system of serfdom, still in force in the Russian Empire, was becoming evident even to conservatives. Bobrowski proposed its gradual abolition, as an 'unusual, abnormal and single' legal step, with the Government guaranteeing compensation to landowners. Even within the committees Bobrowski's position was that of a moderate; and we have to remember that men of more radical persuasion were *ipso facto* excluded from the assemblies invited to address the Russian authorities. In a situation where no open, uncensored expression of political opinion was possible, it is difficult to tell what the prevailing sentiments among the Polish landowning nobility really were. Bobrowski attached great importance to the work of the committees and described it in his memoirs in valuable detail. It is true that they formed a useful and unique platform for socio-economic discourse; however, the Tsarist authorities not only ignored their proposals, but in fact had never intended to consider them. The whole initiative was a ploy to keep Poles talking and divert them from more enterprising ideas.[20]

The abolishing of serfdom apart, Bobrowski – a cautious, soberminded man – did not share many of the lofty illusions of his more idealistic or more impatient contemporaries. He did not hide his disapproval of the ideas of the 'ultra-democrats', like his brother-in-law Korzeniowski, his brother Stefan, his nephew Stanisław, or the popular writer Józef Ignacy Kraszewski. It is worth pointing out, however, that those 'radicals' did not advocate granting the non-enfranchised masses any more privileges than those enjoyed by that time by the subjects of the emperors of Austria or Germany. This is the measure of Bobrowski's 'progressiveness'.

6

The Polish Rising of 1863–4 against Russian rule was the most important historical event Bobrowski witnessed. He condemned it vehemently, although all male members of his family, including his young brother Stefan who was one of the early civilian leaders of the uprising, were involved in this movement.

He accused the insurgents in the Ukraine of foolhardiness and ignorance. He thought they stood no chance of success given the Russian military superiority in numbers and weapons, and the sullen enmity of the local Ruthenian peasantry. He was right. The uprising was suppressed in a matter of days, with hundreds of insurgents killed in action, massacred by peasants or executed by the Russian authorities. There followed massive reprisals: thousands were imprisoned and sent into exile, hundreds of estates were confiscated, open and ruthless persecution of everything Polish set in. However, the uprising in the former eastern provinces ('the Borderlands') of the old Polish Commonwealth was only a spasmodic offshoot of the main movement, a desperate and abortive demonstration of solidarity and of fidelity to the dream of Poland within her pre-partition borders. While Tadeusz Bobrowski expressed his sorrow at the prospect that the former eastern provinces would be lost to Poland but did not intend to do anything about it, the insurgents wanted to re-establish, with their blood sacrifice, the link between Ruthenians and Poles, severed by class conflict.

In the ethnic Polish territories the insurrection continued for nearly two years, and its ultimate failure could not have been considered a foregone conclusion. Bobrowski denounces the entire movement in very harsh terms. One can fully sympathize with his bitterness and grief when he describes the desolation caused by the uprising in his homeland – but his general damning verdict does not convince. He lists the causes of the Rising as: first – false, misleading foreign trends and influences, particularly the intrigues of Napoleon III and the beguiling example of the recent Italian success in the assertion of the 'national principle'; second – the volatile, fickle and credulous character of Poles; third – memories of the Russian oppression of the period 1831–55; fourth – excessive expectations aroused by the more liberal rule of Tsar Alexander II.[21] Most historians would not agree with him, and dismiss the first cause as a real factor. What is, however, most significant is that Bobrowski does not even mention, here or elsewhere, the role of the protest against the lack of national independence! The latent conflict between the democratic traditions of Poland and the autocratic rule of the Tsars is dressed up by him as Polish volatility and fickleness.

For the insurgents, the Russian yoke was an outrage, to be removed as quickly as possible and by the use of all available means. For

Bobrowski, the Tsar's power was a fact, a given; Poles had no chance of overthrowing it and had to wait. For what? His answer: 'after an era of moral and material exhaustion there must come an "epoch of peace and reconciliation", an epoch of reflection on the part of the strong and mighty, that will enable the weak and oppressed to live and rise in the name of the holiest interests of mankind and of nations'.[22] This blatantly ahistorical optimism of the 'rationalist' is no wiser than the romantic enthusiasm of the insurgents; and, one may add, even more dangerous to the existence of the nation. After all, the sacrifice of Stefan Bobrowski and Apollo Korzeniowski pointed to the future: they became national heroes. Tadeusz Bobrowski's unrealistic 'reasonableness' pointed to nothing. He refused to admit that the situation of Poland was tragic. There was simply no hope for a rebirth of national independence without active resistance; and active resistance implied death, imprisonment, exile.

With all his sharp, critical mind Bobrowski had no feel for historical change and no understanding of the need for more far-reaching social reforms. He blamed the Rising for the Tsar's failure to implement the projects of peasant reform prepared by the Polish landowners' committees. Absurdly: we know that such an implementation was never even considered. But in expressing that blame he missed something much more important: in March 1864, prompted by the Polish underground National Government proclamation (of January 1863) which abolished serfdom, the Russian Government changed the rules of the emancipation and made them more favourable to peasants....

Bobrowski imagined (and claimed in his memoirs) that as a law-abiding man, whose anti-irredentist attitude was generally known, he was trusted by the authorities and thus not subject to police supervision. He was deluding himself, as we know today from police archives.[23] This delusion of a man lost in the whirlwind of history looks symbolic.

7

Was his self-delusion the source of his political dogmatism – or rather, as I suspect, its consequence, an attitude assumed in the face of his own isolation and helplessness, political as well as intellectual? There is some evidence to suggest that initially, in the late fifties and early sixties, Bobrowski was not as hostile to Polish irredentism as later, at the time of writing his memoirs.²⁴ With age, he grew more embittered and doctrinaire, frustrated by remaining in the margin, cut off from public life. Conscious of having wasted his life, of having lived below his abilities and ambitions of becoming a diplomat or international lawyer, he put the blame not on the objective circumstances of a foreign oppression, but on the alleged sins of his own compatriots. Why? I think he wanted to bolster his feeling of superiority over his social milieu. He did not wish to admit that his attitude of an appeaser did not make him much different in the eyes of Russian authorities, who saw him as just another Pole.

Even his lack of physical fitness served to isolate him from his neighbours: he never learned to swim, shoot, ride, or drive. 'Physically weak, I was unable to take part in games natural to boys; I preferred to sit quietly on a small stool in the corner and to listen to adult conversation.'²⁵ Nor did he share their religious beliefs: he was apparently an agnostic. His tolerant parish priest gave him, nevertheless, a good testimony: 'Bobrowski ready to help others, would offer best advice to many, generous to the poor, never came to church, never confessed, did not observe fasts.'²⁶

> ... a convinced doctrinaire, deeply confident in the inflexible and unchanging laws and duties of reason, critical judgement and free will which make man a master of his own fate and history, and rejecting all external influences of feeling, passions, and one's environment, possessing for every problem of life a ready formula obtained by abstract reasoning ... I would bring ... my sister [Ewa] to tears. Once, in the heat of discussion, she told me that if I were brought by the strength of my reasoning to the conclusion that she ought to be killled, I would be capable of grasping a knife and slaughtering her!²⁷

This is how Bobrowski presented himself, not without pride, in his memoirs. It seems to be a fair description. 'Abstract reasoning' would not, in fact, induce him to feel a *moral* distinction between those inclined to doubt everything (as himself) and those ready to risk everything (as his sister and brothers). As innumerable other Poles, he had the bad luck of having been born at the wrong time and place. His best qualities destined him to live in an independent country and in peaceful times, with no need to make tragic choices between treason, isolation and self-sacrifice.

He was proud, scrupulously honest and ready to help others – but also cold and suspicious of more emotional persons. In his memoirs he mentions in passing that as a young man he sowed some wild oats, was an object of sexual attention for elder women, and even contracted a 'discreet disease' – but never alludes to being in love. Even the courtship of his wife (who had 'wonderfully beautiful eyes' and a good figure, although 'mouth and teeth not pretty') he described in words more suitable to a marriage counsellor than to a man in love.[28]

8

Bobrowski, early widowed and then left alone after the death of his daughter, spiritually isolated even within his own family, was also a man very unhappy in his personal life. His probity and demonstrative shunning of politics made him a perfect guardian of orphans. He formed a close relationship with only one of them: the future Joseph Conrad.

It was certainly not a case of instant attraction. Bobrowski's early letters to his ward evidence frequent frustrations and disappointments, lack of understanding and irritation. It was only after some ten years of guardianship, and a good few after Conrad had left Poland, that admonitions and remonstrations – usually couched in the terms of a contrast, highly mythological and not substantiated by facts, between the fickle Korzeniowskis and the steadfast Bobrowskis – began to ebb. After a lapse of five years the two men met again in 1883 in Marienbad (now Mariánské Lázně) – Conrad could not come to visit his uncle as he was still a Russian subject without a valid passport – and after that meeting their relations took a turn for more mutual sympathy.

Even Conrad's foibles were made exotic and coloured by his remoteness, while Bobrowski's troubles with other members of his family remained simply commonplace and everyday irritations. Conrad would squander money in an adventurous manner, in bizarre enterprises and mysterious accidents; brother Kazimierz Bobrowski and then his orphaned children needed money for coal and clothes and meat. Conrad progressed in his arcane career as a British seaman, far from domestic entanglements; meanwhile his geographically less-distant cousins would get involved in conspiracies of which Bobrowski disapproved.

And so, with the years, a deepening and reciprocal emotional attachment developed. Bobrowski's personality mellowed; still 'doctrinaire', especially in political matters, he became psychologically more tolerant.

His correspondence with Conrad became his sentimental outlet; the son of his beloved sister brought out the best in Bobrowski. As the years went by, the difference in age between uncle and nephew became less and less important. Two lonely men – although isolated for very different reasons – reached out to each other and saw in each other a depository of their longings. Distance brought them psychologically closer together, helping in mutual idealization.

9

Bobrowski was in fact the 'true discoverer of Conrad's literary talent', *pace* the later conflicting claims of Wilfred Hugh Chesson and Edward Garnett.[29] As early as 1881 he praised his nephew's writing skills and suggested that he begin sending regular correspondence to a well-known Warsaw weekly, *Wędrowiec* (The Wanderer).[30] The letters to his uncle, spanning twenty formative years (1874–94) of Conrad's life, were burned, together with the family manor at Kazimierówka, at the time of the Bolshevik Revolution. This constitutes a great loss not only to Conrad's biographers, but to literature in general: there were probably close to a hundred of them, several apparently concerning the same subjects Conrad would raise later in his fiction and about thirty written at the time he was working on *Almayer's Folly*.

Most of Bobrowski's letters to his nephew have been preserved and they constitute an invaluable – for several years the only – mine of biographical information. We learn from them about epilepsy, from which Conrad suffered as a child, about the uncertain beginnings of his maritime service, his attempted suicide in 1878, his intricate financial schemes, his political opinions, etc.[31]

And not only that: Bobrowski's letters often throw interesting light on Conrad's tales and novels. Thus those from 1881–2 confirm the authenticity of many details, concerning the ill-fated barque *Judea* in 'Youth'; and those of 1876–7 testify that *The Arrow of Gold*, regarded sometimes (according to Conrad's own suggestion in his 'Author's Note') as an autobiographical novel, presents much more fiction than truth.

Bobrowski attentively followed Conrad's African adventure, which would later provide the factual background for 'Heart of Darkness'. He was sceptical from the beginning. His letter of 24 June 1890, written at the time when Conrad was just beginning his trek inland, contains an innocuous but revealing fragment: 'You are probably looking around at people and things as well as at the "civilizing" (confound it) affair in the machinery of which you are a cog.' In 'Heart of Darkness' it is not the narrator, Marlow, but the monstrous Kurtz who goes into the depths of the Congo believing in his 'civilizing' mission; evidently, Conrad had his illusions which his uncle did not share.

Other statements crop up in Bobrowski's letters which sound like unexpected and prophetic commentaries on Conrad's much later work. 'You are obstinate, my dear lad, or is it the professional code of honour or the customs of the country you are living in that account for your sailing on such a miserable ship and risking your neck?' he wrote on 26 May 1882, as if not about second mate Korzeniowski but about one of Conrad's fictional characters. And in the letter of 9 November 1891 (quoted above) which contains Bobrowski's polemic with his nephew's 'pessimism' and his own philosophical credo we read the words: 'I have developed in myself this calm outlook on the problem of life, whose motto, I venture to say, was, is, and will be "usque ad finem" the devotion to duty interpreted more widely or narrowly, according to the circumstances and time.' The analogy with one of the pivotal scenes of *Lord Jim*, where Stein talks with Marlow about the 'romantic' personality of Jim and formulates the answer to his own question – 'How to be?' – is obvious. But there is also a significant difference: for Bobrowski the 'usque ad finem' formula encapsulates his lesson of stoical resignation and obedience to duty; whereas for Stein it points to dreams, which perhaps would never be realized, but which give meaning to our lives: 'That was the way. To follow the dream, and again to follow the dream – and so – *ewig* – *usque ad finem*.[32]

However, the most obvious and important instance of Bobrowski's influence on Conrad's writings is his memoirs, published in 1900 and sent to Conrad next year – curiously enough, not by a member of his family but by a Cracow librarian.[33] He used them as a source both in his reminiscences, *A Personal Record*, and in his tale 'Prince Roman'. The latter borrowing has attracted more attention and has been carefully analysed.[34] The former was noted for the first time by Rafał Blüth in his 1939 study on 'two borderland families'[35] and presented more fully in my paper, published in 1964.[36]

Thus Bobrowski and Conrad write about Conrad's mother Ewa and her sister Teofila:[37]

Conrad:

... the girls took it in turn week and week about ... Driving home one wintry afternoon to keep me company ... they lost the road and got stuck in a snowdrift. She was alone with the coachman and old Valery, the personal servant of our father. Impatient of delay while they were trying to dig themselves out, she jumped out of the sledge and went to look for the road herself ... She made light of the cough which came on next day, but shortly afterwards inflammation of the lungs set in, and in three weeks she was no more! (pp. 29–30)

Bobrowski:

My sisters fulfilled their promise and took weekly turns to keep me company at Oratów. On one journey the sledge in which my younger sister was travelling got stuck and she was forced to get out into the snow; as a result she caught a slight cold and began to cough, but as her health was on the whole quite good, no one paid any special attention. However ... her condition suddenly deteriorated. She developed a galloping consumption and died within six weeks.

She did not shine so much by personal beauty and a cultivated mind, in which your mother was far superior. It was her good sense, the admirable sweetness of her nature, her exceptional facility and ease in daily relations that endeared her to everybody. Her death was a terrible grief and a serious moral loss for us all. Had she lived she would have brought the greatest blessings to the house it would have been her lot to enter, as wife, mother and mistress of the household. She would have created around herself an atmosphere of peace and content which only those who can love unselfishly are able to evoke. Your mother – of far greater beauty, exceptionally

[Teofila's] outstanding qualities were not so much her education and beauty – in which my elder sister excelled, although she had a pleasant appearance and an adequate education – but her common sense, sweet disposition, and an ability to adapt herself to people and situations. Her death was a great moral loss to us all, for it deprived us of that everyday assistance which can only be given by a woman convinced that in family life every occupation is worthwhile as long as it may bring satisfaction to someone. I am certain that if she had lived she would have brought a blessing to her home as a wife, mother, and mistress of the house; and that she would always distinguished in person, manner and intellect – had a less easy disposition. Being more brilliantly gifted, she also expected more from life. At that time, especially, we were greatly concerned about her state. Suffering in her health from the shock of her father's death (she was alone in the house with him when he died suddenly), she was torn by the inward struggle between her love for the man whom she was to marry in the end and her knowledge of her father's declared objection to that match. Unable to bring herself to disregard that cherished memory and that judgment she had always respected and trusted, and, on the other hand, feeling the impossibility to resist a sentiment so deep and so true, she could not have been expected to preserve her mental and moral balance. At war with herself, she could not give to others that feeling of peace which was not her own. It was only later, when united at last with the man of her choice, that she developed those uncommon gifts of mind and heart which compelled the respect and admiration even of our foes. Meeting with calm fortitude the cruel trials of a life reflecting all the national and social misfortunes of the community, she realised the highest conceptions of duty of a wife, a mother and a patriot, sharing the exile of her husband and representing nobly the ideal of Polish womanhood. (pp. 28–9)

have exuded that atmosphere of contentment which she had the ability to create under all circumstances. My elder sister possessed beauty and worldly deportment, her education was above that of contemporary women, her mind very lively and heart very warm; she was not as complaisant [as Teofila] and her demands more difficult to meet, and at that time needed more attention from others than she was able and prepared to give herself.

As she was rather weak in health, the conflict between her love for her future husband and the known will of her father, whose memory and opinion she cherished, naturally upset her inner balance; dissatisfied with herself, she could not give others what she lacked herself. Only once united with her beloved man, was she able to develop fully her unusual qualities of intelligence, feeling, mind, and heart. Amidst the greatest hardships of personal life, beset by all possible national and social misfortunes, she always knew how to choose, and with fortitude adhere to, her duties as wife, mother, and citizen, winning the respect of her own kin and of strangers, sharing her husband's exile and representing Polish womankind with dignity.

Bobrowski about himself:

I was the most frail at birth of all the children. For years I remained so delicate that my parents had but little hope of bringing me up; and yet I have survived five brothers and two sisters, and many of my contemporaries; I have outlived my wife and daughter, too – and from all those who have had some knowledge at least of these old times, you alone are left. It has been my lot to lay in an early grave many honest hearts, many brilliant promises, many hopes full of life. (p. 30)	The years of infancy and childhood did not augur well for my life or health . . . Yet things turned out contrary to human expectations! Among numerous and much stronger siblings I survived four brothers and two sisters and many other contemporaries, as well as my wife and daughter. In my family only one brother and one nephew are left. Thus, many of hopes full of life I had to bury prematurely . . .

The above fragments are the easiest to spot, because Conrad identifies them himself as told by his uncle. However, there are more borrowings and quotations which we find in the main flow of narration, coming ostensibly straight from the reminiscing author. Thus about Mikołaj Bobrowski, Tadeusz's uncle:

Under his taciturn, phlegmatic behaviour was hidden a faculty of short-lived, passionate anger. [p. 47] . . . for grand-uncle Nicholas differed in this from the generality of military men of Napoleon's time (and perhaps of all time) that he did not like to talk of his campaigns . . . His admiration of the great Emperor was unreserved in everything but expression. Like the religion of earnest men, it was too profound a sentiment to be displayed before a world of little faith . . . Proud of his decorations, earned before he was twenty-five, he . . . even was unwilling to display the insignia on festive occasions, as though he	By temperament he was a melancholic and a recluse, and although outwardly phlegmatic he was easily roused . . . Through his life he worshipped Napoleon, without any reserve in the depths of his thought, as he did not like to talk about this; also, unlike other Napoleonic soldiers at the time he never spoke about his own exploits, although he had been decorated with the Legion of Honour and the military cross. Temporarily an officier d'ordonnance to Marshal Marmont, he was the last to ride the bridge in Leipzig before it was blown up, as he himself carried the specific order. He was wounded only once,

wished to conceal them in the fear of appearing boastful. 'It is enough that I have them,' he used to mutter. In the course of thirty years they were seen on his breast only twice – at an auspicious marriage in the family and at the funeral of an old friend . . . he was the last man to ride over the bridge of the river Elster after the battle of Leipzig. (pp. 46–7)

But his phlegmatic physiognomy lighted up when he spoke of his only wound, with something resembling satisfaction. You will see that there was some reason for it when you learn that he was wounded in the heel. 'Like his Majesty the Emperor Napoleon himself,' he reminded his hearers with assumed indifference. (p. 48)

    His nephew (my uncle and guardian) told me that the first lasting impression on his memory as a child of four was the glad excitement reigning in his parents' house on the day when Mr Nicholas B. arrived home from his detention in Russia [p. 56]. In 1831, on the outbreak of the Revolution, Mr Nicholas B. was the senior captain of his regiment. Some time before he had been made head of the remount establishment quartered outside the kingdom in our southern provinces, whence almost all the horses for the Polish cavalry were drawn . . . At the first news of the rising in Warsaw, all the remount establishment, officers,

in the heel like the G[reat] Napoleon himself, a fact he would occasionally mention in moments of good humour. He never wore his decorations, saying that to have them was enough. Yet I saw him twice wearing medals: in 1837 at the wedding of his friend Konstanty Bernatowicz and twenty years later at my own.

My first childhood memories go back to 1833. I was just over four years old at the time and and the first event which struck my childish memory and imagination was my uncle's (Mikołaj Bobrowski's) return from exile in Russia. At the time of the outbreak of the 1831 insurrection my uncle, responsible for remounting the 2nd regiment of horse fusiliers of the P[olish] a[rmy], had been staying at Biłołówka (then Machnów district), the main rallying point of the P[olish] a[rmy] remounts. There all the officers responsible for remounting had been arrested and deported first to Kozielec (Chernikhiv province) and vets., and the very troopers, were put promptly under arrest and hurried off in a body beyond the Dnieper to the nearest town in Russia proper. From there they were dispersed to the distant parts of the Empire . . . Astrakhan was his destination . . . Declining the option offered him to enter the Russian army, he was retired with only half the pension of his rank. (pp. 54–6)

later to the depths of Russia. In my uncle's case it was first Vyatka and later Astrakhan. In 1833 he returned home, having been discharged with only half of the pension he was qualified for, because of his refusal to join the Russian army.

Other borrowings: the sordid story of Bobrowski's grandmother Katarzyna née Błażowska and her second husband, Leon Staniszewski, as told in *A Personal Record* (*APR*, pp. 49–53), follows closely *Pamiętnik* (I, pp. 49–51); the scene of the compulsory return of the ailing Ewa Korzeniowska with her son to exile (*APR*, pp. 64–7) is sketched out in the memoirs (II, pp. 458–9); the description of the pillage of Mikołaj Bobrowski's manor in 1863 (*APR*, pp. 57–63) is based on Bobrowski's note (II, p. 489). Apart from these longer fragments Conrad used also numerous details taken from his uncle's bulky volumes; in fact, we can trace there many if not most of the specific information concerning Polish matters contained in *A Personal Record*. And thus we discover the cousin of Mr Nicholas B., an ex-officer of the Austrian army, proud of his distinctions and official discharge with the word 'unschreckbar' in it, in the *Pamiętnik* (I, p. 64) under the name of Piotr de Biberstein Pilchowski.

Spinning out his narrative, Conrad developed and adjusted Bobrowski's text, making his anecdotes more pointed and adding lyrical or ironic comments. From time to time he would get mixed up, as when he changed the school at Lubar, attended by Mikołaj Bobrowski, from one run by the Dominicans into one directed by Benedictines (*APR*, p. 53) and described it as, to boot, the only one 'of some standing then in the south', which was far from the truth. Generally, the 'Polish' parts of *A Personal Record* offer an excellent example of Conrad's writing method: to ground his story even in the smallest detail on documentary or remembered factual material – and to weave the tale freely, treating this material in the same fashion as he treats elements garnered from other times and places and his own imagination.

10

I opened this chapter by quoting Conrad's general assessments of his uncle's role in his life. The words 'although he did not understand' point to an essential factor in their relationship: it was one of contrasting personalities, first clashing and then becoming complementary; of two men of markedly different ways of experiencing and interpreting reality, who in the course of twenty-five years kept affecting each other. Conrad's influence on Bobrowski we can only guess at, as we observe the evolution of the latter's attitude towards his nephew. Bobrowski's sermons on the need for stability of plans and reliability in work were addressed to a young man whose behaviour notoriously clashed with these postulates.

The uncle-guardian made a strenuous effort to inculcate in his ward the qualities of responsibility and thrift. '... don't idle, learn, and don't pretend to be a rich young gentleman and wait for someone to pull your chestnuts out of the fire – for this will not happen ... do something, earn something, for one cannot be a parasite' (8 July 1878). 'You would not be a Nałęcz, dear boy, if you were steady in your enterprises ... But I would not be myself and your uncle if I did not discourage you from changing professions and did not warn you that such changes make people become déclassé ... Work and perseverance are the only values that never fail' (30 May 1880). 'I am by no means against speculation, providing it is done with one's own money which one has earned and saved, but I am when it is based on borrowed capital. "Hope is the Mother of fools and calculation the Father of the sober-minded"; so goes the proverb' (15 August 1881).

If he did not fully succeed in making the adult Conrad stable in his plans and reasonable in his financial affairs, at least his lessons were fully absorbed in the moral messages conveyed in Conrad's work. On the psychological plane, Bobrowski's gospel of duty to be practised in everyday life kept colliding with the young Korzeniowski's propensity for day-dreaming and recklessness. But on the level of ethics the same gospel overlapped with the legacy of Apollo Korzeniowski and the entire tradition of Polish Romanticism. Polish Romantic writers had preached the supremacy of duty as well – first of all to one's *patria*, home country, but also to the ideals of justice and truth. Thus these very elements of Bobrowski's message which clashed with his nephew's personal inclinations would enrich his philosophical consciousness. Stoicism did not preclude romanticism but added to it a firmer and more complex fibre.

There were, however, in Bobrowski's teachings two salient elements which Conrad never accepted but kept turning over in his mind and his work. The first was his general attitude of a reconciliation with existing reality; the second was his historical optimism. The former was grounded in Bobrowski's quietism, the latter in his rationalistic determinism.

> My dear lad, whatever you were to say about a good or bad balance of the forces of nature, about good or bad social relationships, about right or wrong social systems, about the boundless stupidity of crowds fighting for a crust of bread . . . You will never control the forces of nature . . . you will also never change the roads along which humanity goes, for there exists in social development an historical evolutionary compulsion which is slow but sure, and which is governed by the laws of cause and effect.

And then, in the words quoted above, he asserts that although the world around us is not the best imaginable, it is still 'tolerable' as the only possible one.[38]

There was a political edge to the above 'consolations'. In the Conclusion of his memoirs Bobrowski wrote:

> The reason for this [present], if I may so call it, 'bestialization' of governments and peoples is their mania for grandeur, their exaggerated national egoism, their disregard of principles for the sake of gain, their worship of power and success justifying the use of all available means! Such tendencies are and must be only momentary phases in the general evolution of mankind and it seems to me that this detrimental tide . . . will pass . . . and must pass . . . with this conviction I look to the future . . . in which I trust.[39]

In Conrad's copy of the memoirs this fragment is marked on the margin with a big question mark.

Were Bobrowski to wonder what caused his nephew's doubts, he should have blamed himself. He managed to persuade Conrad of the futility of armed resistance, but failed to convert him to his belief in the inevitability of historical progress. And, specifically, Conrad never shared Bobrowski's illusions about Russia and her designs.* Bobrowski, even when complaining bitterly about Russian persecution of Poles, never analysed and questioned the prevailing system of government; for Conrad the problem of Tsarist political oppression was both national and structural: Russia was not only imperialist, but autocratic.

To sum up: while Bobrowski failed to eradicate Conrad's romanticism, he infected him with scepticism. And the most important result of this influence was a strengthening of the tragic tensions that form the base of Conrad's best work: the tensions between enthusiasm for man's abilities and a merciless exposure of the hidden weaknesses of the noblest heroes; between the protest against injustice and disbelief in the possibility of change; between the romantic urge to improve this world and the conviction of the futility of all great human endeavours; between patriotic fidelity and despair in the chances of the Polish struggle. All Conrad's major works vibrate with these tensions: with the conflicts between the consciousness of a necessity of unquestionable norms and ideals – and a sceptical awareness of human frailty, of the absolute moral indifference of nature, of the crushing powers of cupidity and ignorance.

Continued internal strife was for Conrad a painful, exhausting and necessary element of his greatness as a writer. I think that Tadeusz Bobrowski was the initiator of this gnawing, troublesome and priceless demon. If so, then Conrad was right to confess, when he learned about the death of his uncle, that he felt: 'as if everything has died in me. He seems to have carried my soul away with him.'[41]

---

* He apparently had some about Panslavism, but we know about them only from Bobrowski's response. I supppose that he stumbled upon the idea of Panslavism when he looked for something consoling on his political horizon.[40]

5

The Sisters: a grandiose failure

Joseph Conrad did not finish two of his novels: one at the beginning of his writing career, the other at its very end. *The Sisters* and *Suspense* differ in many ways. The former was quickly dropped for good, the latter occupied Conrad's mind for at least twelve years, and he kept returning to it over and over again. Compared with *The Sisters*, *Suspense* shows signs of its author's age and weariness. The narrative form of the two works is quite dissimilar. Even the faults of both stories lie at opposite poles: while the language of *The Sisters* errs in the direction of recherché rhetoric, that of *Suspense* occasionally veers into banality and glibness.

Still, the two unfinished novels have a couple of things in common. Both are thoroughly European in their background and subject, and both are imposingly ambitious in their thematic sweep. Among Conrad's completed works only *Nostromo* and perhaps *Under Western Eyes* can match the scope of *Suspense*.

The grandness of the design of *The Sisters* has been little noted so far. It was Conrad's third story; he began it immediately after completing *An Outcast of the Islands* in the latter part of 1895. After the two exotic tales, *Outcast* and *Almayer's Folly*, *The Sisters* was an attempt at a completely different theme: Europe and the modern world. The actual writing of the piece was not easy. Edward Garnett, an experienced critic and Conrad's first 'literary' friend, was negative in his appraisal of the manuscript's beginning. He advised Conrad to abandon his tale of the 'land' and instead make use of his experiences in the tropics and on the high seas. As a result Conrad ceased working on *The Sisters* and began *The Rescue*, with which he also had great difficulties, finally finishing it only in 1919. His next novel, however, *The Nigger of the 'Narcissus'*, turned out to be one of the greatest achievements in the genre of the sea story.

We find the last mention of the abandoned *Sisters* in a letter from Conrad to Garnett written on 9 April 1896.[1] The extant chapters of the novel appeared in 1928, after Conrad's death, and remained relatively unknown. The fragment of *The Sisters* is short, about forty pages in manuscript. It consists of seven chapters and contains two completely different plots. The first four chapters deal with a young Ruthenian painter from Russia travelling through Western Europe and becoming increasingly disillusioned. The remainder of the narrative presents the lives of two orphaned Basque sisters; one of the sisters is reared by her uncle in a Parisian suburb – the same suburb in which the young artist, Stephen, comes to live. These two plots (chapters I–IV and V–VIII respectively) do not converge. Every student of Conrad can immediately see the correlation between the 'Basque' sections of *The Sisters* and *The Arrow of Gold* – a late (1919) and weak novel, commonly though with scant justification considered to be an autobiographical piece. In both novels there are two sisters, Rita and Theresa. Both pairs of sisters have an uncle who is an austere Basque priest. In *The Arrow of Gold* Rita is the lover of a wealthy French painter, Henry Allègre.

English and American critics have given little attention to *The Sisters*, in particular to its 'Russian' sections. Their interests have centred mostly on biographical issues and particularly on the question why Conrad never completed his story. There have been several hypotheses offered on this point; however, all theories seem to have one element in common: *The Sisters* is considered to have little artistic value. Most critics agree that Conrad's portrayal of his protagonist is vague and banal; Stephen is presented in a stereotypical and unfocused way. Furthermore, the style is belaboured and unexpressive; artificial and confused phrases often lapse into grammatical error.

The pompous awkwardness of style can be seen as a sign of the more profound difficulties Conrad was having with the subject. (We find a similar style in 'The Return', begun immediately before *The Sisters* and always disliked by its author.) Conrad himself confessed eighteen years later that he had abandoned *The Sisters* 'in despair of being able to keep up the high pitch'.[2] Ford Madox Ford contends that Conrad wanted to develop *The Sisters* into a dramatic tale of incest culminating in the murder of the lovers by the fanatical uncle-priest, but that the character of the ascetic Basque curate was basically too similar to the character of the priest in Maupassant's *Une vie* for Conrad to handle.[3] However, even apart from Ford's notorious unreliability, his theory concerns only the hypothetical conclusion of the book, which Conrad could, after all, have ended differently. It is also possible that Ford never talked with Conrad about *The Sisters* and that all he says about the story is sheer fabrication. Ford's hypotheses bear little relation to the existing text; he even fails to notice the analogies between *The Sisters* and *The Arrow of Gold*.

Jocelyn Baines supposes *The Sisters* was put aside on the advice of Garnett who found the text 'stilted and lifeless': it 'reads like a painstaking exercise in the art of fine writing'.[4] Albert Guerard, also analysing the style, concludes that neither the subject-matter nor the method of writing suited Conrad. Guerard believes that the beginning of the story contains obvious ingredients of a clumsily camouflaged and youthfully naive autobiography and that Conrad had enough critical sense to see that he was writing 'with the monotony of one blowing up balloons of the same kind, one after another'.[5] Thomas Moser, author of the classic psychologically oriented study of the 'achievement and decline' of Conrad's art, sees in the discarded novel additional evidence that a convincing and non-ironic description of love between two normal European people was a goal which Conrad could not achieve. Moser directs our attention to the surprising echoes of the tropics in Conrad's description of Parisian suburbs:

> Below in the damp and uniform gloom the grass sprang up vigorous and conquering, over that desolate remnant of beauty; covering the ground thickly with a prosperous, flourishing growth in a triumph of undistinguishably similar blades that pressed thick, low, full of life around the foot of soaring trunks of the trees; the grass unconquerable, content with the gloom, disputing sustenance with the roots, vanquishing the slender trees that strove courageously even there to keep their heads in the splendour of sunshine.[6]

Moser suggests that the character of Rita is associated with the images of narcotic fragrances and flourishing vegetation, images which prepare us for Stephen's subjugation.

Moser's theory that Conrad put *The Sisters* aside because he was unable to manage the erotic elements of the plot seems to me unconvincing. First, it is based on the assumption that a 'normal' love story was to form the skeleton of the entire plot; it is difficult to consider this as more than just a possibility. Secondly, it does not explain in the least the striking weakness of the opening chapters. Thirdly, it does not answer the question why Conrad abandoned the novel before even beginning to write about love. If love was really to have been the theme of *The Sisters*, then it is safe to assume that Conrad was aware of this from the very beginning; however, the text abruptly halts before any erotic action begins. I think the reason why Conrad did not continue his story must be sought in the novel itself, not elsewhere.

Moser concludes that

> Whatever the reason for Conrad's inability to continue with *The Sisters*, there can be little doubt that his decision was right. Even as a first draft, this is a most unpromising fragment. The prose exhibits great uncertainty of tone; it virtually collapses under the weight of abstract nouns: 'the western life captivated him by the amplitude of its complicated surface, horrified him by the interior jumble of its variegated littleness.' Although Conrad throughout his career almost never completely escapes the cliché, *The Sisters* reaches a low point in banality. 'He thought: It is dark now but tomorrow is another day.' *The Sisters*, then, would have been a step backward when Conrad was really on the threshold of great things; only a few months later he was to begin one of his most nearly perfect works, *The Nigger of the 'Narcissus'*.[7]

Such an unequivocal interpretation and assessment contrasts with the only Polish study of *The Sisters*, 'An Island in the Polish Gulf' by Kazimierz Wyka, an eloquent and attractive piece, published in 1964.[8] Wyka considers *The Sisters* a great work: 'this solitary arm of the statue remains a masterpiece'.[9] He finds Conrad's story closely connected with Polish literature: 'a story consistent in its reflection of the Polish romantic tradition and in more than one aspect a story also indicative of this tradition's contemporary [to Conrad] trend in Polish literature'.[10] Wyka's commentary concentrates exclusively on the first four chapters of *The Sisters* – he does not discuss the remainder of the novel, as if it did not exist. He evidently assumes that the novel was to develop the plot of the life of an East European living in the West, although the existing fragment does not support such an assumption and the title, *The Sisters*, seems even to contradict it. Wyka deeply regrets that Conrad never completed his novel.

What are the causes of such a radically different assessment? First, Wyka bases his opinions on a Polish translation of *The Sisters* rather than on the English original. This translation, the pet project of the Conrad enthusiast Wit Tarnawski, is clearly better than the original; it is better because of its firmer style and more precise use of language – but it is also better in other respects. In smoothing the style and enlivening the tone the translator supplants those suggested by the original with different literary and intellectual associations. For example, by simplifying Conrad's sentence about life in the West ('at the same time it startled one with its inner disorder and smallness'), Tarnawski tones down the blatant abstraction of the novel's style. By giving the translated text a particular temper, which brings to mind Stefan Żeromski,* Tarnawski raises the fragments with reflections about life from a level of empty wittiness to one of rhetorical sublimity and a concern with the deeper meaning of human existence. In any event, it should be noted that in Polish, which is saturated with the romantic tradition (as German is saturated with philosophical idealism), grandiloquent sentences seem sensible even when they actually make little sense.

Such stylistic improvement, however, does not suffice to hide the banality of ideas and the artistic frailty of *The Sisters*. Stephen's vague musings ('I want to know... don't ask what – what some other knew and died without telling'); the lameness of metaphors ('They also [the deserts] would speak in glorious promises only to cast him down at last from the pinnacle of his expectations'); the emptiness of Stephen's aesthetic endeavours (how much more real in this respect are his literary cousins, Teobald in Henry James' *The Madonna of the Future* or Pellerin in *L'Education sentimentale*!); the entirely non-painterlike sensitivity which this 'painter' exhibits; and the absence of any references to contemporary or past art all serve to render Stephen an indistinct, papier-mâché protagonist.

Still, in spite of all its faults and weaknesses, *The Sisters* succeeded in attracting the attention and sympathy of Kazimierz Wyka, one of the

---

* A leading Polish prose writer of the turn of the century (1864–1925).

most outstanding Polish critics of the twentieth century. Why? There was another, more significant reason for his interest. The only well-written sections of the novel are those which portray the Ukraine, Stephen's homeland.[11] These descriptions strike a familiar chord in any lover of Polish literature. In these scenes, and also in Stephen's meditations, Wyka heard clear echoes of Mickiewicz's poetry, as well as – although more vague – reminiscences of other Polish poets. Wyka's interest in and partiality to *The Sisters* stem from these sections, and he concentrates his attention only on the elements he favours. Hence his opinion that *The Sisters* 'is permeated in its tiniest stylistic components not only with the romantic tradition of Polish literature, but also with its present'.[12]

Unfortunately, those clear echoes are mainly illusions, and Wyka's flattering vision of *The Sisters* is a result of his wishful thinking. Conrad was a better judge of his art than is his Polish admirer.

Wyka finds the 'path' to the 'Polish tissue' of *The Sisters* in the lines, 'He resolved to return to the cities, amongst men; not because of what the poet said about solitude in a crowd; but from an inward sense of his difference from the majority of mankind', in which he sees an allusion to the opening section of Mickiewicz's 'Great Improvisation' in *Dziady* (The Forefathers' Eve).[13] Can this be so? It is hardly possible that at this time in his life – a period of particular sensitivity about his non-English background – Conrad would make an allusion to a specific poet, Mickiewicz, whom he was certain no reader would recognize. The fragment quoted refers to Stephen at a time when, after a period of real loneliness in mountains and at the sea-shore, he decides to return to the company of people and settle down in Paris. Thus, the 'poet' mentioned probably contrasts an 'external' solitude with the more profound 'solitude in a crowd'. Mickiewicz, on the other hand, refers to a different form of solitude: the real lonelines of prison, which does not affect his hero ('what do people matter'), and from which he is able to learn (his hero says earlier: 'loneliness is the master of sages'). Both the context and the sense are quite different here.

In any event, was Mickiewicz the first romantic to discuss loneliness? Which poet of the period kindled the 'fashion' of solitude? Who popularized the pose of the misunderstood and alienated hero-wanderer? Let's consider: Stephen leaves his native country and wanders about Europe; he has no friends and cannot find his place in society. He is affluent and exploited, and spends time thinking about the relationship between Art and Nature... It should not surprise us that Conrad is in fact alluding to Byron's *Childe Harold's Pilgrimage*:

> To sit on rocks, to muse o'er flood and fell,
> To slowly trace the forest's shady scene,
> Where things that own not man's dominion dwell,
> And mortal foot hath ne'er or rarely been;
> To climb the trackless mountain all unseen
> ....
> This is not solitude; 'tis but to hold
> Converse with Nature's charms, and view her stores unroll'd.
> But midst the crowd, the hum, the shock of men,
> To hear, to see, to feel, and to possess,
> And roam along, the world's tired denizen,
> With none who bless us, none whom we can bless
> ....
> This is to be alone; this, this is solitude.[14]

This thought is repeated many times over in Byron's poetry, once even in the context of 'being different from the crowd':

> I have not loved the world, nor the world me;
> ....
> They could not deem me one of such;
> In the crowd I stood
> Among them, but not of them; in a shroud
> Of thoughts which were not their thoughts...[15]

Since there are several motifs in *The Sisters* which are characteristic of Byron (leaving one's parents – Canto I; farewells, being tired of life – I, 4–5; misunderstandings and lack of friends –I, 8–9; a cult of Nature – II, 48, II, 87, III, 13; independence of spirit – III, 12 etc.), we can assume that Conrad had *Childe Harold's Pilgrimage* fresh in his mind at the time he was writing his novel.[16]

Thus, Wyka's 'path' proves spurious. His other forays are not more successful. Wyka writes that the technique of describing a 'landscape in motion' was characteristic of 'Mickiewicz and only of Mickiewicz' and that a horse or a horse-drawn vehicle were the only 'means of quick transportation available at the time'.[17] This is not quite true: one could move quickly over water as well. In the first chapter of *L'Education sentimentale* – a book which Conrad knew very well and whose echoes can be heard in *The Sisters* – Flaubert offers an excellent description of a 'moving' landscape as seen from the deck of a ship on the Seine. And although Conrad's landscapes remind us of Antoni Malczewski* and Mickiewicz rather than of Flaubert, the origin of this particular convention in Conrad is of little significance. It does not account for the inner structure of Conrad's works and does not clearly point to their literary sources. In other words, if we were unable to decode the poetics of Conrad's novels without knowing Mickiewicz's techniques of description, then and only then would the 'Polish' origins of Conrad's literary method be something more than a curiosity. But since Conrad wrote in prose at the end of the nineteenth century and because he was evidently continuing the tradition of the French masters, for a literary historian his descriptive technique is neither surprising nor mysterious.

The same can be said of Conrad's anthropomorphic and theriomorphic stylistic devices, which Wyka analyses. Again, Conrad's methods do not have a specifically Polish source here. We find the same devices in the Bible as well as in Homer, Shelley, Blake, Sterne, Dickens, Flaubert and Zola. In addition, the opposition between Truth and 'formulas' is a romantic stereotype (frequently found as early as in Goethe).

Does all this mean that *The Sisters* does not contain any undoubtedly Polish elements? Not exactly. A couple of Polish proverbs which appear in the novel may serve as an example: 'wszystko można, lecz z ostrożna'[18] and 'wilcze oczy, popie gardło'.[19] And although Wyka's claim that the central elements of Conrad's art in *The Sisters* 'can only be explained in terms of the Polish literary tradition' cannot be substantiated, it is more than likely that during his work on *The Sisters* Conrad's imagination was under the pressure of Polish artistic and intellectual traditions. However, contrary to Wyka, I believe that this influence was not beneficial to *The Sisters* and made it harder for Conrad to continue the story.

No one to date has asked why Conrad began writing *The Sisters*. Unfortunately, we can only form hypotheses since none of Conrad's

---

* Author of *Maria* (1825), a masterpiece of the 'Ukrainian' school of Polish Romantic poetry.

letters of this period to his closest friend and literary confidant of the time, his 'aunt' Marguerite Poradowska, has survived. This is the more regrettable since it is very likely that the origins of *The Sisters* are somehow linked with Poradowska.

Poradowska wrote – in French – regional short stories about Poles and Ruthenians ('il y a l'espace, le souffle du vent dans Votre description des champs ukrainiens', wrote Conrad in praise),[20] and Stephen chose to live nowhere else but in Passy, an elegant Parisian suburb where Poradowska lived. She also lived there in the company of birds, 'parmi les oiseaux', as Conrad mentioned in a letter.[21]

The end of 1895 and the beginning of 1896 was a time when Conrad frequently travelled to the Continent, especially to Paris. This was also a period when he had multiple contacts with French intellectual life and with the French financial world;[22] he experienced both the splendour and the sham-brilliance of the West. This was also the time of his continued literary apprenticeship, of his first acquaintances and friendships within the literary circles of London, and of his growing creative ambitions; it was a time of searching for new themes and of experimenting with new techniques. Doomed to be considered 'foreign' – if we do not take into account 'The Return', which was a failure, it was to be ten years before Conrad tried to write about land-life in England – and at the same time afraid of being consistently labelled an exotic-tropical writer (which always irritated him), Conrad wanted, in one way or another, to try writing about the Europe with which he was familiar. The Basque sisters, members of a family of Carlist royalists, are connected with the Marseilles period of Conrad's life, 1874–8, the time in which the action of *The Sisters* possibly was to take place.

Why did Conrad choose not to write about things Polish? Probably because he was not familiar with them (when leaving Cracow in 1874, Conrad had spent only five years of his life in ethnic Polish territories); because to do so would, in the eyes of his readers, have made him a writer of folkloristic or political curiosities;* because it would have been difficult for him to write about Polish problems in English; and also because

---

* As was Poradowska. The time when Polish themes attracted serious international interest (as in the 1830s and 40s) had long passed, especially in England.

in all probability Polish matters were painful or at least awkward for him to handle.[23]

Hence, with a *naïveté* as striking as that he showed in giving his elder son the name 'Borys' – allegedly an all-Slavonic name, also used by Poles[24] – Conrad chose for his protagonist in *The Sisters* a Ruthenian wandering over Western Europe. In both cases he demonstrated not his knowledge but his ignorance. It is doubtful that he wanted his novel to be autobiographical: perhaps he made his hero a painter because as a painter searching for visual beauty Stephen did not force Conrad to deal with literary matters with which he himself was most deeply concerned. This, however, was an unfortunate decision because Conrad was consequently compelled to discuss – in vague and unconvincing terms – issues with which he was not familiar. The results of choosing a protagonist of the given ethnic origin were even more troublesome: the only thing Conrad and Stephen had in common was the landscape of their native land. Symptomatically, there is a contrast between the liveliness of the scenes with Russian merchants and officials (Conrad's own memory was here assisted by his uncle Bobrowski's stories and memoirs) and the stilted presentation of Stephen's life as student and traveller. It is obvious that Conrad had only the vaguest idea about what Stephen's family relations, thoughts, emotions and interests should be like. To make up for this gap in knowledge with the resources of his own experiences evidently turned out to have been impossible for Conrad; the differences were too great. The themes that Polish Romantic poetry or later Polish prose (if he was at all familiar with it) could suggest were not helpful either and in fact pushed Conrad in the wrong direction, drawing him away from concrete description.

In addition, Stephen's disenchantment with the West, expressed in cliché phraseology of the *fin de siècle,* is both banal and abstract. Whatever Konrad Korzeniowski had managed to learn from Polish literature or from his father's and Stefan Buszczyński's political journalism must have been a handicap rather than a help to him. The traditional motif of Polish disenchantment and bitterness stemmed from resentment against Western opportunism, trivial materialism, political *naïveté* and moral insensibility in the face of Russian autocratic imperialism as well as against the indifference to the suffering and struggles of less fortunate peoples. However, these of course were not the feelings of a young Ruthenian wanderer with a peasant and Orthodox background.

In each paragraph Conrad had to face the dilemma: should he breathe life into the hero, making him more real by making use of his own memories and experiences but at the same time transforming Stephen's identity and thus basically changing the entire story, or should he hold firm to his plans and continue to plod ahead with maladroit generalities? The dilemma was insoluble. This book did not let itself be written. In spite of what Thomas Moser claims, Conrad could have coped with the sisters themselves as he later coped with the Viola sisters in *Nostromo*. But the Basque part of the plot, while apparently based to a greater extent on Conrad's reminiscences, was at the same time thematically more restricted, and the 'Russian' part, which opened broad vistas – artistic, cultural, philosophical – was less tangible, being less familiar; and Stephen himself, who might have been handled from a distance while meditating in Munich or while travelling around Europe, now, in the close-up presentation at his Paris home, demanded concreteness.

Many years later, Conrad declared that he did not like to leave behind the evidence of having bitten off more than he could chew.[25] When beginning *The Sisters* he let himself go, heedlessly. But even so, he surely never realized how succulent were the morsels of which he did not manage to get a fuller taste.

Let us consider: European painting was just at that time undergoing a profound change, through post-Impressionism towards abstraction. Conrad, rather conservative in his visual taste, was not unaware of that process. His interest in Zola must have led him to know something about the Impressionist theory, and in the collection of Dr Paul Gachet – which he saw and did not like – he came across the canvases of Cézanne, Van Gogh and other innovative painters of the time.[26] The reaction against realism, a search for the mystery hidden behind the façade of things – which Conrad mentions in *The Sisters* writing about Stephen – were at that time widespread tendencies.

Stephen was not alone in moving westwards in his pursuit of artistic inspiration and understanding. Had he been more fully described, he would have been the earliest novelistic presentation of one of the long row of either talented, or merely ambitious, artists from Eastern Europe who about the turn of the century wandered to Germany and France:

from Constantin Brancusi to Marc Chagall, Jules Pascin or Chaim Soutine. They brought along their artistic restlessness, their childishly bold colours, their thirst for the mythical. Many of them came from Russia itself, where – as Conrad also mentions in *The Sisters* (p. 51) – there was not much of an indigenous interest in painting.

At the very moment Conrad was struggling with the manuscript of his hapless novel, two Russian painters decided to move to Munich, just where Conrad's hero lived and studied. One of them, Alexei von Jawlensky, had abandoned the same kind of career Stephen's parents had planned for their son: that of an officer in the Imperial Guard. The other, Wassily Kandinsky, was to become one of the founders of modern non-figurative painting. Both decided to leave their homeland for the same reason; as Valentine Marcadé writes, they felt they were wasting their lives in Russia, and thirsted for a quicker rhythm of life, broader horizons and an immediate contact with the new trends in art. Conscious of their capabilities, they wanted to give themselves a better chance of development.[27] In a word, they felt much as Conrad's Stephen did. And they decided to go to Munich because it was less of a whirlwind (I am quoting here Leonid Pasternak, father of Borys), better suited for the study of what is basic in painting, and because, to quote Pasternak again: 'Paris – c'est une femme, Munich – c'est la bière.'[28]

For Conrad also, evidently, Paris meant women: this is clear even in *The Sisters*. But he could not have known anything about Jawlensky, Kandinsky and their decisions. What he knew about Munich came probably from his Polish acquaintances: a Polish 'Munich School' of historical and decorative painting had been well known since the 1870s. Nevertheless, the fact remains that writing about a young painter moving from Russia to Munich and then to Paris he was tracing the route simultaneously followed, unbeknown to him, by several painters who were to secure for themselves an important place in the history of modern art. He came, in other words, pathetically close to a great subject.

To sum up, *The Sisters* is unfortunately not 'the lovely arm of an imposing statue'. It is a dramatic document on Conrad's wanderings and strayings; it is a testimony to the difficulties he encountered in finding his place in life and in literature.

It is also a grandiose failure; a stunted and stillborn work of impressive design and bold thematic reach; a work which showed that its author possessed a feel for what is essential and problematic, even if he could not yet handle his material adequately. Only later in his career did Conrad in fact write two 'European' novels based on his unique experiences: *The Secret Agent* and *Under Western Eyes*.

6
Lord Jim: a Romantic tragedy of honour

I

'He was an inch, perhaps two, under six feet...' Considering that Jim's height has no bearing on his story, perhaps no other great novel begins so nonchalantly. This manoeuvre is characteristic. At the very opening of the novel we encounter an example of the play of shadows which the author will carry on to the end. Right at the outset we are given a meticulous description of Jim's physical appearance, but his psychology will remain undeciphered until the end – undeciphered, that is, for the main narrator, Marlow, though not necessarily for the reader, whose knowledge throughout is broader than Marlow's. The reader knows, for instance, something about Jim's past. She or he knows of Jim's unrealized jump off the deck of the training-ship, in time to help save the shipwrecked sailors. She or he has learned, too, of Jim's day-dreaming about the courage and efficiency which he assumed himself to be ready to display in case of need; and knows that it was just this day-dreaming which prevented him from showing real courage and readiness for action when the opportunity to do so actually arose. This knowledge helps the reader to see more distinctly the psychological circumstances of Jim's fatal jump from the deck of the apparently sinking *Patna*. In addition, the reader will have formed her or his own opinion of Marlow and be therefore in a better position to interpret, even through the veil of Marlow's uncertainties, Jim's behaviour and motivation.

However, the atmosphere of persistent scrutiny and tantalizing uncertainty is rendered so suggestively in the novel that even Douglas Hewitt, in his excellent study, keeps stressing the impossibility of 'judging' Jim, who – to him – remains mysterious to the end. Hewitt contends that 'we expect Marlow to give us a final explanation' but instead Marlow continues 'ruminating to obscure the issue' by throwing new veils and introducing new riddles.[1]

Hewitt's charges seem to result from an insufficient grasp of the novel's structure. *Lord Jim* has two main protagonists, not one; and it is at the same time a narrative about certain physical and psychological facts as well as a description of the process of acquiring knowledge about these facts. At times this description sounds like a text taken from a treatise about the philosophy of knowledge written by a thinker bred on Romantic poetry.

Jim's entire story could have been related in a few pages, but in this book, not short but not prolix either, the author's strategy includes exhibiting the processes by which other people learn this story, and their reactions to it. The most striking example of this technique is the story of Captain Montague Brierly, unanimously regarded as '*the* fortunate man of the earth',[2] who commits suicide soon after taking part in the court of inquiry into the *Patna* (and Jim) affair. Several other characters in the novel, albeit their lives are in no way linked with Jim's, serve as foils, helping to throw light on him by their own behaviour. Such is the case, for example, of the steward, Bob Stanton, who drowns while trying, unsuccessfully, to save a panic-stricken woman. Various characters in the novel express their opinion of Jim: sailors, merchants, villains, models of virtue. One may say that Jim is like a cane stuck into an anthill – the author is interested in the cane, but he devotes more space to his description of the reaction of the disturbed ants.

Only two men seem fully to understand Jim's behaviour: the artless lieutenant of a French gunboat and Stein, the old romantic ex-revolutionary, a veteran of the 1848 Revolution. Marlow himself till the end considers Jim 'inscrutable' and 'obscure'. Marlow's doubts, however, are not at the heart of the book. The uncertainty of interpretation is only one element of the novel, not its essential message.

Admittedly, the first chapters seem, at least initially, rather puzzling within the structure of the novel as a whole. It is not clear, to the reader, from whose perspective the action is being viewed. These opening chapters consist of a montage of episodes from different periods in Jim's life and of information on various aspects of Jim's past. Jim's thoughts are related to the reader by an omniscient narrator, and it is not until the fourth chapter that the novel's true world, the world of Marlow's tale, emerges from the seeming chaos of the pre-narration. But even then the reader is not told a continuous tale which will carry her or him to the end of the book, for in the last nine chapters one of Marlow's past listeners steps forward reading Marlow's notes which report on the last stages of Jim's story.

Lord Jim has been accused of wobbliness in composition, of excessive dragging on of the subject, and of artificiality in the inclusion of the whole Patusan story. Answering these charges, Robert Haugh has shown that the composition of the whole is planned and consistent. The Patusan chapters form an integral part of the novel and bring all the major issues to their conclusion.[3] For example, Jim's two first 'jumps' mentioned above have their counterpart in his third jump: over Rajah Tunku Allang's courtyard palisade in the second part of the novel. The evil personified by Gentleman Brown echoes the earlier indifferent malevolence of the sea, while the keen and boundless trust of the inhabitants of Patusan reflects the earlier passive, blind trust of the *Patna*'s passengers. In the last chapter the passionate voice of Jewel appealing to Jim in the name of love echoes the seductive cries of the terror-stricken officers of the damaged *Patna*, calling Jim to escape.

Undeniably, in the latter part of the book the pace of narration changes, the action becomes faster and there is more of it. This shift in technique is a result of the change in perspective from which the reader views Jim. First he was studied from within; now the attention is focused on his behaviour, on his feats. No new brush strokes are added to Jim's psychological portrait; but he is subjected to new trials. We learn more about him, not through authorial introspection but only by inference based on his actions. The second part of the novel is needed as a practical testing ground for Jim as the protagonist.

Any arbitrariness of construction will be found only in the opening part of the novel. In the later chapters, the story of Jim's plight and the musings of his philosophizing friend gradually transform the book into a coherent whole. Complications in the development of the plot are a function of time shifts and of changes in the narrative perspective. These complications are both natural and effective. A Polish critic, Kazimierz Wyka, noted that Conrad had been the first novelist to stress intentionally the difference between the time of action and the time of narration.[4] This disparity between narrative and dramatic time creates the effect of a slow, incremental approach through which the reader draws gradually closer and closer to the protagonist.

I have said that *Lord Jim* is a novel about personal cognition, about the ways and means of acquiring knowledge of another person. But perhaps it would be more exact to say that it is a novel in which the cognitive process, the quest for truth, is concurrent with the narrative thrust itself. There are only a few theoretical remarks scattered in the text on the problem of cognition. Instead, the reader follows the process itself, the arduous and burdensome pursuit of a faithful description – through many eyes and minds – and just evaluation of Jim. The difficulties which this quest presents for the reader do not, however, spring from the particularity and complexity of Jim's character. Although his behaviour is uncommon and the course of his life complex, his character itself is not complicated or obscure. Jim's personality stands out primarily because of his dogged obstinacy and his obsessive and even desperate consistency, after the *Patna* disaster, in pursuing his goal.

2

Marlow refers to Jim repeatedly as 'one of us', but the grounds for this statement are not immediately clear, since Marlow's listeners seem to be distinctly unlike Jim. Marlow's sense of spiritual affinity with Jim, however, is spontaneous, instinctive and unrelated to his problems with understanding him. That Jim is 'one of us' means in the context of the novel that Marlow, his listeners, and implicitly we, the readers, and Jim, all belong together. Thus the main function of Marlow's reminders is to turn Jim into a character who is not only symbolic (this is what Marlow thinks of him, p. 265), but also in a way typical. Since he is 'one of us', his fate is not unique but significant to us all.*

---

* This interpretation is supported by the fact that the words 'one of us' can be read also as an allusion to the Bible, where God says to the angels about Adam, who has eaten the forbidden fruit: 'Behold, the man is become as one of us, to know good and evil' (Genesis 3:22). However, it has been pointed out – most clearly by John Batchelor in his comprehensive study of *Lord Jim* – that Marlow uses the term 'one of us' also in a restrictive sense, as referring to Europeans only.[5] To me this is yet another example of the contrast between Marlow's personal vision of things and the image of them which emerges from the novel as a whole.

There are in its text other indications that the action of *Lord Jim* is to be understood as endowed with a broader, more general sense. For instance, the *Patna* and her destiny appear in some fragments as an allegory for all humanity, left to the mercy of the indifferent elements, and to the honesty of a few conscious and responsible individuals: 'as though she had been a crowded planet speeding through the dark spaces of ether behind the swarms of suns, in the appalling and calm solitudes awaiting the breath of future creations' (pp. 21–2).[6]

Conversely, one comes from time to time across the opinion that Jim can be fully understood only as a Pole,[7] perhaps someone like the crazy colonel in Franz Werfel's play *Jacobowsky and the Colonel*. Such a notion is difficult to concur with despite the fact that the type of hero represented by Jim and the kind of problems raised in the novel appear far more frequently in Polish than in English literature. But it is enough to remember William Faulkner – Conrad's greatest disciple and follower – to see that Poles have no literary monopoly on quixotism. All one can say is that in Poland the chivalric ethos survived, as an element of social and moral reality, longer than in most other Western European countries.

Anyway, Jim could have learned his principles from Shakespeare, whom we hear he read with enthusiasm: 'Best thing to cheer up a fellow' (p. 237). There he might have found an exalted cult of honour, analysis of its loss, and the Homeric idea that the fear of disgrace can be greater than the fear of death.[8] Perhaps he might even have found the glorious description of his own end:

> Nothing in his life
> Became him like the leaving of it. He died
> As one that had been studied in his death
> To throw away the dearest thing he ow'd
> As 'twere a careless trifle.[9]

Jim's behaviour, which puzzles the narrator, may be illuminated by reference to certain moral and literary antecedents. Gianbattista Pigna, one of the Renaissance theoreticians of honour, offers a precise interpretation of Jim's situation: a momentary cowardice caused by a lack of experience brings disgrace and awakens suspicions that it may be a sign of a permanent fault; a single act of cowardice should not, however, be regarded as necessarily resulting in an irreversible loss of honour, for this may be brought about only by habitual behaviour.[10] Jim seems to be instinctively aware of this ethical idea and looks for an opportunity to prove that this cowardice was indeed an isolated mishap. His situation is well understood by the lieutenant of the French gunboat; he views Jim's momentary weakness with understanding (which does not mean leniency) but is unable to imagine a life 'when the honour is gone' (p. 148). The Frenchman's final words are often interpreted as expressing a final and irrevocable condemnation of Jim. Marlow is the first victim and perpetrator of this misunderstanding. In his conversation with the lieutenant he pleads Jim's case in personal, psychological terms ('a lenient view', '[Jim's] feeling in the matter' etc.), and misses the gist of the Frenchman's ethical analysis, presented in terms of facts, not of intentions. He realizes the failure of their communication ('a thing of empty sounds'), but resorts lamely and outrageously to a suggestion that the whole moral issue could perhaps be reduced 'to not being found out'! The Frenchman, surprised, answers with condescending irony: 'this, monsieur, is too fine for me' (p. 149). Indeed, we may assume that the lieutenant's view of Jim's plight overlaps with Jim's own: his life has been deprived of worth but not of hope, because honour can be regained.

3

The French lieutenant and Stein are, as I have said, the only characters in the novel who do not appear to have much difficulty in understanding Jim's behaviour. Nor are they surprised or indignant at the 'impracticality' of the principles to which he wants to adhere; they know that the ethics of honour is neither pragmatic nor utilitarian. It is in their conversations with Marlow that the key concepts defining Jim's personality appear. The dialogue with the lieutenant concerns honour. Stein simply calls Jim a 'romantic'.

If I am to believe standard dictionaries of English, in the mind of the Anglo-Saxon reader the term 'romantic' may perhaps evoke misleading associations. Here it signifies by no means egocentrism or freakishness, but rather an exalted sense of responsibility. Jim is a 'romantic' of the same stripe as some Byronic heroes, and particularly as Father Robak, the moral protagonist of Adam Mickiewicz's great epic poem, *Pan Tadeusz*.[11] They share a like fate: of losing their honour by an act committed in the state of frenzy, regaining it by years of service to a community, and confirming it in the moment of a heroic death.

Placing *Lord Jim* within the context of the classic works of Polish Romantic literature helps us to notice and understand a most important and up to now neglected element in this novel: imagination and dream, both 'typically Romantic' concepts, are here opposed to each other. In *Lord Jim* imagination is shown as a dangerous faculty, debilitating and destructive. This same (personified) Imagination, 'the enemy of man, the father of all terrors' (p. 11), brings the hero of Juliusz Słowacki's drama *Kordian*, a rebel Polish officer on his way to assassinate the Tsar, to a state of nervous breakdown and insanity.[12] Imagination makes Jim first passive and then frightened, both on the deck of the training-ship and on the wrecked *Patna*. It is a peculiar excrescence of psyche, a growth of its tissues; in a person sensitive to external impulses imagination produces an uncontrolled internal explosion of visions and emotions.

The 'dream', on the other hand, about which Stein talks in answer to Marlow's question on 'how to live', appears as something positive: 'To follow the dream, and again to follow the dream – and so – *ewig – usque ad finem...*'[13] The dream, which shares with imagination the quality of transcending that which is immediately real, propels the dreaming person towards external goals and ideals. In the course of realization of the dream reality gets transformed: this is the very essence of the dream. One succumbs to imagination; dream forces one to do something.

The opposition imagination–dream constitutes in *Lord Jim* a critical rejoinder to Romantic literature. In the structure of the novel itself, the contrast is linked to a subtle and gradual evolution in Jim's moral attitude.

In the first stage – which includes the court of inquiry – when talking about his flight from the damaged *Patna* Jim explains away his jump not only by his dulled consciousness, but also by his belief that to remain on board was pointless. Thus he tries to justify his instinctive action by an implicit reference to rules, which tie the norms of behaviour to their practical effectiveness. Obviously, the rules of honour are of a quite different kind: they are binding irrespective of the consequences. More importantly, Jim keeps stressing his good intentions and his basic decency. His explanatory protestations are grounded in a stubborn claim to innocence. Jim's attitude is reminiscent of Jean-Jacques Rousseau's, when he describes in the *Confessions* how he blithely disposed of his five illegitimate children and then parries possible accusations:

> is it possible that my warmheartedness, lively sensibility, readiness to form attachments ... my natural goodwill towards all my fellow-creatures, my ardent love of the great, the true, the beautiful and the just; my utter inability to hate or injure ... the sweet and lively emotion which I feel at the sight of all that is virtuous, generous, and amiable; is it possible, I ask, that all these can ever agree in the same heart with the depravity which, without the least scruple, tramples underfoot the sweetest of obligations? No! I feel and loudly assert – it is impossible.[14]

Jim's explanations follow the same pattern: for exculpation, the accused points at his own sensibility. The association with Rousseau is the more natural here because the concept of imagination played an important part in both his writings and his heritage.

Marlow comments on Jim's attempts at self-justification: 'no man ever understands quite his own artful dodges to escape from the grim shadow of self-knowledge' (p. 80). But Jim, in time, enters this shade of his own will. After chapter XIII, in which the French lieutenant in his dialogue with Marlow introduces the concept of honour, we cease to hear about Jim's 'dodges'. Jim comes to recognize that he has broken a rule which is binding irrespective of the circumstances. He begins to talk in different terms, stressing the idea of his 'paying off' (p. 178) and of 'a chance to get it all back again' (p. 179). To his beloved girl he presents his flight from the *Patna* simply as a result of fear (p. 315); initially he kept rejecting this admission and claiming that he had not been afraid (e.g., p. 87), although the reality intrudes from the very first chapters of the book with the recurring words 'fear' and 'terror'.

Marlow makes several attempts to characterize that 'fixed ideal of conduct' which forms the novel's standard of reference. He describes its effect as 'an unthinking and blessed stiffness before the outward and inward terrors, before the might of nature, and the seductive corruption of men – backed with a faith invulnerable to the strength of facts, to the contagion of example, to the solicitation of ideas' (p. 43). He points at its psychological function: 'an individual trying to save from the fire his idea of what his moral identity should be, this precious notion of a convention, only one of the rules of the game, nothing more, but all the same terrible by its assumption of unlimited power over natural instincts, by the awful penalties of its failure' (p. 81). He talks about the anxiety evoked by 'the most obstinate ghost of man's creation ... the uneasy doubt uprising like a mist, secret and gnawing like a worm, and more chilling than the certitude of death – the doubt of the sovereign power enthroned in a fixed standard of conduct' (p. 50). These belong among the most striking and precise characterizations of the modern crisis of the secular moral norms – those rules which make 'humanity' a normative concept, as they impose on human beings certain mutual obligations. 'The real significance of crime', says Marlow, 'is in its being a breach of faith with the community of mankind' (p. 157). And the French lieutenant – presented as an embodiment of timeless tradition – encapsulates in a few pithy phrases both a rejection of Rousseau's libertarian optimism and an Aristotelian stress on the social nature of man: 'Man is born a coward (*L'homme est né poltron*) . . . But habit – habit – necessity – do you see? – the eye of others – *voilà*. One puts up with it' (p. 147).[15]

Marlow perceives correctly the basic attributes of the ethics of honour: its inflexibility, anti-emotionalism and anti-pragmatism. Still, he is amazed and sometimes even confused by its implications. He never calls into question, as Jim seems to during the first few encounters with him, the validity of a 'fixed standard of conduct', but he seems surprised at the consequences of adherence to this standard. They both adhere to the same moral principles; but of the two men Jim has been more severely tested, has passed through deeper doubts and graver internal strife – and has emerged as the more radical in his adherence. Marlow is perplexed by the – to the modern utilitarian mind, anachronistic – rigorous exigencies of the ancient ideal of honour. He does not question its theoretical validity, but his attitude reflects a change of temper: does it really have to be so painfully demanding? Marlow has probably become, unconsciously, so saturated by the 'reasonable' bourgeois pragmatism of the life ashore that he has ceased to think about those rigours.

This is why, unlike Stein and the French lieutenant, he experiences to the end occasional difficulties in interpreting Jim's behaviour. However, his vacillations must not be regarded as the final verdict of the novel. Just the contrary: they accentuate Marlow's role as a co-protagonist. By endowing him more distinctly with individual qualities they make Marlow even more unlike a *porte-parole* of the 'author'. He is by no means an 'ideal observer', but a spectator-participant, like any other character limited in his possibilities of perception and understanding.

4

Still, some critics ascribe Marlow's doubts and imprecisions to the underlying message of the book as a whole, and accuse *Lord Jim* of a lack of internal congruity. I suppose that one of the causes of this charge is an erroneous identification of the novel's psychological subject-matter. It embraces more than just the issue of Jim's ignominious flight and his later moral regeneration. At its core stands the (typically romantic, again) conflict between the individual's notions and ideas – and empirical reality.

Before the *Patna* incident, this conflict appears in the form of a discord between Jim's imaginings and his practical capabilities. His attitude is a typical example of 'measuring one's strength by one's goals',[16] and is here mercilessly exposed. Subsequent events and Jim's psychological evolution (*Lord Jim* is also a *Bildungsroman*, a novel of experience or education) do not lead to an abandonment of the contrast between ideas and reality, but to a change in its form: to a replacement of the imagination by the dream. Thus two romantic attitudes in life are juxtaposed. While the first type of 'romanticism', an egocentric engrossment in the world of imagination, leads the hero to a moral defeat and infamy, the latter type, of following 'the dream', and of a stubborn fidelity to the ideals of duty and honour, leads him to a tragic death. The Polish reader recognizes here easily an analogy to the transformation of Gustaw into Konrad (to whom Joseph Conrad owed his given name) in Adam Mickiewicz's drama *Dziady* (The Forefathers' Eve, 1832); there, a young poet, egocentric and endowed with fantastic imagination, under the impact of political persecution which falls on his friends and his country, turns into a national poet, writing in defence of justice and freedom.[17]

Beginning with chapter XIV, the basic psychological thread of *Lord Jim* takes the form of a contrast between, on the one hand, Jim's acute self-awareness and his urge to regain his lost honour, and, on the other, the opinion of the people who regard him as a fool, a fraud, or at best an eccentric. His concern is not simply to win other people's confidence, which may after all be based on appearances. He wants to achieve a concurrence between his own vision of himself and the judgement of other men. This is characteristic for the ideal of honour. This concept, as we know, has two aspects: of social esteem and of self-esteem; the discrepancy between the two is a source of dramatic conflicts, typical for the ethics of honour.[18]

This need for the understanding and approval of one's moral environment explains the frantic insistence with which Jim confides in Marlow and the importance he attaches to his friendship. In Patusan, however, while Jim can prove himself and pass all the tests of courage and selflessness, he cannot find the coveted accord between his own idea of himself and his image in the eyes of others. The people who place their absolute trust in Jim either disbelieve his confessions about his past (as Jewel does), or neither know anything about it nor understand his moral motives and categories of thinking. And so, although surrounded by people who adore and love him, and to whom he is genuinely devoted, Jim remains a solitary. Perhaps this makes it easier for him to abandon them all: 'He goes away from a living woman to celebrate his pitiless wedding with a shadowy ideal of conduct' (p. 416).

5

I have spoken about the 'epistemological' function of Conrad's narrative stratagems used in *Lord Jim*. The other – and not less important – function of time shifts and changes in points of view is the achievement of a tragic effect. The very construction of the plot of *Lord Jim* – introduction, development, suspension of the final catastrophe, and the pathetic finale – reminds us of a classical tragedy. One of its basic features was the inevitability of fate: the course of events was irrevocable, it could be neither stopped nor changed. But effects relatively simple to obtain in the ancient Greek or the French or Spanish classical drama have become almost unattainable in the modern realistic novel, which opens out too many vistas, revealing a multitude of possibilities and a free play of chance. (When in the novels of a Hardy or a Zola inevitability gets inserted in the form of naturalistic determinism, by the same token their protagonists are deprived of a sufficient degree of free will to make them tragic heroes, not simply victims of forces beyond their understanding and control.)

In *Lord Jim* the action rolls on with the inevitability of an avalanche; we are conscious of the necessity of nearly everything which happens, as if, indeed, a merciless fate had decided it all. And indeed Marlow occasionally mentions 'fate'; but even the most careful examination of the described course of events does not reveal in the novel the workings of any external determining forces. The sense of a tragic inevitability is produced by Conrad's mastery of narrative technique, not by his resorting to the supernatural. The entire course of events is based on realistic causes and motivations. Mystery and elusiveness, whenever present, do not cover up anything arbitrary: they add, as in real life, to the general impression of the tragic.

Not until the end of chapter IX does the reader learn what Jim did, what was his infamous act to which several vague allusions have been made. But by that time we know enough about Jim and about the circumstances of the whole affair to accept his fatal jump as unavoidable. More than Marlow, the reader is ready to believe Jim's assurances that he fled the ship only half-conscious of what he was doing and that once in the saving boat he wanted to commit suicide.

Close-ups, time shifts and changes in narrative perspective help to eliminate from the reader's mind any assumption that what happens has happened by chance. Of course, this effect is connected with the very technique of a novel-tale, in which the teller confers upon his story the quality of consistency – simply by weaving, amidst the multitude of random events, a sequence bound by real or apparent cause-and-effect links. This selection of facts, made by the story-teller, impresses itself upon our consciousness all the more forcibly as Marlow's musings frequently stray from the main subject. His digressions enhance the reader's feeling that the tale in its entirety is full and 'objective'.

At the very end of the novel Conrad applies an entirely different method to obtain the same objective: the effect of inevitability. We learn about Jim's death and about the dramatic events leading to it from the accounts given to Marlow by different sources and from Marlow's letter to one of his former listeners. Thus the reader is given a bare outline of the facts, devoid of a broader context and representing a closely knit whole.

Jim's final fate is a consequence of his principles. The saviour and benefactor of Patusan did not forget his earlier defeat. While preserving the memory of his former weakness, he did not feel elevated, purified, entitled to pass a final judgement on other people. The voice of his conscience, a source of his honesty and humility in dealing with others, was the noblest trait of Jim's character, and also the direct cause of his débâcle. The murderous Brown was quick to spot the weak point in Jim's defences: pity aroused by the memory of his own fall.* If he, Jim, was permitted to redeem his old error by later perseverance and sacrifice, Brown must not be denied a similar chance. To avoid the trap, Jim would have had to betray his principles. But he did not waver.

When Tuan Jim, one-time chief mate of the *Patna* and the present ruler of Patusan, stops before Doramin saying, 'I am come in sorrow', we feel that this is the way it had to be. In the sudden flash of the Malay's ancient pistol the truth about Jim appears complete and clear. The tragic catharsis, a rare guest in modern times, responds to the call of a twentieth-century writer.

But this scene, full of pathos, does not close the novel. Our last look falls upon Jewel and Stein, withered by sorrow. Jim's moral victory has been purchased not only with his own life but also with the pain and sorrow of those closest and dearest to him. Moreover, we know that after his death Patusan has plunged into chaos of internal strife.

This does not mean, however, that the ending ought to be understood as putting in question the ideals to which Jim had adhered with such determination. The final scenes of *Lord Jim* ought to be interpreted within the framework of the traditions of literature concerned with chivalric ethos: there, after the hero's death follow usually scenes of grief and mourning. Happy endings are most unusual in this tradition, with its recurrent motif of physical demise and moral victory. From the *Iliad* down to *Chanson de Roland* and Calderón's tragedies, death is the fate of the defenders of honour and mourning the fate of their families and friends. Having lifted his hero onto the tragic pedestal, Conrad shuns any simple-minded illusions.

One other leading – and romantic – theme of the novel is brought to the fore in its final fragments: loneliness and its most cruel companion, lack of understanding. Neither the faithful Tamb' Itam nor the beloved Jewel can comprehend the reasons for Jim's actions. On the penultimate

---

* I think only a lack of psychological insight can lead to the suspicion that Jim felt – as some critics assume – a kind of criminal solidarity with Gentleman Brown: this was what Brown himself aspired to, but why should we take his fantasies seriously? Critics of Jim's decision to let Brown go tend to overlook another factor as well: if not for Cornelius' treason, Brown himself would not have had a chance for his revenge.

page we read about his 'egoism'; Jewel charges him even with falsehood (p. 350), and her accusation is the saddest result of Jim's final decision. Old Stein was the only one who understood him, but was Jim aware of it? He was denied the satisfaction of the wish, wistfully expressed in the novel's motto: 'It is certain my conviction gains infinitely the moment another soul will believe in it.' Apart from everything else, *Lord Jim* is a tragedy of incomprehension.

7
The Mirror of the Sea

Conrad's first volume of essays, *The Mirror of the Sea: Memories and Impressions*, published in 1906, garnered immediate eulogies in the letters he received after its publication from Bennett, Galsworthy, Henry James, Kipling and Wells[1] – it has not, however, attracted much critical attention since. This is a pity, since the collection offers valuable insight into the workings of Conrad's mind and writing method. While the best overall assessment remains that by Morton Dauwen Zabel in his Introduction to *The Portable Conrad* (New York 1947), the only comprehensive critical studies devoted especially to *The Mirror* are in Polish[2] and in French.[3]

To appreciate it fully, it is best to read *The Mirror* not knowing, or else forgetting, how the volume originated and its parts were assembled: simply, to read the book as a whole.

Ostensibly, this is a collection of 'memories and impressions', as its subtitle says, concerning the sea; and the most obvious understanding of the title is probably that the author intends to hold to the sea the mirror of his prose. But, as often in Conrad's works, the title has another and more important meaning. The sea may be understood as being itself a mirror. The motto, from Boethius' *On the Consolation of Philosophy* – a book in praise of philosophical thinking – seems to enforce this interpretation. The motto talks about a 'miracle or wonder' (there is here a hidden allusion to the title, as both 'mirror' and 'miracle' come from the same Latin *miraculum*) which 'greatly troubles' the author. But what is the sea a mirror of? Perhaps of Nature in general, of the universe. Thus the book turns out to be a mirror of what is in itself a mirror. Such an understanding is repeatedly confirmed by the text. As one instance of this, the other key word of the motto, 'wonder', returns in section XXXVI in a telling context. In what is in fact a biblical allusion to the Lord's 'wonders in the deep' (Psalm 107:24), we read: 'the most amazing wonder of the deep is its unfathomable cruelty'.

Thus at the very beginning an alert reader is given a hint that the series of memories and impressions he or she is presented with contains as well elements of a philosophical parable. Once we have registered that signal, we shall be less surprised to find in this book so many statements of the author's essential beliefs, sometimes springing up quite unexpectedly.

From the third sentence on (with its gibe at 'a vain people of landsmen'), we keep also receiving signals that we are being addressed by a specialist, who relies not only on his theoretical knowledge but on his personal experience as well. We are made to feel privileged to have an expert – above the ordinary ranks of landlubber scribes – to introduce us to the world of seamen and ships. This stress on personal expertise seems at times overdone, but Conrad's insistence was possibly occasioned by the fact that most of the sketches appeared initially in popular magazines, and he wanted to accentuate their difference from the ordinary journalistic staple.

A look at the thematic range of the volume reveals that it is not so much the sea as the ship which is the initial focus of attention. The ships leaving port and returning, their anchors, sails and loads, their wrecking and their 'captivity' in docks are treated in six (out of fifteen) essays, and a seventh contains a eulogy to a particular ship, the balancelle *Tremolino*. Seamen take, as it were, the second place behind their vessels; and it is they, not the ships, who are apt to make mistakes and to fail. '... ships are all right; it's the men in 'em . . .'[4] who are not always dependable; the ships are their testing instruments. They are looked at from the vantage point of their work: of the duties they perform, the obstacles they must overcome, the weaknesses they have to master. There is little in *The Mirror* of the spirit of adventure for adventure's sake, and the thrills of pleasure-sailing are mentioned with a certain condescension.[5]

Seamanship is regarded as an art of navigation – that is, of going from one place to another with a concrete, useful purpose; but still an art, which develops its special skills. Such attainment of skills forms 'the moral side' of any 'breadwinning industry'. And it 'is more than honesty; it is something wider, embracing honesty and grace and rule in an elevated and clear sentiment, not altogether utilitarian, which may be called the honour of labour'.[6] This non-utilitarian view of the moral aspects of work is characteristic of Conrad's ethics. And it is worth remembering that statement, thrown in by Conrad as if only in passing, because its underlying idea – that utility is not a sufficient ground of moral worth – illuminates the hierarchy of values implicit in most of Conrad's fiction.

The work of a sailor is shown in *The Mirror of the Sea* to be distinguished by two other factors, which make it particularly 'art-like'. One is the special relationship between the man and the vessel he works in, 'a disinterested sentiment', a love 'untainted by the pride of possession';[7] the other, even more important – and mostly gone with the disappearance of sailing-ships – consists in the direct engagement of natural elements, water and wind, as adversaries. This engagement makes man not just an object of more or less accidental fate, but a protagonist, a fighter in the battles of his existence. Such an image of man participating in an *agon* with the elements is most visible in 'The Character of the Foe' and 'Initiation'. The nostalgic idealization of past forms of seamanship serves in *The Mirror* a double purpose: it adds a romantic sheen to the author's reminiscences and strengthens his moral message.

In his guide to ships and seamanship, rich in technical detail and in anecdote, and ranging from a disquisition about the proper stowage of a cargo to glimpses of the history of naval warfare, Conrad uses two methods of presentation: one generalizing, the other reminiscential. It is evident that he feels more at ease with the latter, but, since his objective is not only to recall his own memories but to give an overview of seamanship at the time of the great historical change from sail to steam, he has to draw synthetic pictures. They tend to be stiffish, and it is here that he resorts to facile anthropomorphism, most striking in his overdrawn images of the 'rulers' of East and West winds (amusingly tailored to fit Conrad's anti-Russian slant). This anthropomorphism is actually in conflict with one of the basic ideas of the book: namely, that Nature is quite indifferent to Man, that indeed these two have nothing in common.

The exposure of the sea's 'cynical indifference' to man's courage and endurance is the subject of the best piece in the volume, 'Initiation'; and the discovery that the sea – an enchanting sight though it may be – is essentially 'impenetrable and heartless', oblivious of 'good and evil', constitutes the philosophical point of arrival of *The Mirror of the Sea*. The sketches about 'The Nursery of the Craft' and 'The "Tremolino"', which follow 'Initiation', show the sea at its most attractive and enchanting – but we read them having been warned, and we perceive their raptures from the perspective of a sobering experience which has peeled off naive illusions. The 'Tremolino' tale looks in this perspective what it is: a romanticized story of a youthful and foolhardy adventure.

When we try to sum up the essential content of *The Mirror* – its 'message' – we arrive at a paradox. The book may seem to promise to be a collection of sketches about the glamour and romance of the sea; in fact it argues that 'the sea has never been friendly to man'.[8] Sailing's ultimate aim is shown to be a safe landing; and the 'Emblems of Hope' in the title of the second sketch are anchors, which make a vessel stationary. This paradox is highlighted at the beginning of section XXXVIII (in 'The Nursery of the Craft'): 'Happy he who, like Ulysses, has made an adventurous voyage.' One does not even have to know Joachim Du Bellay's famous sonnet, from which the above is a quotation, to realize that Ulysses was happy not because he travelled (much against his wish), but because, after all his adventures, he finally returned home. Conrad does not carry the quotation to its original – and logical – conclusion, where Du Bellay states that he prefers the sweetness of his home village to sea air:[9] that would have put him personally in a painful spot, as he himself, while a sailor, did not have a home to return to.

This evasion is superbly characteristic of the author's personal presence in *The Mirror*. The book is not an autobiography in the sense of a factual report. When we try to pin down biographical data and connect the events described as Conrad's reminiscences with documented facts, an identification often turns out to be impossible. Many 'remembered' events simply do not have plausible counterparts in Conrad's life. Neither the risky berthing of a ship at the Circular Quay in Sydney,[10] nor the putting another one off ground after an accidental stranding (pp. 69–70), nor many other events, including the rescue of the crew of a Danish brig in 'Initiation', can be traced to facts in Conrad's biography. He was, in spite of his protestations to the contrary (p. 64), several times a passenger on a ship; and was master of only one seagoing vessel, although he uses the plural when mentioning his 'commands' (p. 69). Even 'The "Tremolino"', the most insistently autobiographical piece, verily bristles with details which appear to have no basis in his own experience, or which at best are lifted from some other time and place.

All that is, however, of interest mainly to Conrad's biographers. For the common reader *The Mirror of the Sea* emanates a vision of its author and his life: not reconstructed, but re-imagined, re-created; a life emotionally and intellectually coherent and meaningful. It is a vision of a man attracted to the sea by its romantic glamour; who took his work in ships seriously both in the professional and in the moral sense; who viewed the sea as a testing ground of himself – and of man in general.

The sea of *The Mirror* is enchanting, cruel and unlovable. Its fascination consists in the challenge it poses to man's courage and fidelity. And man's relation to it grows into a metaphor of the human condition in general: the sea mirrors Nature, oblivious to human ideals and sacrifice, testing man coldly and mercilessly. It constitutes an immense stage for his achievement and failure, for his moral greatness or villainy – which are solely of his own making, not connected with any universal order of things.

The Mirror is an uneven book. There are fragments, as in the sketch 'Rulers of East and West', which may serve as demonstrations of Conrad's perilous stylistic propensities: flights into sheer rhetoric, overdrawn metaphors, more pomp than substance. There is occasional padding, with words taking lead of ideas and images rather than images and ideas dictating words. Also, the composition of the volume looks – and is – partly accidental, with the last essay evidently tagged on artificially. However, the degree of intellectual consistency indicates how representative of and integrated in Conrad's thought *The Mirror of the Sea* is, how deeply rooted in Conrad's philosophy is the basic imagery of the sea as a mirror of the Universe. There are three fine chapters ('The Character of the Foe', 'Initiation', 'The Nursery of the Craft') and many fine fragments, which provide an excellent introduction to Conrad's typical motifs and ideas – such as this remarkable sentence: 'Faithfulness is a great restraint, the strongest bond laid upon the self-will of men and ships on this globe of land and sea' (p. 111); or another about 'some particle of the mob spirit, of the mob temperament' lurking 'in each of us' (p. 29).

Conrad's idea of a series of 'sea sketches' originated in late 1903; it seems most likely that it was suggested by Ford Madox Ford, with whom

Conrad had collaborated on *The Inheritors* (1901) and *Romance* (1903). Writing to his literary agent, James B. Pinker, Conrad reeled off a list of planned titles: 'Gales of Wind', 'Up Anchor', 'Yards and Masts', 'The Cut of the Sails', 'The Web of Ropes', 'Old Timbers', 'Round the Compass', 'The Chance of Landfalls', 'The Run of the Seas'[11] – most of them were later changed, some dropped altogether. Ford assisted Conrad in writing, or rather dictating, the first six sketches ('Landfalls and Departures', 'Emblems of Hope', 'The Fine Art', 'Weight of the Burden', 'Overdue and Missing', and 'The Grip of Land'), which were begun in the first days of 1904 and ready by the beginning of March. The work was done in London, where both Conrad and Ford came to stay for three months. Conrad's attention and energy were at that time concentrated on ending *Nostromo*, which cost him an enormous effort.

In late March Conrad returned to Pent Farm, his cottage in Kent; Ford's assistance ceased.[12] By 18 April 1904 he had written three more 'papers' (as he now called the sketches): 'The Character of the Foe', 'Rulers of East and West' and 'In Captivity'. Then a long break occurred. Although in May Conrad assured the patient Pinker that 'I am confident that from the word *go* I could get the Mirror of the Sea ready in six weeks',[13] in summer and autumn 1904 only two more essays were written: 'The Faithful River' and 'Cobwebs and Gossamer'. Conrad returned to the series only in July 1905, adding 'Initiation', and in autumn that year the last three: 'The Nursery of the Craft', 'The "Tremolino"', and 'The Heroic Age'.

The volume collecting these sketches – which appeared in various magazines, under different headings and in a sequence other than in the book – turned out to be not too easy to assemble. Doing the job took Conrad more than a fortnight: 'It is surprising how much time was taken up in putting it into shape', he complained to Pinker on 5 March 1906.[14]

The Mirror of the Sea was published on 4 October 1906. It was well, sometimes enthusiastically, received by critics and some of Conrad's fellow-writers. Henry James outbid them all in effusiveness:

> I read you as I listen to rare music – with deepest depth of surrender, & out of these depths I emerge slowly and reluctantly again ... Nothing you have done has more in it. The root of the matter of *saying*. You stir me in fine to amazement & you touch me to tears, & I thank the powers who so mysteriously let you loose with such sensibilities, into such an undiscovered country – *for* sensibility.[15]

Conrad must have read these words of 'the Master' with pleasure tempered by frustration. Surely, he did not want to be assessed, as a writer, on the strength of these sketches. I think they show his true stature at a point of departure, not of arrival; they may be seen as a document of temptations he had to resist in becoming a great writer. We understand Conrad's real measure when we remember that he wrote *The Mirror* at the same time as he struggled with *Nostromo* and *The Secret Agent*.

8

A Personal Record

In 'A Familiar Preface', which Conrad wrote to *A Personal Record* in the late summer of 1911, he says that 'this little book is the result of a friendly suggestion'. Even if true, this certainly is not the whole nor the essential truth. While it is highly probable that Ford Madox Ford encouraged Conrad to write his autobiography (he was to produce several autobiographical books himself), it is also evident that Conrad had his own very strong reasons. And, ironically, what Ford wanted to publish in his *English Review* – the monthly he started in December 1908 – was not 'this little book', but a much longer text.

The earliest mention of the project we find in Conrad's letter to James B. Pinker of 18 September 1908: 'These are to be intimate personal autobiographical things under the general title (for book form perhaps) of the Life and the Art... they will be concerned with Polish life and life at sea, intimate thought and sensations.'[1] By that time, however, the first section had already been written, to appear in the opening issue of the *English Review*. Five weeks before that letter, on 10 August 1908, Robert Lynd – then a well-known critic – had published in the *Daily News* a review of Conrad's recent volume of short stories, *A Set of Six*. He attacked Conrad for not writing in his native language:

> Mr Conrad, as everybody knows, is a Pole, who writes in English by choice, as it were, rather than by nature... To some of us... it seems a very regrettable thing, even from the point of view of English literature. A writer who ceases to see the world coloured by his own language – for language gives colour to thoughts and things in a way that few people understand – is apt to lose the concentration and intensity of vision

without which the greatest literature cannot be made ... Mr Conrad, without either country or language, may be thought to have found a new patriotism for himself in the sea. His vision of men, however, is the vision of a cosmopolitan, of a homeless person.[2]

Initially, Conrad reacted with dejection. 'It is like abusing a tongue-tied man, for what one can say. The statement is simple and brutal; and any answer would involve too many feelings of one's inner life, stir too much secret bitterness and complex loyalty to be even attempted with any hopes of being understood', he complained in a letter to his close friend, the literary critic Edward Garnett,[3] the man who had accepted his first novel for publication fourteen years before. But then he decided to do just what he had apparently rejected: to deal in print with his complex feelings and loyalties. *A Personal Record* became his considered reply.*

Privately and publicly, Conrad tried to play down the importance to himself of *Some Reminiscences* (the title under which *A Personal Record* originally appeared), and stressed Ford's role in prevailing upon him to take up the idea. He wrote to H. G. Wells:

> Ford has persuaded me to give some personal stuff for the [English] R[eview] ... But I was thinking of doing something of that kind for the boys, yet fearing that I would never do it from mere horror of writing, and this seemed an unique opportunity to pull myself together for an effort in that direction. But I fear it is a silly enterprise besides (what with the stirring up of all these dead) being a somewhat ghoulish one. I explain to you so that you should not suspect me of incipient softening of the brain.[4]

In his 'Author's Note' to *A Personal Record*, written in September 1919, Conrad claimed even – in sharp contrast to Lynd's criticism – that the comments on his not writing in his native language 'had been of the most flattering kind'. These were, however, attempts at covering up his tracks. The repeated insistence on both the painful subjects raised by Lynd – the choice of England 'over' Conrad's own home country and the writing in a foreign language – reveals the psychological impulse behind the series. The fact that an analogous accusation, expressed in the shape

---

* The fragment about the critic 'who, metaphorically speaking, jumps upon me with both feet' (*A Personal Record*, pp. 106–7) seems to refer directly – and sarcastically – to Lynd.

of a charge of 'desertion', had been made earlier (in 1899) by a prestigious Polish novelist, Eliza Orzeszkowa,[5] is an indication that Lynd expressed, in an aggressive way, thoughts and doubts which Conrad must have encountered many times before.

And he decided to reply, in the form not of a defence or an explanation, but of an imaginative autobiographical statement. The result is a splendid piece of personal mythology.

A few weeks after the first announcement, quoted above, Conrad described for Pinker his design in greater detail:

> To make Polish life enter English literature is no small ambition – to begin with . . . To reveal a very particular state of society, bring forward individuals with very special traditions and touch in a personal way upon such events for instance as the liberation of the serfs . . . is a big enterprise. And yet it presents itself easily just because of the intimate nature of the task, and of the 2 vols. of my uncle's Memoirs which I have by me, to refresh my recollections and settle my ideas . . . A mere casual suggestion has grown into a very absorbing plan . . . I have been thinking of a title something like 'The Art and the Life', or The Pages and the Years, Reminiscences.[6]

To his literary agent, to whom he was heavily in debt, Conrad presented the reminiscences as an easy piece, which would not distract him from the more demanding (and paid in advance) work on *Under Western Eyes*. But he was, as usual with him, deluding both himself and his creditor. Writing, or rather, dictating (to Ford, Miss Lillian Hallowes and Conrad's wife Jessie*), did not go all that easily; also, Conrad had to spend much time on revisions.[8] The contributions to the *English Review* did interfere with other work more wanted by his publishers, who evinced a marked lack of interest in the *Reminiscences*. 'Too much about life in Poland and about Mr Conrad's uncle, and very little about himself and about how he came to write', complained Pinker's American correspondent.[9] Hopes for serialization in the US fell through.[10] Pinker

---

* Ford claimed that he had written *A Personal Record* from Conrad's dictation, but the claim can be only partly true. The evidence in Conrad's letters is not always conclusive, but it seems that he may have dictated to Ford chapters I and III; Miss Hallowes certainly wrote down chapters II and IV; the remaining three were in all likelihood dictated to Jessie (neither Ford nor Miss Hallowes being present at Aldington); at least a part of the last and shortest chapter VII, was written by Conrad himself.[7]

himself 'didn't think much' of the text.[11] Still, for many months Conrad kept planning to develop his autobiographical essays into a book between two and four times its present size.[12]

By April 1909 Conrad had written seven chapters. He then fell ill with a heavy attack of gout, while at the same time his conflict with Ford, simmering for the last couple of months, boiled over, mostly because of Ford's irresponsibility and even arrogance. Conrad refused to contribute anything more to the *English Review*. The fate of *Some Reminiscences* hung for some time in the balance. Conrad considered the possibility of continuing the work.[13] Finding no encouragement on the part of prospective publishers and in need of money for his son's school, he finally decided to publish the text as it stood; it came out in book form in January 1912. But even afterwards Conrad would come back to the project, outlining a plan of a follow-up 'under the general title of Some Portraits family and others – my uncle the conspirator, two marriages, episodes of the liberation of our peasants and of the '63 rising'.[14] Nothing came out of this; doubtless the general lack of readers' interest in Polish themes played a role.[15]

The narrative structure of *A Personal Record* has evoked expressions of puzzlement and even an accusation of 'incoherence';[16] but while it is true that the literary convention Conrad uses has been more common in Polish than in English literature, its origins are undoubtedly English: in Lawrence Sterne's *Sentimental Journey*. That finely fanciful little book had been greatly admired in Conrad's native country and inspired many highly accomplished successors, which developed Sterne's artfully loose associative construction. In his youth, Conrad certainly read some of these books, and the Sternian parentage of his technique is at times fairly obvious, as at the beginning of chapter IV. We can also discern in *A Personal Record* a touch of *Tristram Shandy*: apparently rambling associations sprinkled with specialist excursuses (e.g., pp. 90–1) hark back to the traditions of learned wit.[17] In fact, there is in this book, in spite of its casually conversational air, little of randomness (with the one exception of the story about the greedy 'X' in chapter III, told for no discernible reason). Changes of subject-matter and of points of view, sometimes playfully flaunted, serve specific artistic and emotional purposes.

The tone of narration is seemingly debonair, with here and there harder glitters of wry humour and sarcasm (which Arnold Bennett particularly praised). This tone forms a screen, tinged with self-irony, through which the reader perceives subjects personal, intimate, puzzling, even embarrassing, sometimes intensely emotional: Conrad's memories of his parents; his leaving Poland with its demanding patriotic heritage; his writing in an alien language; his wish to become a seaman; his turning into a professional writer. But there is little of direct intimacy, with the exception of a few sentences about Conrad's mother and father. When one of his friends criticized the conversational reserve of *A Personal Record*, Conrad defended himself by saying: 'this defect saves the pangs of my shyness'.[18] The real motive was pride, however – as he himself suggests in 'A Familiar Preface', when professing his 'repugnance' to open displays of emotions (p. XVI). Conrad specifically scorned the 'confessional' form of reminiscences and taunted its most eminent practitioner, Jean-Jacques Rousseau. His own principles of restraint and sober self-possession, as laid out in the same 'Preface', were grounded in a distrust of unbridled emotionalism, which may 'enchant' others but carries with itself the danger of falsehood: 'The effort to bring into play the extremities of emotions' is tainted with a 'debasing touch of insincerity' (p. XVII). This justification of the way in which his reminiscences are written contains a salient element of Conrad's artistic credo: he placed himself firmly at the opposite pole to not only Rousseau but also Dostoevsky.

The associative mode of his reminiscences allows Conrad to pass easily from a particular subject in hand to the general problem it poses. Events of his life are shown in sudden flashes of reflection, sometimes beguilingly playful, more often serious and definitive. Several memorable passages express his beliefs: that the 'aim of creation cannot be ethical at all' (p. 92), and thus all human values are of man's own making; that 'the temporal world rests on a few simple ideas; so simple that they must be as old as the hills. It rests notably, among others, on the idea of Fidelity' (p. XIX); that art's true source is 'imagination, not invention' (p. 25). His views on the role of imagination (which for Conrad is basically reconstructive, re-imagination in fact) in art and on the prose art of fiction, which 'is but truth often dragged out of a well and clothed in the painted robe of imaged phrases' (p. 93), are a continuation of thoughts expressed in his celebrated 'Preface' to *The Nigger of the 'Narcissus'*, written in 1896. And the words about 'that spirit of piety towards all things human which sanctions the conceptions of a writer of tales' (p. 25) can be regarded as developing Conrad's old idea of human solidarity which binds the writer of fiction to his readers, and as a variation of his statement (in the said Preface) about art 'rendering the highest kind of justice to the visible universe'.

The most vividly evocative fragment of *A Personal Record* is Conrad's description of his meeting with Almayer; and appropriately so, because it serves the double purpose of illustrating the author's artistic principle of 'imaginative and exact rendering of authentic memories' (p. 25) and providing an additional justification for his becoming a writer.

The feeling of distance which Conrad keeps between himself and his subject, and thus also between himself and his readers, is intensified by the fact that so many of the stories told in *A Personal Record* are reported after another source, namely his uncle Tadeusz Bobrowski's memoirs. Indeed, several fragments of the book are recapitulations or direct translations of Bobrowski's text. Thus – to give only the more important instances – the characteristics of Conrad's mother and her sister, the story of Mr Nicholas B. (the heroic dog-eater), the sordid tale of Conrad's paternal grandmother and her second husband, and the descriptions of the pillage of Mr Nicholas B.'s house and of Conrad's sick mother being compelled to return to exile, are all taken, in various degrees of exactness, from Bobrowski's memoirs, published eight years earlier.[19]

Professing that 'in these personal notes' there was no 'drapery of fiction' such as the 'veil' which separates the novelist from his reader (p. XIII), Conrad wove a different fabric, less obviously conventional but not less artful, protective and decorative at the same time. It exhibits the unity of artistic and psychological principles on which the book is built, and enables Conrad to create his private mythology – an artefact of his life, as it were – without blatant distortion of facts.

And there are many distortions, but blunted and obfuscated by the way of telling, to be exposed only by an inquisitive researcher. They are of scant importance for the appreciation of *A Personal Record*, but they are significant in pointing at the book's fundamental idea. This idea was formulated by Conrad himself: to give the vision of 'a coherent, justifiable personality both in its origin and in its action' (p. XXI). All departures from factual truth are explainable by reference to this basic idea, to that underlying need: to impress coherence on his life, with all its anomalous passages, unusual decisions and sudden changes, with all its uncertainties, typical of a man prone to depression, the most severe bout of which, confining him to bed for many weeks, occurred only a few months after the writing of *A Personal Record*. This search for consistency, the real need of it, is shown not only in various omissions of events which would put it in question, and by adducement of events imagined, but, most visibly, in the avoidance of any suggestion, typical in the autobiographies of writers close to Romanticism, of internal tensions within his mind, of the Faustian 'two souls in one breast', of hesitancy, conflicting desires and aspirations. Conrad wants to and does present himself as being of one piece.

To call this fictional, 'created' Conrad 'public' as opposed to 'private' (i.e., real) is, I think, misleading. It is not the private and public faces that are in question here, but rather the actual Conrad and Conrad as he wished himself to be. Writing about himself was for Conrad a way of dealing not only with his readers, but first with himself. He wanted to be, not only to be seen, like that.

When he looked back at his life, there loomed in it a few especially sensitive and painful issues: those 'questions, some of which have remained unanswered to this day', as he had written a few years before in *The Mirror of the Sea*.[20] Leaving Poland had evidently impressed itself on his conscience as an act to be explained and somehow justified, especially in the light of his parents' sacrifice for their country. He declares his own 'fidelity to a special tradition' and even 'love' for Poland's memory, and shows his compatriots in a nimbus of romantic heroism, but repeatedly stresses the tragic hopelessness of Polish national aspirations: 'It has been the fate of that credulous nation to starve for upwards of a hundred years on a diet of false hopes' (p. 46). He could thus, while preserving his natural pride, portray his departure as combined with a tragic awareness of the futility of continuing his ancestors' exertions. And the images of his native land are like memories of a long-submerged Atlantis, as if his own leaving meant that it ceased to exist at all.

His resolve of going to sea presents Conrad as unswerving, wilful and absurdly unusual; in fact it was none of these. His joining the British merchant marine was a matter of accident, not of primary design.

Conrad is quite right in claiming that he did not consciously 'choose' English as the language of his works; yet writing in English was for him pre-eminently not a consequence of some inherent determinism, but a result of the force of events. Similarly, Conrad adjusts many other, less essential elements and aspects of his life. The final sentences, in which the Mediterranean land- and seascape appears as grey, livid and drab in contrast to the brightness of the Red Ensign, are perhaps the most glaring example of this wizardry.

In conclusion, *A Personal Record* is a captivating and moving book, which tells us something about Joseph Conrad's real past, about his family and national background, and much about his persistent quest to impose on his life a meaning – a meaning consistent with the stern demands of the moral principles he had formulated and in which he believed.

9
Joseph Conrad's *The Secret Agent,* or the melodrama of reality

Melodrama may be most generally defined as a sequence of events for which 'normality' (or verisimilitude, if it is represented or described) is claimed, but which is too spectacularly dramatic, too extravagant to be taken as 'normal' or realistic. It is, of course, a culturally and historically relative concept: what is melodramatic for a reader of *The New Yorker* is not so for a reader of *True Stories*; a novel by Smollett or Balzac is, for us today, inherently more melodramatic than one by Sinclair Lewis or Roger Martin du Gard.

There is the melodrama of events and the melodrama of presentation; the two often overlap, but not necessarily. On the one hand, a straightforward description of the plight of the nineteenth-century immigrants to the United States, of the trenches in Flanders in 1916, or of a Soviet labour camp may strike us as melodramatic by the sheer force of facts related. On the other hand, it is possible to describe hidden psychological developments in a manner which has to be called melodramatic; Henry James would sometimes do that, as has been pointed out by several critics.

In its developed literary and dramatic forms, melodrama rests on the principle of unabashed emotionalism. It strives to call forth unambiguous and strong feelings, plays on polarities of moods, selects plots abounding in emotionally loaded situations, uses starkly contrasted characters and impassioned speech; there is hardly any withholding of anticipated emotional gratification and the denouement is psychologically unequivocal. These 'ontological' rules tally with the fundamental axiological principle of melodrama: it operates on black-and-white contrast of moral values, or, to put it more adequately, enacts violent conflicts of moral extremes.[1]

The words 'melodrama' and 'melodramatic' are often used with reference to the work of Joseph Conrad. Usually this is done in an accusatory manner, pointing at his apparent weakness for popular artistic clichés. Thus it is not superfluous to point out that melodrama appears in Conrad's work in many functions and guises. We find in his stories both the melodrama of events, as in 'Typhoon' and the unfinished *Suspense*, and the melodrama of presentation, as in 'The Black Mate' and *The Arrow of Gold*. And, of course, there are novels where melodramatic events are melodramatically described, as in the early *An Outcast of the Islands*, in *The Rescue*, and in the late *Victory* and *The Rover*. It is widely agreed that the appearance of melodramatic conventions mars the structure of these ostensibly realistic novels, and in the case of *Victory* makes the symbolism of this novel obtrusively evident and garishly simple.

That Conrad was not irresistibly and passively drawn to melodramatic conventions is shown by the example of 'Typhoon', where he skilfully deflates the latent emotionalism of the plot by detachment and parries black-and-white simplifications by display of gentle irony. It is only in *The Secret Agent* (1907), however, that Conrad demonstrates his dexterity in employing the techniques of melodrama for very different and by no means simply parodistic ends. *The Secret Agent* is also Conrad's only piece with reference to which he himself used the concept of 'melodrama': he wrote to R. B. Cunninghame Graham that the novel was 'a sustained effort in ironical treatment of a melodramatic subject'.[2]

As aesthetic categories, melodrama and irony are polar opposites. While melodrama blows up, irony deflates. But what Conrad does, in fact, is not only to present a melodramatic subject in a non-melodramatic manner but also to put certain typical melodramatic conventions to a fresh use. And he does all that, I shall be trying to show, not as an artistic experiment or exercise in skills, but to obtain his unusual aesthetic effects and, above all, to convey, in this distinctive fashion, a specific intellectual message. *The Secret Agent* was supposed to be, in Conrad's words in the same letter to Graham, 'a new departure in genre', an intentionally meaningful departure.

The events forming the plot of *The Secret Agent* are sensational and gory enough: a double, or rather treble, agent serving the anarchist movement, the Russian embassy in London and the British police; a scientist producing explosives for terrorist purposes; a half-wit blown to pieces by a bomb; a husband knifed to death by his wife; there is provocation, betrayal, robbery, suicide; among the principal characters are anarchists, policemen, foreign diplomats, a statesman, a devoted mother, a loving sister and an idiot. The narrative, however, goes against the melodramatic grain of the subject-matter. The course of action does not resolve the conflicts but makes them more complex and ambiguous; instead of simple contrasts we are faced with manifold deceptions, misunderstandings and ambiguities. The story does not end with a final triumph of good over evil but on scenes of moral confusion and desolation.

The only pure emotions are those of an idiot – and these are cynically aroused and perversely exploited. (By the way, Stevie does not – *pace* Professor Irving Howe – escape Conrad's irony.[3] And he is a literary cousin not so much of Dostoevsky's Prince Myshkin – the standard association of critics – but of the Romantic 'fools', simpletons and madmen who understood the world in the terms of their hearts. Stevie is even, ironically, called an 'artist'.) And the stronger the emotions of other characters, the more muddle they cause. Thus emotions are not, as in melodrama, the locus of a clear distinction between good and evil but a domain of chaos and hopelessness.

The last conversation of the Verlocs, ended by Winnie stabbing her husband, is, as a subject, pure melodrama – but it is written as an anti-melodramatic *tour de force*. The Verlocs express their raw, deepest feelings: fear and hatred, disillusionment, weariness and despair. But there are no effusions, no overstatements; the dialogue is languid and convincingly naturalistic, and the pace of the scene is the slowest in the whole book. And in spite of the mutual frankness of the couple, contrasting with their earlier reticence, and total in that they are now not hiding anything intentionally, the scene is a piling-up of confusions and misconstructions. Winnie Verloc's thought, 'what were words to her now?' (p. 250),[4] is revealing: contrary to the melodramatic principle of a final disclosure of facts and feelings, what does not meet the eye is deemed important. 'What could words do to her for good or evil in the face of her fixed idea?' (p. 250). Winnie does not try to deceive her husband, but there is nothing in her words and behaviour that would warn her husband about his impending doom; in Adolf Verloc's perorations there is nothing intended to fool Winnie or to arouse her fury. Thus full sincerity may be fully deceiving; what is on both sides intended and perceived as a moment of truth, turns out to be a scene of thickening confusion that leads straight to murder.

While in melodrama the initial mysteries and muddles are finally and triumphantly resolved, in *The Secret Agent* mysteries keep multiplying. The perplexities reach their dramatic peak some fifteen pages from the end in the scene where Comrade Ossipon mistakes the corpse of Verloc for the living man. Unlike this last case, most of these mysteries remain ultimately unresolved – for the characters, that is, not for the readers. Robert D. Spector believes that the whole irony of *The Secret Agent* consists in a gradual exposure of the ignorance the novel's characters display concerning each other's motives, plans and actions.[5] This, however, is only one of the ways in which Conrad's irony works.

Making dynamic use of a secret is, of course, one of the commonest conventions of melodrama. In *The Secret Agent* this convention is blithely and brilliantly transmogrified. Secrecy is used not to heighten the tension, to play on opposites, or to dramatize the basic good–evil contrast; we do not have characters who are overtly good and secretly evil, or apparently evil and in fact good. The thrills of this thriller do not come from unexpected developments and suspense: most of the plot's events are clearly foreshadowed. Secrecy is used to expose the intricate connections and interplays between *good* and *evil*. More importantly, what is secret in the novel is shown to be soothing and stabilizing; to disclose too much or to investigate too deeply – in other words, to blow the cover of secrecy – is imprudent, disturbing, risky. Winnie Verloc believes, in the often-quoted phrase, 'that things do not stand much looking into' (p. 177). Her attitude amounts to the tacit acceptance of a web of secrets around her. It also makes her more 'secret' than her husband: being incurious, she does not provoke any questions about herself either. When the death of her brother compels Winnie to 'look into' things, she flies into a murdering rage.

The stabilizing role of the 'uninquiring acceptance of facts' (p. 153) and tolerance of secrets is demonstrated by several other characters: Mr Vladimir and the Assistant Commissioner, Stevie and Inspector Heat.

As long as they do not show too much inquisitiveness, things keep to their steady, unobtrusive (and corrupt) course. The acceptance of secrets also forms a part of the irony in *The Secret Agent*. Secrecy is obviously a degeneration of human intercourse and of communal life in general; if it is shown to be a condition of relative peace, then, by the same token, the existing order of things is shown to be degrading.

The 'natural' progress of a sensational plot is from secrets and obscurity to discoveries, revelations and clarifications. In *The Secret Agent* the course is different: we pass from secrets and simplicity to confusion and ambiguity. And while in melodrama such events as murder, suicide and treason are understood to represent reality, in *The Secret Agent* they are shown to hide it: they are just its visible outward manifestations, misleading if taken at their face value. This is why Conrad does not bother to keep us in suspense, does not hesitate to describe the reasons and preparations for a crime, to presage the most dramatic events of the story. Again, what does not strike the eye is most important.

The high-pitched language of melodrama is sometimes used in *The Secret Agent* but ironically to deflate, not to build up the mood. When Conrad says that Mr Verloc 'descended into the abyss of moral reflections' (p. 52), or when a flicker in the eyes of Mrs Verloc is compared to 'a ray of sunshine heralding a tempest of rain' (p. 297), the effects are mock-heroic.

A mock-heroic poem or novel (like *Joseph Andrews*), however, is not a burlesque and requires a standpoint from which the heroic is being mocked. Irony consisting of a determined effort to expose shams, to blow covers, to reveal deceptions, implies an assessing authority that commands these devastating actions. It is sometimes assumed that this authority is in *The Secret Agent* a thoroughly nihilistic one, that it undermines and destroys without any positive reason or value in the background, that Conrad does not evaluate but only derides. Such an interpretation puts Conrad on a level with the bomb-producing Professor, the only 'perfect' anarchist of the novel.

Is *The Secret Agent* a nihilistic book, a work in which irony turns its corrosive force upon itself, a novel lacking – to quote Irving Howe – 'a moral positive to serve literary ends'? Or is it, in J. Hillis Miller's words, a novel in which 'Conrad's voice and the voice of the darkness most nearly become one'?[6]

There are two characters, one minor and the other fairly central, with whom the reader may easily sympathize or even identify: the old lady patroness of Michaelis and the Assistant Commissioner. Neither of them is immune to ironic treatment: in the case of the old lady it is, however, counterbalanced by a dose of respect; and in the case of the Assistant Commissioner it is reduced to the vestigial level of good-humoured jokes about his foreign appearance. From neither of these do we fear any duplicity; in the presence of the latter we feel relaxed and confident: here we have, for a change, somebody who is not morally suspect – and who is clever to boot.

But for the vindication of Conrad's claim that *The Secret Agent* 'may even have some moral significance',[7] the end of the novel is more important. The final paragraphs show two characters: Comrade Ossipon, who twelve days before took all her money from Winnie Verloc, and the Professor. Considered in the terms of their own designs they ought to feel successful, and the Professor sounds very sure of himself. But are they presented as victors? Ossipon, supposedly 'scientific' and 'free from the trammels of conventional morality' (p. 297), is brought to his knees by nothing more than remorse for having caused Winnie's suicide. Just when he has achieved what he always wanted – money and with it practically unlimited leisure and access to women – he finds himself incapable of enjoying the fruits of his cunning. He cannot bring himself to face other people and is heading straight for the gutter, the punishment for his betrayal of trust.

The Professor ostensibly fares better. The novel closes on him walking 'unsuspected and deadly, like a pest in the street full of men'. But the Professor feels compelled to avert his eyes 'from the odious multitude of mankind' (p. 311). The multitude impresses this Stirnerian hero with fear because it is 'invincible'. 'The resisting power of numbers, the unattackable stolidity of a great multitude, was the haunting fear of his sinister loneliness' (p. 95). It is only when he is fully swathed in his 'astounding ignorance of worldly conditions' that the Professor feels confident. When we see him last, he is walking ahead, grotesquely ill-matched to the immensity of his self-appointed task: 'His thoughts caressed the images of ruin and destruction. He walked frail, insignificant, shabby, miserable – and terrible in the simplicity of his idea calling madness and despair to the regeneration of the world' (p. 311). He is dangerous, but freakish.

Thus both these characters are ultimately exposed as humbugs: as men of false consciousness at best, despicable frauds at worst.

It is the historical experience of mankind that has shaped the moral ideas to which the Assistant Commissioner turns when balking at Inspector Heat's double-dealings and exposing Mr Vladimir's plotting. It is this moral tradition from which the irony of the novel takes its fibre – and on which it bases its appeal.

The essential seriousness of *The Secret Agent* – a novel which is much more than an 'entertainment' – is sometimes put in question because of the treatment accorded to anarchists. It is true that anarchists in *The Secret Agent* look primitive and one-dimensional when compared with the central personalities of the novel – the Verlocs, Winnie's mother, Stevie, or for that matter even the Assistant Commissioner. We do not, however, have to see this as an artistic failure; it seems more appropriate to consider it an element in the general design of 'ironical treatment of a melodramatic subject'. The anarchists in *The Secret Agent* are characters of a melodrama; they are physical images – embodiments – of their ideals. Thus Michaelis' obesity and consequent immobility signify his optimistic determinism; the cadaverous Yundt represents the staple of terrorism; the Professor's meagre figure contrasted with the strength of his monomaniacal passion points at the monstrous abnormality of his designs. If they are grotesquely overdrawn, simplified and maligned, this is because the ideas and socio-political attitudes they stand for are also grotesque, crude and malevolent. Their arch-enemy, Mr Vladimir, is treated in much the same way – which should acquit Conrad of the accusation that he was particularly unjust to anarchists. In the case of all these characters, melodrama equals realism, just as for Winnie 'the very cry of truth was found in a worn and artificial shape picked up somewhere among the phrases of sham sentiment' (p. 298).

The contemptuous treatment of 'revolutionary' anarchists in *The Secret Agent* does not mean that the social injustice and political oppression that give rise to revolutionary movements are dismissed in the novel as non-existent or unimportant. On the contrary, causes for social and economic grievances are plainly in evidence. 'Bad world for poor people' (p. 171) stands here as a documented statement, though the context of this verdict may be bizarre. Demands for civil liberties are also quite obviously regarded as well founded. If Conrad ridicules his anarchists, this is not because he considers them rebels without a cause; he only thinks they are either wrong-headed, or impostors, or both. Take Comrade Ossipon, the 'ex-medical student' (p. 44). This professional educationist and writer of leaflets treats education and knowledge with utter contempt. All he believes in is emotional rabble-rousing. 'What the people knows does not matter' (p. 50). The terrorist Karl Yundt would like to harness 'the suffering and misery of poverty...all the hopeful and noble illusions of righteous anger, pity, and revolt' (p. 48) to his programme of 'no pity for anything on earth...death enlisted for good and all in the service of humanity' (p. 42).

They are outside the mainstream of the conflicts between the rich and the poor, the idle and the exploited, the oppressors and the oppressed. They are the lunatic fringe of these conflicts. But marginal as they may be, they are both symptomatic and dangerous. Symptomatic, because they show that the divisions listed above are not identical with the good–evil demarcations, that evil breeds evil – in the form of 'sinister impulses which lurk in the blind envy and exasperated vanity of ignorance' (p. 48). Professional oppositionists are at least as prone to moral degeneration as professional rulers. Dangerous, because it is easier to provoke hatred than compassion, to destroy than to reform, to kill than to co-operate. Today, when one reads the Professor's theorizing, 'To break up the superstition and worship of legality should be our aim. Nothing would please me more than to see Inspector Heat and his likes take to shooting us down in broad daylight...what's wanted is a clean sweep and a clear start for a new conception of life' (p. 73), one is struck by Conrad's uncanny gift of prophecy.

The anarchists as portrayed in *The Secret Agent* may be atypical as revolutionaries or even as anarchists – although nobody can deny that there were, and are, many like them – they are certainly, as I have said, outside the mainstream of social and political movements; but they can influence the course of events. They can influence it not by giving to it a fresh impetus, by subjecting it to some new organizing principle – but by derailing it, by making the existent structures malfunction or even collapse.

Therefore, these melodramatic heroes are both grotesque, almost absurd – and real, significant, portentous. A lunatic fringe represents here some essential socio-political issues. And this very fact, that a melodramatic subject-matter and melodramatically construed characters are so uniquely suited to expressing serious truths, forms an inherent artistic reason for Conrad's irony. Look here, he seems to be saying, if this is our situation, if such people, such grotesque people as Mr Vladimir or Mr Verloc or Comrade Ossipon or the Professor can influence our life or cause our death, if we are defended by such men as Heat and governed by such as Sir Ethelred – then irony is indeed the only attitude worthy of a serious person.

10

Conrad, Russia and Dostoevsky

Immediately after its publication *Under Western Eyes* was granted the label of an anti-Russian book, and it stuck: such has been the prevailing view of Western critics and scholars since. Indeed, its text abounds in sharply critical remarks about the Russian national character, which can be used to support this view. The issue of whether it has either a Western, or a Polish bias has been raised and discussed innumerable times. Only the evident limitations of the horizons of the somewhat stuffy narrator, the Geneva-based English teacher of languages, save the novel's general perspective from being simply identified with the 'Western eyes' of the title. Still, a common critical assumption is that Russia as a whole is here viewed from the outside – and summarily condemned.

Under Western Eyes was one of Conrad's first works to be translated into Russian: in 1912, almost immediately after its publication.* In 1925, eight years after the Bolshevik Revolution, a new translation appeared. Both were well received by the critics, who commented about the obvious analogies with Dostoevsky's *Crime and Punishment* as well as echoes of *The Devils*, but did not complain of anti-Russian prejudice: on the contrary, Conrad was repeatedly praised for his knowledge of Russian realities and for his psychological perspicacity.[1]

Why was it so? First, the very fact that *Under Western Eyes* received in 1912 the approving stamp of official censorship indicates that the

---

* Conrad's claim in his 'Author's Note' to the 1920 edition of the novel, that 'six years' after its original publication he 'heard that the book had found universal recognition in Russia and had been re-published there in many editions', cannot be substantiated.

atmosphere in Russia had changed from the period described in the novel. It changed even more after 1917; and while in the first years after the Revolution the communists' ideological vigilance was still sufficiently lax to allow the publication of this radically anti-revolutionary book, the very difference in the political situation inserted a protective distance between the text and its interpreters. (In later years Conrad was condemned and banned as a rabid anti-communist; this last classification he had certainly deserved.)

Secondly, in Conrad's novel a 'bad' Russia is not openly contrasted with a 'good' West; Switzerland, the emblematic representative of Western 'bourgeois' democracy, is itself an object of sarcastic gibes.

However, the main reason is more substantial: most of the 'anti-Russian' statements found in *Under Western Eyes* echo or even repeat the opinions about Russian autocracy, political traditions and social attitudes which had been expressed earlier by Russian liberal, democratic and radical thinkers.

A telling example is the image of Russia (appearing in the mind of Razumov, the main protagonist) as 'a monstrous blank page awaiting the record of an inconceivable history'.[2] It has been pointed out that these words echo a fragment in Adam Mickiewicz's *Dziady* (The Forefathers' Eve).[3] However, Mickiewicz's lines are in their turn a reflection of an image found in the famous 1829 *Philosophical Letter* of the early Russian 'dissident' Pyotr Chaadaev (1793–1856), in punishment for writing which the author was declared insane by the Tsar.[4]

In the *Letter* Chaadaev writes that Russia has never known the basic Western moral ideas 'of duty, justice, law, and order'. '[W]e never advanced along with other people; we are not related to any of the great human families; we belong neither to the West nor to the East, and we possess the traditions of neither.' '[I]solated by a strange destiny from the universal movement of humanity, we have absorbed nothing, not even traditive ideas of mankind.' 'What is habit and instinct to other people must be forced into our heads with hammer blows.' '[W]e are strangers to our own selves.' '[W]hat renders us indifferent to the hazards of life also renders us indifferent to good and evil, to truth and falsehood.' 'Even in our glances I find there is something strangely vague, cold, uncertain.'[5]

Twelve years later Mikhail Lermontov, one of Russia's greatest poets, considered subversive by the authorities, wrote before his second exile to the Caucasus: 'Farewell, unwashed Russia / Land of slaves, land of masters / And you, blue uniforms [of the police] / And you people, devoted to them.'[6]

The verdict of the most important Russian émigré political writer Alexandr Herzen was calmer but no less critical:

> What is then this monster called Russia, which demands so many offerings and which leaves to its children nothing but a sorry choice of either moral perdition within an environment hostile to everything humane, or death at the beginning of their lives? A bottomless pit where even the best swimmers disappear, where the greatest efforts, the greatest talents, the greatest abilities perish before they manage to accomplish anything.
>
> ... a strange soil has been prepared by the Tsar's paternal government and imperial civilization in our 'kingdom of darkness'. It is the soil on which seedlings of great promise have grown, on the one hand, into worshippers of the Muravëvs and the Katkovs and, on the other, into the bullies of Nihilism and the impudent Bazarov free lances.*[7]

Nikolai Chernyshevski, a leading radical thinker whose theories were fiercely attacked by Dostoevsky, encapsulated his judgement in a pithy phrase, quoted later by Lenin himself: 'A wretched nation, nation of slaves: from top to bottom – all slaves.'[8]

What the puzzled English–Swiss teacher of languages says about Russia and the Russians in *Under Western Eyes* does not sound more damning but carries with it less authority. In any case, most of these ideas were already familiar to Russian readers. In fact, Conrad repeats, both in Razumov's interior monologues and in the narrator's commentary, many arguments of a debate which went on throughout the whole of the nineteenth century. It was the debate between, on the one hand, the apologists of Holy Russia and Tsarist autocracy, and, on the other, the liberal-minded 'Westernizers', who saw Russia as the centre of barbaric despotism in Europe, a nation strangled by a monstrous political and spiritual tyranny.

---

* Mikhail Muravëv, nicknamed 'the hangman' for his brutal suppression of the Polish uprising of 1863; Mikhail Katkov, a reactionary and chauvinist journalist; Bazarov, the nihilist protagonist of Turgenev's novel *Fathers and Sons*.

2

Conrad was a Russophobe: this seems to have been the conventional wisdom for many years. And there is, again, ample evidence to support this thesis, coming from both Conrad's biography and his work. In one of his earliest preserved letters (of 1885) to another Pole, Spiridion Kliszczewski, Conrad speculates about the possibility of Great Britain entering 'an Anti-Russian alliance'.⁹ Thirteen years later, writing to the same addressee, Conrad complains about England's missed 'last chance to assert itself in the face of Russia'.¹⁰ In 1904, in a letter to *The Times*, he fulminated about Russian warships firing upon English fishing boats.¹¹ This last instance was an exceptional and brief occasion for Conrad's attitude to overlap with the prevailing mood of his adopted country's public opinion. To his disgust, Great Britain remained Russia's ally till the end – that is, till the Bolshevik Revolution of November 1917. And fourteen months after its outbreak Conrad complained to Sir Hugh Clifford that 'The mangy Russian dog gone mad is now being invited to sit at the Conference [Peace Conference in Versailles] table, on British initiative!'¹²

Conrad was certainly aware that his feelings and opinions about Russia were not shared in his British political environment. This awareness was probably most acute in the years 1919–21: David Lloyd George (Prime Minister 1916–22) was hostile to Poland as a reborn state; in summer 1920 English dockers refused to load munitions destined for Poland, fighting at the time for her life against a Soviet invasion. Conrad himself knew that his 'unfavourable view of Russia' was notorious:* 'I would have been abused if I had voiced' the predictions of Russian behaviour towards their Romanian allies.¹⁴ Generally, when reading his pronouncements on Russian subjects we have to remember that their occasional aggressiveness could in fact have been a self-defensive manoeuvre.

A good example is Conrad's letter to Edward Garnett, in which he charges his friend with having learned his history 'from Russians no doubt' and thus forgetting that Conrad, as a Pole, has been 'used to go to

---

* And at least once used this notoriety for his own convenience, when he peremptorily explained away his break with Ford Madox Ford, writing: 'A Russian [David Soskice] has got hold of the E[nglish] R[eview] and I can not [*sic*] contribute any more.'¹³

battle without illusions'.[15] Indeed, when Conrad mentions Russia, it is more often than not in the context of Poland: whether in his letters to friends, such as Cunninghame Graham, John Quinn, and Christopher Sandeman,[16] or in his political essays, 'A Note on the Polish Problem' and 'The Crime of Partition'. In 'Autocracy and War', Conrad's longest and most ambitious political statement, Poland is mentioned only once but in a crucial passage, which links together German and Russian imperialism in their 'common guilt'.[17]

'Autocracy and War', published nine years before the outbreak of the First World War, ends with a prophetic warning – 'Le Prussianisme, voilà l'ennemi!' – but Conrad's attention is focused on Russia. He begins his essay with an analysis of the consequences of Russia's defeat in her war with Japan. That distant war, fought thousands of miles away, so brutal and bloody that its massive atrocity eludes our imagination, had direct implications for Europe. It put an end to the old myth of Russian might and exposed the internal decrepitude of the Tsars' empire.

Interwoven there is another argument, concurrent but less explicit. It is the argument against historical optimism, which finds its expression in the belief in a positive, shaping force of abstract ideas. Simultaneously with his assault on the spectre of Russian tyrannical power, Conrad attacks with derision the 'essentially mediocre phenomenon' of 'the glorious French Revolution' – which, according to him, had at its roots 'the degradation of the ideas of freedom and justice', a degradation made manifest in the person of 'its heir' Napoleon, 'a vulture preying upon the body of Europe'.

Conrad then takes a closer look at the Russian Empire. He presents it as a monster, born from an arbitrary fantasy of Peter the Great. It is therefore a gigantic freak, which possesses no historical justification grounded in 'the constructive instinct of the people'. Russian despotism 'has neither an European nor an Oriental parentage ... it seems to have no root either in the institutions or the follies of this earth'. Russia belongs neither to the West, nor to the East; she remains 'outside the stream of progress'.* She is alien to the conception of legality, grown in

---

* Some of Conrad's opinions, such as the contention that Russia belongs neither to the West nor to the East and that she exists outside history, echo the words of Pyotr Chaadaev. Conrad learned about him either from Astolphe de Custine's famous *La Russie en 1839* or from Anatole Leroy-Beaulieu.[18]

'the shadow of old monarchies of Europe'; she presents an enormous void, 'the negation of everything worth living for'. Russian autocracy is separated by a 'black abyss . . . from the benighted, starved souls of its people'; having no natural historical past, it 'cannot hope for a historical future'. But this very autocracy, which precludes any spontaneous development of the national spirit, is the essence of Russia: 'autocracy, and nothing else in the world, has moulded her institutions, and with the poison of slavery drugged the national temperament into the apathy of a hopeless fatalism'. The Russians are thus seen as victims and helpless hostages of their system; autocracy 'seems to have gone into the blood'. Suppression of all liberty and 'the brutal destruction of dignity' disqualify Russia from giving 'her voice on a single question touching the future of humanity'.

Is there any hope for Russia? Conrad is unable to define it. Of one thing he is certain: the empire will fall apart ('there must be . . . a shattering . . . of the territorial unity'). He predicts that 'the throes of Russian resurrection will be long and painful'. Evolutionary reforms are not possible, because of 'the political immaturity of the enlightened classes' and 'the political barbarism of the Russian people'; anyway, 'There can be no evolution out of a grave.'

Revolution, then? Revolutions in Europe were 'the uprising of the people against the oppressive degeneration of legality'. Since Conrad sceptically opines that 'Every form of legality is bound to degenerate into oppression', a revolution can be seen as 'a short cut in the rational development of national needs in response to the growth of world-wide ideals'. (As he has already condemned the 'Great' French Revolution, Conrad probably has in mind the revolutions of 1830 and 1848.) In any case, such a revolution is impossible in Russia, since no intellectual ground has been prepared for it and there 'never has been any legality in Russia'. Therefore a revolution in Russia 'cannot be anything else but a rising of slaves' which will lead to another 'tyranny, assuming a thousand protean shapes'.

Thus the final dismal verdict sounds, that the revolution in Russia will be both inevitable and fruitless. However, a few months later Conrad greeted with hopeful enthusiasm the changes, such as the convening of the first parliament ever, brought in Russia by pressures of the revolutionary movement; he even mentioned the possibility of an 'orderly rational programme [of a general reform of the state] in accord with the national spirit'.[19] But evidently his hopes were quickly dashed by the dissolution of two consecutive Dumas and a return to the official policy of Russification. The Tsarist system confirmed its fundamental unreformability and Conrad did not need to revise his catastrophic prophecies. After the 'October' Revolution his main concern was 'to keep the Russian infection, its decomposing power, from the social organism of the rest of the world'. That was a prophetic diagnosis, as were his words 'In this Poland [at that time still divided under foreign rules] will have to play its part on whatever lines her future may have to be laid.'[20]

'Autocracy and War' spells out, with a rhetorical flourish, the political reasons for Conrad's animosity towards Russia. It is a damning assessment, which was later expanded and sharpened in fictional form in the pages of *Under Western Eyes*. The condemnatory attitude seems confirmed in Conrad's introductory note of 1920; although he insists on the 'scrupulous impartiality' displayed in the novel, he winds up with the statement that 'all these people are not the product of the exceptional but of the general – of the normality of their place, and time, and race. The ferocity and imbecility of an autocratic rule ... provokes the no less imbecile and atrocious answer of a purely Utopian revolutionism' (p. X). However, more pertinent than Conrad's protestations of his 'absolute fairness' is the fact that all his arguments are political in kind: Russia is, again, condemned for specific reasons, which concern her lawlessness and negation of civic traditions. In other words, Conrad's attitude is hostile but explained in concrete and rational terms.

Does then the epithet 'Russophobe' indeed accurately and fully describe Conrad's complex attitude towards 'things Russian'? The young Russian in 'Heart of Darkness', who from a later historical perspective could be seen as a prophetic portrait of a naive enthusiast of the 'new, better world', is anything but repulsive. In *Under Western Eyes* itself there are several Russian characters who attract our sympathy or at least respect: the Haldin trio, Sofia Antonovna and Tekla.[21] And we have also 'the humane Tomassov', the protagonist of 'The Warrior's Soul' (written in 1916), a young officer of the Russian army at the time of Napoleon I, chivalrous and idealistic.

If these instances, and the memory of Conrad's reaction to the reforms of 1905, should make us hesitate to stick the label 'Russophobic' on his work, still they do not counterbalance the venom of much of what he said and wrote about Russia. To see the problem in full requires yet another approach.

3

Russia was for Conrad not only a country, a system of government, and a people; it was also, and very importantly, a literature. Of course, his friendship with Edward Garnett, who had many Russian friends and whose wife was the most eminent translator of Russian prose into English, played a role. As a result, Russian literature is the third – after English and French (and very far behind, to be exact) – most frequently mentioned in Conrad's letters.

For Conrad, the Russian 'national spirit' did not preclude greatness in art. He considered Ivan Turgenev a great writer, 'an incomparable novelist', an 'incomparable artist'; and wrote, 'Never was a writer so profoundly, so whole-souledly national.'[22] Conrad praised him repeatedly and once described the planned 'sketches' of *The Mirror of the Sea* as 'being in the spirit of Turgenev's *Sportsman Sketches*' – a most ambitious but misplaced claim.[23]

Lev Tolstoy Conrad treated with reserved respect, considering him 'perhaps worthy' of Constance Garnett's translation, but also with hostile suspicion: he was repelled by Tolstoy's theoretical 'anti-sensualism', railed against the 'gratuitous atrocity' of *The Death of Ivan Ilyitch* and the 'monstrous stupidity' of *The Kreutzer Sonata*; and declared that Tolstoy's 'base from which he starts – Christianity' was 'distasteful' to him.[24]

And so while Turgenev was praised although he was a Russian national writer, and Tolstoy blamed for qualities having nothing to do with his nationality, the detested Dostoevsky was for Conrad practically identified with Russianness. 'I don't know what D stands for or reveals, but I know that he is too Russian for me. It sounds to me like some fierce mouthings from prehistoric ages', he commented about *The Brothers Karamazov*. And asked by Garnett for a preface to his study of Turgenev he took the opportunity to contrast the author of *Fathers and Sons* sarcastically with 'the grimacing terror-haunted creature' of Dostoevsky.[25]

Fyodor Dostoevsky, in his youth a radical, imprisoned and sentenced to hard labour for taking part in a juvenile conspiracy, accepted his punishment as an atonement, repented and became a leading reactionary thinker and vocal supporter of the Tsarist regime and religious Orthodoxy. His ideological conversion seemed to validate the repressive methods used by Tsar Nicholas I. Of Poles and their national aspirations he was openly contemptuous.[26] Conrad may have known from his uncle that Dostoevsky repeatedly attacked in his articles and lampooned in *The Brothers Karamazov* Tadeusz Bobrowski's good friend Włodzimierz Spasowicz, a well-known St Petersburg lawyer.[27]

Thus Conrad had sufficient political reasons for considering Dostoevsky an enemy. But Dostoevsky's ethical beliefs were equally unacceptable. Both writers were passionately concerned with moral issues – but the Russian saw them in the light of his religious beliefs. For Dostoevsky, God was necessary for the existence of a moral order: 'If God does not exist, everything is permissible', says his Ivan Karamazov. Moral failures he would treat in terms of pity and forgiveness; moral crimes in terms of penitence and expiation; self-abasement was a typical attitude of his sinful heroes. Conrad, an agnostic, believed that moral norms are man-made, shaped and passed on by tradition, and binding irrespective of the fact that the universe within which we live is morally indifferent. Atonement was for him possible only by way of action, as in *Lord Jim*. His ethical dramas were played out in the categories of duty, fidelity and honour; the contrast between the rigidity of the code and the fragility of man was for him a tragic but unavoidable fact, a necessary concomitant of man's dignity. The deeper Dostoevsky – more explicit than was Tolstoy in his attachment to Christianity – probed the souls of his heroes, the more vividly he presented his 'accursed problems' of suffering and sin, the more memorable were his characters – and the more dangerously seditious must he have appeared to Conrad.

That was not all: Dostoevsky was a powerful, bewitching writer – but a writer of a completely different persuasion. Verbose, disorderly in construction of his stories, wallowing in exhibitionist introspection and endless perorations, he was the very antithesis of Conrad's master Flaubert, he was all the things Conrad warns against in *A Personal Record* when he declares his repugnance at the 'open display of sentiment' and preaches restraint.

Thus there were enough factors political, ethical and artistic to pitch

Conrad against Dostoevsky. That these reasons did not stem from Conrad's national or personal prejudices or obsessions, witness the fact that half a century later a brilliant Russian émigré writer, Vladimir Nabokov, justified his distaste for Dostoevsky in very similar ideological and artistic categories.[28]

Yet there were still other, additional, personal reasons which seem to have made Conrad see Dostoevsky as a personal enemy. As his letters to Garnett indicate, he considered Dostoevsky sick and abnormal. He must have known about Dostoevsky's epilepsy; but he must have also remembered that he himself had suffered from the same affliction. Dostoevsky's gambling mania must have reminded him about his own youthful casino débâcle in Monte Carlo, which ended with an attempted suicide. The Russian monster was a provocation in both the public and personal spheres.[29]

4

Conrad took up the challenge in *Under Western Eyes*. I think that when the pre-eminent Dostoevsky specialist, Joseph Frank, writes that 'Conrad's bitterly anti-Russian animus probably did not allow him to acknowledge how much he learned from Dostoyevsky. (That he knew *Crime and Punishment* by heart is clear to any reader of *Under Western Eyes*)',[30] he falls victim to a misunderstanding. Conrad did not attempt to hide the references to *Crime and Punishment* in his own novel; he flaunted them, beginning with the name of his hero – a 'telling' name, like the name of Dostoevsky's Raskolnikov. But quite irrespective of Conrad's own intentions we have to read *Under Western Eyes* as a text linked to another text, as a response to *Crime and Punishment*, a response in the form of an elaborate replay of several motifs and issues.[31] The borrowings from *Crime and Punishment* which we are going to note are of a different order from most of the 'hidden' borrowings and filiations traced by Ives Hervouet in *The French Face of Joseph Conrad*. They are meaningful: their function and sense consists in that they are recognized by the reader as allusions, gibes, retorts, parodies. When in reading *The Nigger of the 'Narcissus'* we notice that the description of the death of Wait is partly translated from Maupassant's *Bel-Ami*, the effect may be jarring (because of a possible suspicion of plagiarism), but our interpretation of Conrad's novel won't change; nor does it if we realize that the painful words of Natalia Haldin after she hears Razumov's confession repeat the words of Mme de Renal in Stendhal's *Rouge et noir*.[32] But an identification of analogies with *Crime and Punishment* makes the semantic texture of *Under Western Eyes* richer: the latter text refers to the former, and Dostoevsky's novel becomes an auxiliary means of representation of Russian reality.[33]

Let us begin by listing the most obvious parallels. 'Razumov' suggests a man with 'razum', reason; the name of Dostoevsky's 'Raskolnikov' suggests rebellion, but he demonstrates his rebelliousness by the unrestrained use of his mind. Both protagonists commit odious crimes; both produce rational justifications for their acts; both confess them to women they love; and both do it in a situation when the suicide of another possible culprit can dispel all suspicions concerning themselves. Both consider themselves intellectually superior to their environment. Before and after their acts both wander aimlessly around St Petersburg, and are afflicted by a strange illness. In both cases accident plays a role in pushing them to their crimes: in the case of Raskolnikov it is his meeting with Lizaveta; in that of Razumov, the drunkenness of Ziemianitch. Both find it difficult to control themselves at the slightest allusion to their acts; but both tend to play with fire.

Analogies do not concern only the protagonists. The city quarter 'of the very poor' in *Under Western Eyes* seems to be the same district where live the Marmeladovs of *Crime and Punishment*. One of the most memorable scenes of *Under Western Eyes*, when Razumov asks Natalia Haldin if she conceives 'the desolation of the thought – no one – to – go – to?' echoes Marmeladov's words: 'do you realize when you have nowhere to go to?' Raskolnikov's mother goes mad, as does Mrs Haldin. And so on.

There is also a visible parallelism in the development of action: after the fast initial pace of events there follow long sequences of reflections, talks and rencontres; the second part of *Under Western Eyes* contains a high proportion of conversations recorded or reported more typical of Dostoevsky than of Conrad. And then come dramatic accelerations and rather hasty endings.

The main difference between Dostoevsky's novel and Conrad's is that the subject of the latter is more specifically Russian – and political, not primarily moral. Although Raskolnikov's resolve to murder the old woman moneylender is ideologically motivated (and Dostoevsky points an accusing finger at the dangers of social radicalism coupled with Chernyshevsky's 'rational egoism'), his crime is in fact committed for money and could take place in any country. The crimes of *Under Western Eyes* are political and are committed in a characteristically Russian situation: this is the starting-point of Conrad's duel with Dostoevsky. Haldin kills Mr de P– because he sees no other way to give his country a chance of freedom. Razumov betrays Haldin because he is afraid that his career will be ruined ('There goes my silver medal!' is his first thought when Haldin confides in him) and then (in reversal of Raskolnikov's reflections) rationalizes back his denunciation.

Raskolnikov's act was in his original intention supposed to be a protest in the name of social justice, a corrective action. It is shown as sordid and morally devastating. In *Under Western Eyes* an analogous act of protest is Haldin's assassination of Mr de P–, an ideologue and strong man of autocracy. Whatever the reader may think about the general sense of terrorism, Haldin remains a hero and a selfless martyr. Razumov's betrayal of him is practically an act of confirmation and strengthening of the existing system. Here Conrad's novel enters the debate not only with Dostoevsky the moralist of *Crime and Punishment*, but also with the conservative and even reactionary Dostoevsky the politician (of the 'Diary of a Writer' and *The Possessed*). However anti-revolutionary Conrad may have been, he presented the reality of Russian autocracy as unbearable and more repulsive even than the dangers of revolution.

I think we may see the Russian sections of 'Autocracy and War' as an ideological blueprint of *Under Western Eyes*, not in the sense of Conrad's intentions, but in the sense of general political and historical formulas applied.[34] There also exists a textual link between the essay and the novel, and that link concerns Dostoevsky (although he remains unnamed): in 'Autocracy and War' Conrad writes that 'Some of the best intellects of Russia ... ended by throwing themselves at the feet of that hopeless despotism as a giddy man leaps into an abyss', while in *Under Western Eyes* we read, 'many brave minds ... have turned to autocracy for the peace of their patriotic conscience' (p. 34); and again, Councillor Mikulin puts it even more bluntly, 'You shall be coming back to us. Some of our greatest minds had to do that in the end' (p. 295).

In *Crime and Punishment* Porfiry Petrovich, who investigates the murders of the old woman and her sister, is a kind, relaxed, voluble man, anything but sinister; there can be no doubt that not only the law but also justice is on his side. In Conrad's novel the faces of law and order are different. They are cold and ruthlessly efficient; and if Councillor Mikulin stresses – as Porfiry Petrovich also does – that he understands his interlocutor very well and in fact sympathizes with him, the function of this intellectual 'bond' is made very clear: it is a ruse used to facilitate the manipulation of Razumov by the police for their own purposes. It is also clear that the institutions of law and justice are regarded by their official defenders as purely instrumental; for instance, Mikulin does not say it openly but leaves no doubt that Haldin was repeatedly tortured before his death.

Razumov is an illegitimate son of Prince K–. He is thus like the hapless Nejdanov, the protagonist of Turgenev's *Virgin Soil*, son of Prince G., who cannot force himself to live by the principles of social radicalism which he has embraced and commits suicide. Nejdanov's illegitimate birth places him in between social milieux (he is a student, like Razumov). Conrad goes a decisive step further. While endowing his hero with a distinct and memorable individuality, he makes him at the same time a symbolic figure: as the son of a prince and an Archpriest's daughter, Razumov is an offspring of Power and Orthodoxy. More importantly, he feels he belongs to Russia's 'immensity' as a whole; he is thus a loose atom in a swarming mass of the empire's inhabitants, a man without concrete roots, environment and obligations, a perfect embodiment of the nameless, non-personal relationship between autocracy and its subjects.

Razumov is yet another example of Conrad's warnings about the dangers of social alienation; frequently compared to Jim, in his readiness to establish moral rules for himself he makes one think even more of Nostromo. He does not wish to remain lonely, he wants to belong – but to belong only generally (somewhat in the spirit of *The Social Contract* of his patron Rousseau), not concretely. In other words, he wants to belong but without specific societal commitments and responsibilities.

A key statement in *Under Western Eyes*, made before the action starts to develop, is: 'A man's real life is that accorded to him in the thoughts of other men by reason of their respect or natural love' (p. 14).

This is why Razumov, betraying Haldin's trust, has indeed betrayed himself (p. 361) and later, 'living in lie' (thus living an unreal life), he finds himself unable to establish a personal relationship with anybody – and especially with Natalia, with whom he falls in love.

Crime and Punishment is a cautionary tale about a student who commits a crime, led astray by subversive theories and his own intellectual arrogance. *Under Western Eyes* is a tale about a student, intellectually very sure of himself, who commits a crime which he then justifies by his loyalty to Russia (he rejects with scorn the very theories under the influence of which Raskolnikov fell). The whole relationship between Razumov and the government officials is fraught with ironies. He inspires confidence in Haldin, and that is the undoing of both of them. General T– also repeats that he has confidence in Razumov, but in fact does not trust him at all. Razumov calls his denunciation of a trusting colleague 'an act of conscience', wants to do it 'with outward dignity' (pp. 38–9), but quickly becomes an accomplice to torture, execution, and provocation – to end his career as a police agent at the punishing hands of another agent. In the light of 'Autocracy and War', his case is exemplary: in the country without 'law, order, justice, right, truth' loyalty towards the state is a sordid mockery.

The epigraph of *Under Western Eyes*, which quotes Natalia Haldin's words 'I would take liberty from any hand as a hungry man would snatch a piece of bread', also harks back to 'Autocracy and War': 'freedom . . . to Russia must seem everything'. It is not difficult to notice that Dostoevsky plays down in his works the importance of political liberties (as does Razumov, who accepts injustice as a fact of life), if anything stressing the new dangers they create. In his famous Legend of the Grand Inquisitor (in *The Brothers Karamazov*) he transfers the question of freedom onto the metaphysical plane of the human condition in general. Neither 'Autocracy and War' nor *Under Western Eyes* (nor for that matter *The Secret Agent*) contains any simple-minded glorification of the use which the peoples living in Western democracies have made of their civil liberties. Conrad does not sentimentalize freedom, rather the opposite. Still, he shows freedom as clearly preferable to its lack.

There is little of sentiment in *Under Western Eyes*. When it may be expected – as in the relation between Razumov and his father – it is conspicuously absent. When emotions are displayed, as in the Château

Borel sequences, they are shown to be fraudulent. This anti-emotionalism can be seen as another element of Conrad's polemic with Dostoevsky. It is bolstered by the repeated diagnosis that the essential characteristic of the Russians is their 'naive and hopeless' cynicism, typically clothed in 'mystic phrases' (p. 104) and displayed not only by Razumov and the government officials, but even by Natalia Haldin. Jacques Berthoud correctly identifies this cynicism as 'the antithesis of rationality'.[35] It is shown to consist in a voluntarist and irreverent approach to established conventions and in an implicit contempt for the traditional forms and norms of human behaviour. Insistent display of emotions is its favourite cloak.

Jocelyn Baines, who was the first to have a closer look at the parallels between *Under Western Eyes* and *Crime and Punishment*, summed up their differences:

> Raskolnikov's confession is the begining of a process which leads to full repentance and to spiritual regeneration, whereas Razumov's confession is a culmination and is conclusive; Raskolnikov finds his god, but for Razumov, as for Conrad, there is no god ... *Under Western Eyes* is an indictment; its mood is fatalistic, and Conrad's compassion is controlled by a predominantly ironical approach. *Crime and Punishment* is an assertion of ultimate human goodness and the mercy of God, ending with a note of hope and faith.[36]

All this is true; but I would add that Baines' summary places both novels outside history and political geography and in so doing limits their significance.

5

Even apart from the parallels with *Crime and Punishment*, *Under Western Eyes* is a novel abounding in references to Russian literature and history. Most of them have been traced and described several times.[37] Three conclusions can be drawn from all those allusions to real personalities such as General Dmitry Trepov, or Father Gapon, gibes at Mikhail Bakunin, Lev Tolstoy, and Prince Pyotr Kropotkin; details meant sometimes as sarcastic jokes, like in the case of the 'exquisite' bronze of a running adolescent by 'Spontini', who was in fact a composer and not a sculptor (p. 43), and so on. Firstly, the dialogue with Dostoevsky is carried out not simply between two texts, two novels, two novelists –

but within an environment densely populated with more or less clearly identifiable cultural and political figures. Ivan Turgenev (and particularly the Turgenev of *Virgin Soil*) stands at Conrad's elbow, with his women, selfless victims of both autocracy and rebellion, and with his similar if less sombre and tragic assessment of Russia's plight. Secondly, it is neither possible nor necessary to decipher all these allusions, gibes and sarcasms; but we have to remember that for an informed contemporary reader the referential web of *Under Western Eyes* was very rich. And thirdly, it is futile to search for a precise identification and a coherent reconstruction of personalities, movements and events presented in this novel, which is not a piece of fictionalized journalism. As Eloise Knapp Hay argues in her pioneer study of Conrad's political novels, *Under Western Eyes* is a book about generalities, not specifics.* Conrad himself claimed that he was 'concerned with nothing but ideas'.[39]

Two examples: first, Razumov places himself on the side of history as against theory (p. 66). But it is not any theory, any abstract idea of Liberty (p. 50), which has made Victor Haldin and Tekla opt for the revolution – it is their nation's historical reality; and it is the theoretical doctrine of the necessity of autocracy in Russia which provides Razumov with a justification of his betrayal of Haldin. Secondly, Razumov presents himself proudly as a 'thinking reed' (p. 89) but, unlike Pascal whose famous formula he repeats, he negates and wants to escape the tragedy, inherent in such a vision of human existence – the tragedy which Victor Haldin accepts.

6

The reader of *L'Education sentimentale* will not understand much of Flaubert's masterpiece unless she or he is acquainted with French history of the middle of the nineteenth century. Most political novels present the same difficulty. *Nostromo* is from this point of view easier, since the story of Costaguana is told on its very pages; the plot of *The Secret Agent* is comparatively self-contained; but *Under Western Eyes*, with its action not only on the Russian but generally on the European plane, requires for its interpretation a fair amount of knowledge about

---

* She also observes, with pardonable exaggeration, that in comparison with historical sources 'Conrad's novel presents a picture of the Russians as paragons of sanity and civility.'[38]

recent history: not only to discern the signs of irony (as in Peter Ivanovitch's sobriquet of 'Russian Mazzini'), but to realize that the narrator's 'eyes' are looking from an angle which is not quite representative of the European West of the time. Switzerland was the quietest nook of the continent; Britain its oldest parliamentary democracy; and if Razumov chooses to consider Geneva typical, he simply exposes his own ignorance. Ten years before the murder of de P–, the President of France was killed; four years before, the King of Italy; in July 1909 (thus while Conrad was writing his novel) in Catalonia, Solidaridad Obrera staged a virtual uprising, with hundreds killed and many churches destroyed – a violent suppression and the fall of the Spanish Government followed. Anyway, it would have been enough for Razumov to take a slightly longer walk westwards from the Boulevard des Philosophes, across the French frontier, for him to find himself in a country torn by internal strife in the aftermath of the Dreyfus affair, between the Radicals who dissolved and exiled most religious orders and Charles Maurras' xenophobic Catholics of the Action Française. French socialists were quickly becoming the second party of the Republic; the Radicals forged an alliance with Russia. Anything but self-satisfied and placid! At the same time, Germany was growing into the strongest nation in Europe, and the first to enjoy the benefits of social security.

But even more important is the awareness that the division between East and West was in fact as stark as is suggested by the narrator, although he may be, in his fussiness, not always convincing: it was a division between societies which were, to use Karl Popper's terminology, rather (even if not quite) 'open', and Russia, which was a quintessential closed society.

From the point of view of its narrative structure *Under Western Eyes* is a simpler and more consistent novel than *Lord Jim*: the whole story is told by one person, the old teacher of languages. At the same time, however, the narrative perspective is more blurred. The actual contents of Razumov's diary are anything but clear; and, unlike Marlow, the nameless teacher is often vague in identifying the sources of both his information and his thoughts.[40]

This causes even perceptive critics to look anxiously for, in Eloise Knapp Hay's phrase, 'the missing centre' of *Under Western Eyes*: a 'central point of view' which would provide an overall ordering perspective.⁴¹ But, as usual with Conrad, that 'missing centre' is supposed to be filled by nobody else but the reader. Neither in *Lord Jim*, nor in 'Heart of Darkness', nor for that matter in *Nostromo* is there in the text itself an identifiable 'central point of view' which would sum up the 'message' of the story. It is an integral and essential element of Conrad's art that it forces readers to synthesize that message for themselves.⁴²

It has to be admitted that in *Under Western Eyes* Conrad makes this task particularly hard, not only by a certain fuzziness of the narrative structure (and adjacent doubts about the personality of the narrator), but also because the novel has in fact two protagonists: one individual – Razumov – the other collective – Russia. And to make the matters worse, both of them are tragic.

It seems that tragedy resulting from a biological determinism (as in Zola's or Hardy's novels) is in our time more readily understood and more easily accepted: probably because the reader can distance her- or himself far from the determined sequence of events. In Conrad's world there are no internal deterministic mechanisms at work. Razumov's lot is tragic not because of his genetic code; it is tragic because 'under the paternal sceptre of the tsars there are no other means of opposition than dynamite and nitroglycerine' and because the logic of Russian autocracy collides with the logic of his own conscience.⁴³ But being a tragic figure he is not a tragic hero: he does not perish while defending, as Jim does, values greater than himself.

Russia's tragedy has been defined by Conrad in 'Autocracy and War': once propelled down its path outside the normal run of history, and deprived by despotic governments of any possibility of natural development, the country can change only by way of a suicidal revolution. But Russia's situation is made desperate also by the fact that nobody can help her: 'It would be in vain for Russia to hope for the support and counsel of collective wisdom.' Europe, self-absorbed and torn by the rivalries of 'industrialism and commercialism', can offer her neither guidance nor succour. On the contrary (as Germany on the one hand and Britain and France on the other in fact did), it is eager to exploit Russia's internal problems for its own benefit.

Conrad's vision of history, most fully presented in *Nostromo*, finds in *Under Western Eyes* its last and grimmest expression. He scoffs at the Hegelian 'logic of history' (p. 35). History is made by men, not gods; it remains at the mercy of human greed and thirst for power. It is fraught with catastrophes against which there is no certain defence. Between the curse of Russia's internal contradictions and Western Europe's 'supremacy of material interests', Conrad did not see much hope. His scepticism did not allow him to imagine that the resolve of Haldins (not necessarily throwing bombs, but ready for sacrifice) would finally prevail over the ruthlessness of General T–s and the cunning of Mikulins; he could more easily visualize the unavoidable, convulsive and cruel pathologies of revolutions than the unsteady, groping progress of the human rights movements.

The 'West' – the largely mythical West – in *Under Western Eyes* is criticized from two positions. Razumov's traditional Russian contempt for the West (Conrad described it earlier in *The Sisters*) is an expression of his complexes and misunderstanding: he wants, like a typical Dostoevskian hero, everything or nothing. The teacher's self-effacing remarks ('Western ears . . . are not attuned to certain tones . . . even of moral distress already silenced at our end of Europe', pp. 163–4) express his occasional awareness that 'his' West is not what it ought to be. And this is why I think that the ideal reader's 'central vision' would be myopic if it confused the limitations of the horizons of the narrator's 'Western eyes' with a negation of Western *values* (even if not always implemented in the West). Democracy may be dull, but it is preferable to autocracy; freedom may be misused in the West, or forgotten, but it is preferable to slavery.

To put it differently, the epithet 'Western' has in *Under Western Eyes* two referents. One is a set of standards explicitly used by the narrator; the other is a set of ideals and traditions, which have been necessary for the development of civil society but are fraught with the risks of indifference, moral obtuseness, superficiality, unjustified feeling of superiority, and thus are not absolutely unquestionable, not 'ideal'.

Under Western Eyes ends with a whimper, not with a bang. This signals that whatever moral and political judgements and messages the readers' 'central point of view' can arrive at, some of them may well be hesitant and inconclusive.

7

As I have tried to argue, there were many factors which made Conrad identify Dostoevsky with Russia and Russia with Dostoevsky. This identification strengthened his animosity; but whenever 'things

Russian' were not covered by Dostoevsky's shade, Conrad could be fair, or even enthusiastic, as he was about Turgenev.

Although his attitude towards Russia and towards Dostoevsky was unambiguous, its consequences turned out to be paradoxical. Did Conrad realize that when he castigated the Russians in 'Autocracy and War' and *Under Western Eyes* he was to a large extent repeating their own self-criticism? Probably not; but that it was so is a part of the public meaning of his writings. It is sad to think that he was certainly not aware that in several fragments of his works he stood side by side with Alexandr Herzen, a leading émigré writer, who in 1852 started his 'Free Russian Press in London' with the assistance of Polish political exiles and who later supported the Polish 1863 insurrection. In fact, both in 'Autocracy and War' and in the 'Author's Note' to *Under Western Eyes* we find thoughts which Herzen expressed years earlier in his *Du développement des idées révolutionnaires en Russie*: that autocracy runs in the Russians' blood; that there has never been a tradition of respect for legality in Russia; or that the lack of all civic institutions makes the Russians prone to resort to violence.[44]

Another paradox: in *Under Western Eyes*, where he wanted to vanquish Dostoevsky both artistically and intellectually on his own ground, Conrad also paid homage to his enemy. Taking up Dostoevsky's motifs he replayed them brilliantly in his own orchestration.

11
Conrad and Rousseau: concepts of man and society

The objective of this chapter is not a quest for sources. That Conrad read Jean-Jacques Rousseau does not need to be proven; how well he remembered his works and how strongly he felt Rousseau's influence when writing his own novels does not concern me here. What I am attempting is not a genetic enquiry, but an exploration in the history of certain ideas. Nor is this a comprehensive study of the Conrad–Rousseau relation, which would require a fuller discussion of various aspects and diverse components of Rousseau's thought and means of expression.

Rather, comparing Conrad with Rousseau is here supposed to serve three purposes: firstly, to elucidate, by way of a contrastive analysis, Conrad's concepts of man and society; secondly, to place Conrad within the context of the history of European moral and socio-political thought which, in turn, will make it possible to determine his position on the map of philosophical and political tendencies of his day; and, finally, to clarify the intellectual structure of those works of Conrad which can be interpreted in terms of his opposition to Rousseau's ideas.

The political issues raised in Conrad's fiction attracted scant notice during his lifetime. He was also gravely disappointed by the lack of public response to 'Autocracy and War', his longest piece of political journalism. But within the last thirty years Conrad as a political writer has been given a growing consideration. Still, the conceptual framework of his thought, the sources and implications of his basic ideas of man, society and historical process, and the relation of his beliefs to the main currents of European political philosophy have not been much explored. Conrad's political convictions thus remain to a large extent insufficiently defined.

In the thirties the label 'conservative' was affixed to Conrad – and it stuck. In spite of what Irving Howe and Arnold Kettle wrote later on Conrad's incisive, disillusioned presentation of social and political conflicts,[1] 'conservative' is still an epithet used almost automatically in characterizing Conrad's views. Avrom Fleishman was the first to challenge this simplistic opinion, but I believe he did not do it on well-chosen grounds. Fleishman places Conrad within what he calls 'the Burke tradition'. And indeed, there are evident affinities between Conrad's and Edmund Burke's attitudes. But there are also serious differences both in their views and in their conceptual apparatus. For instance, where Conrad writes about 'nation' or 'humanity', Burke has 'state' or 'society'; in fact, in his understanding of the nation Burke is closer to his near-contemporary Rousseau than to Conrad. Moreover, to place Conrad within the 'Burke tradition', that is within the tradition of the thinker generally considered to have been the father of modern conservatism, makes it rather awkward to account for, or even to point at, those elements of Conrad's thought which do not belong to and indeed clash with this tradition.[2]

Two other objections may be raised. The very concept of 'the Burke tradition' is rather vague, because Burke was a polemicist, not a systematic thinker. Also, interpreting Conrad in terms of Burke and his followers leads us away from the more immediate, continental sources of Conrad's ideas – which, even if we leave aside his Polish background, account I believe for most of the analogies with Burke's 'organic' approach to society. It was certainly no accident that Conrad would switch to French almost invariably when writing on philosophical or political problems; there can also be no doubt that he knew French history more intimately than English.

Besides Rousseau, the only other thinker with a similar scope of interests Conrad knew and referred to was Carlyle. But, in spite of superficial resemblances, Conrad was even more radically opposed to Carlyle and less influenced by him than by Rousseau.[3] More importantly, Carlyle is too shallow, flashy and idiosyncratic a thinker to be really useful as a comparative counterpart. Also, he was not the father to but only a stepson of a certain political and intellectual tradition, and therefore a juxtaposition with him would drive us into a side-alley of the history of ideas.

Not that a comparison with Rousseau himself is without difficulties. It is well known that he was a man of split personality and that his writings, even his developed theories, abound in contradictions. Rousseau the sentimentalist disappears with hardly a trace in his *Social Contract*; his philosophy of the individual seems to conflict with his philosophy of the state. Moreover, the Rousseau of the *Considérations sur le gouvernement de la Pologne* is much more outspoken than his later adversary Burke on the issue of national feelings and traditions; but the Rousseau of *The Social Contract* understands the nation in purely abstract terms as an agglomeration of the loyal inhabitants of a state. I am not, however, going to dwell on these contradictions (of which Conrad might have been completely unaware) and shall conveniently talk only about those theories and aspects of Rousseau which have exerted the strongest influence and thus can be taken, at least in the historical sense, as most characteristic of him.

Explicitly, Rousseau appears twice in Conrad's works: in *A Personal Record*, with reference to *The Confessions* and *Emile*, and in *Under Western Eyes*, where a reference to *The Social Contract* is made and where an island monument of Jean-Jacques in Geneva plays quite an important role: one exile keeps a symbolic watch on another exile. Commenting upon *The Confessions*, Conrad ironically shrugs off Rousseau's 'thoroughness in justifying his own existence' and calls him – also ironically, I presume – 'an artless moralist'.[4] And indeed, to a writer so passionately concerned with problems of moral responsibility, *The Confessions* must have appeared as primarily an exercise in self-exculpation. The theoretical foundations of this auto-apology are laid in one of the opening sentences of Rousseau's memoirs: 'I am not made like any of those I have seen; I venture to believe that I am not made like any of those who are in existence.'[5] Why is Jean-Jacques different? Because he is exceptionally sensitive, has natural good impulses, 'worships freedom, abhors restraint, trouble, dependence'. The outspoken advocate of equality assures us that he is not 'one of those low-born men' without 'a real sentiment of justice'. The claim to uniqueness is thus coupled with a claim to goodness. The seat of goodness is his heart, whatever the evidence of his actions may say. The man who has told us the memorable story of how he accused a girl who was in love with him of stealing a ribbon he had stolen himself, replies in this manner to criticism of the way in which he has disposed of his five children:

> Is it possible that my warmheartedness, lively sensibility, readiness to form attachments ... my natural goodwill towards all my fellow-creatures, my ardent love of the great, the true, the beautiful, and the just; my utter inability to hate or injure ... the sweet and lively emotion which I feel at the sign of all that is virtuous, generous, and amiable; is it possible, I ask, that all these can ever agree in the same heart with the depravity which, without the least scruple, tramples underfoot the sweetest of obligations?
>
> No! I feel and loudly assert – it is impossible.

(Still, his children died of neglect in orphanages for the destitute.) Rousseau's position boils down to this: I am unlike anybody else, and therefore I should be judged by special standards; I am well intentioned and sensitive, therefore I cannot do evil. Any account of the moral principles advocated by Conrad must include the exact opposite of Rousseau's stance, and the moral position of many Conradian heroes represents the antithesis of Rousseau's peculiar 'great moral lesson': 'to avoid those situations in life which bring our duties into conflict with our interests'. This, Conrad would say, is stark moral cowardice. In his life, Conrad also made compromises; but to proclaim such a programme would, in his eyes, amount to making evasion a norm.

Conrad's gibe – in the quoted section of *A Personal Record* – at confessions as a 'discredited form of literary activity' acquires a peculiar significance in view of his own frequent use of this very convention. His heroes quite often indulge in confessions of two different types. The first is a straightforward disclosure of a painful or otherwise important experience, an 'opening of one's heart to a friend', as we have in 'The Lagoon', 'Karain', 'An Anarchist', in the case of Jukes' letter in 'Typhoon', repeatedly in *Chance* and finally in *The Shadow Line*, which is subtitled *A Confession*. The function of such a confession is to unburden one's soul by communing with another person. The frequency and the psychological role of this type of confession derives possibly, as Thomas Moser suggested to me, from Conrad's Catholic background.

The other type is an apologetic confession: its objective is not so much to communicate information as to justify oneself. Chapters IV to XI of *Lord Jim*, 'Falk', and large parts of *Under Western Eyes* contain, or are based on, confessions of this kind.[6] In fact, in *Under Western Eyes* we have as well a third type of 'confession': Razumov's secret report to the Russian police, the scornful and conceited missive which this 'man of reason', driven by best intentions, composes under the benevolent effigy of Rousseau. He feels perfectly safe when he writes it on a solitary islet devoted to the philosopher who maintained that man is innately good and that democracy is an excellent system but suitable only for people who are sufficiently mature.

Different as their subjects are, Jim's confessions to Marlow in the first part of the novel and Razumov's confessions in his diary have in common not only their self-exculpating objective, but also the way in which the arguments are developed. Both Jim and Razumov point at the peculiarities of their respective situations, which make it nonsensical to demand from them a 'conventional' kind of behaviour. Both stress their good intentions and their reasonableness. In the early chapters of the novel, Jim explains away his desertion of the *Patna* by arguing that to remain on board was practically pointless and that he never intended to shirk his duty. Razumov's explanation of his betrayal of Haldin follows a different course – he uses historical, political and philosophical arguments to support his decision – but the essential argument is the same: he was tricked by the circumstances, he did the only reasonable thing, his motives were pure and non-egoistic. Thus in both cases we encounter a characteristically Rousseauian type of self-justification by reference to the exceptionality of one's situation and (in Razumov's case) personality, and to one's good intentions.

In the latter part of the novel, Jim changes his attitude and simply admits that he was afraid. Razumov as well in the end throws away his mantle of self-righteousness and makes a true, non-apologetic confession to Miss Haldin, in this way bowing to the demands of 'conventional conscience'.

Conrad's ethics of fidelity and constraint, of duty, honour and human solidarity, was directly opposed to that of Rousseau, and was rooted in a fundamentally different concept of human nature.

Bertrand Russell was the first to comment on this contrast:

> His [Conrad's] point of view, one might perhaps say, was the antithesis of Rousseau's 'Man is born in chains, but he can become free.' He becomes free, so I believe Conrad would have said, not by letting loose his impulses, not by being casual and uncontrolled, but by subduing

wayward impulses to a dominant purpose ... Conrad's point of view was far from modern. In the modern world there are two philosophies: the one, which stems from Rousseau, and sweeps aside all discipline as unnecessary; the other, which finds its fullest expression in totalitarianism, which thinks of discipline as essentially imposed from without. Conrad adhered to the older tradition, that discipline should come from within. He despised indiscipline, and hated discipline that was merely external.[7]

The first of the cited sentences contains a glaring misquotation: *The Social Contract* begins with the words: 'L'homme est né libre et partout il est dans les fers.' 'Man is born free but everywhere he is in chains.'[8] Also, Russell misses the fact that in Rousseau's thought both mentioned 'modern ... philosophies' exist side by side. Still, the point he makes is valid and deserves amplification.

'Man is born a coward (*L'homme est né poltron*)', says Rousseau's compatriot in *Lord Jim*, a lieutenant of the French navy. 'It is a difficulty – *parbleu*! It would be too easy otherwise. But habit – habit – necessity – do you see? – the eye of others – *voilà*. One puts up with it.'[9] The 'older tradition' voiced here goes far back to ancient Greece. Man is naturally, spontaneously, neither virtuous nor strong; he has to be educated and given examples to follow; he must work on himself, but cannot be morally self-reliant. To Aristotle's dictum that man outside society is either god or beast, Conrad adds in 'Heart of Darkness' that a man who wishes to be a god becomes inevitably a beast. Kind emotions and good intentions have a limited ethical value: were not Kurtz and Charles Gould (of *Nostromo*) men of good intentions? And though a man can rise to greatness, he cannot put a simple trust in himself because of his inherent frailty.

In *The Social Contract* Rousseau admitted that his main problem in describing the desirable state of society was how to preserve the ideal of freedom and at the same time to impose discipline. His extreme moral individualism and emotionalism made constraint in the form of a strongly authoritarian social doctrine virtually a necessity, while his hypothesis of the noble savage and his optimistic idea of the innate goodness of man made an absolutist approach easier and seemingly safe. The outcome was his ideology of a totalitarian democracy: totalitarian because it presupposed a sole and exclusive truth in politics, democracy because it left, at least ostensibly, the search for this truth to all citizens at once. But when a counterbalance to the excesses of individualism was established, it led, both in Rousseau's theory and in the later revolutionary practice, to a total abrogation of the rights of the individual and to state mechanism.[10]

Although *The Social Contract* does not lack contradictions, the general drift of its arguments cannot be mistaken. Regrettably, many readers become so fascinated by Rousseau's rhetoric, so enchanted by the famous and superbly demagogic opening sentence, that they miss the more sinister but inevitable implications of the treatise. What are the main points of Rousseau's doctrine?

Contrary to what might be expected from an apologist of individualism, the concept of society used by Rousseau is quantitative rather than qualitative: a society is simply an agglomeration of units, not an organic whole, and men's powers, will, interests, and personalities are conceived of and represented quantitatively, in form of numbers and fractions. They can be added or subtracted, multiplied and decreased without apparently undergoing an essential change. His vision of society is therefore one of a multitude of atoms. This multitude enters into a social contract which consists of the 'total alienation by each associate of himself and all his right to the whole community'. This community of ciphers is capable of possessing a 'general will'. The general will is described in terms which are at the same time mathematical and metaphysical. It does not represent an opinion of the majority, nor does it have any empirical counterpart – but it is, nevertheless, composed of a sum of all interests, from which the conflicting individual interests have been subtracted. The general will cannot err and is absolutely binding on all citizens of the state. 'Whoever', says Rousseau in one of his more remarkable statements, 'refuses to obey the general will shall be constrained to do so by the whole body, which means nothing other than that he shall be forced to be free.' (We have here an archetypal instance of political double-speak.) No parties, representing divergent opinions, should be permitted. For different peoples different types of government are appropriate; the more populous a state, the stronger ought to be its government. No wonder that Hegel, the philosopher of the Prussian authoritarian state, thought highly of Rousseau's political teachings; but it is only in our century that Rousseau's programme of social atomization combined with a powerful central government was fulfilled.

Rousseau's belief that a removal of institutions will bring about a change, and a change for the better, seems to have been particularly disturbing to Conrad. He makes at least one overt allusion to this theory, in his 'Author's Note' to *Under Western Eyes*, where – referring to the Bolshevik Revolution of 1917 – he writes about 'the strange conviction that a fundamental change of hearts must follow the downfall of any given human institutions'. And his notorious dread of anarchy may be traced back to his knowledge of the influence of Rousseau's doctrine on the events of the French Revolution. The vision of a mob 'liberated' from all traditional constraints and authorities, unruly and heedless but easily swayed by ruthless demagogues, appalled Conrad.

But it would be a gross distortion to present Conrad's relation to Rousseau only in terms of a negative reaction. In his attitude towards Rousseau's ideas we can discern rather an opposition–obsession syndrome: although his reaction to Rousseau was predominantly negative, the ideas he condemned left on him an indelible imprint. It is obvious that the doctrine of the general will must have been repugnant to Conrad; but no less important is that he saw radical social change, the modern nation-state and democracy itself in characteristically Rousseauian terms. Although he chose to become a British subject, he understood democracy neither in the way in which most English theorists saw it – as a system gradually introduced from above, with the electorate broadened out step by step – nor in the Jeffersonian manner – as a system of government by equal and fully enfranchised individuals. Rather, democracy meant for him (like for a typical French conservative) a mechanistic government of the mob, with an inbuilt tendency to autocracy. Only by taking this into account can we explain, for instance, Conrad's vitriolic outburst against the Reform Bill and the results of the 1885 elections in his letter to Spiridion Kliszczewski.[11] I do not know whether he ever read *Democracy in America*, but he apparently took as a *fait accompli* the threat of a new kind of democratic oppression which had troubled Alexis de Tocqueville.[12] To use modern terminology, he tended to equate all democracy with its totalitarian form. And in the contemporary social democrats he saw direct exponents of Rousseau's pernicious ideology – minus any national sentiments the author of *Emile* might have had.*

Characteristically, Conrad criticized the modern democratic or semi-democratic state on two counts. Firstly, in a way Rousseau would agree with, for depersonalizing and emasculating its citizens, for turning them into cogs of a huge socio-economic machinery; and secondly, for achieving what Rousseau had demanded: getting rid of traditional bonds and institutions, atomizing the human community. The typical products of modern society, Conrad suggests, are economic robots and moral anarchists.

Under Western Eyes provides ample evidence of Conrad's opposition–obsession syndrome in regard to Rousseau. To begin with, Rousseau figures there in two roles: as a distinguished native of Geneva, an illustrious patron of Swiss democracy, exiled during his lifetime but now honoured by the monument which plays such an important part in Razumov's actions; and also as a patron of the revolutionary emigrants. Both roles are well grounded in fact, since Rousseau signed his *Social Contract*, later to become a theoretical basis for revolutionary movements, 'a citizen of Geneva'. The first Rousseau is treated with a double-edged irony. The scoffing remarks about Swiss democracy have to be referred to him; also, he provides a symbolic shelter for the *agent provocateur* Razumov. The ideology of revolutionary upheaval induced by terror and destruction is an object not only of implicit irony, but also of direct criticism, raised somewhat naively by the narrator but given additional support by the fact that most professional revolutionaries are presented as rather despicable figures.

Although the career of their leader, Peter Ivanovitch, owes something to that of Mikhail Bakunin, he also represents Rousseau – an 'inspired man' as well – not only in his irrationalism and declared femi-

---

* Conrad seems to have been fairly well read in political philosophy of the eighteenth and early nineteenth centuries; it is more difficult to say how much he knew of contemporary political writers. That he understood the Marxist vision of history (and its difference from anarchism or populism) is clear from what he put in the mouth of Michaelis in *The Secret Agent*. But when he banded together Jean Jaurès and Wilhelm Liebknecht as socialist annihilators of the national idea, he showed his ignorance both of Jaurès' position and of Marx's own outspokenly pro-Polish attitude.[13]

nism (combined with ruthlessness towards those women who depend on him), but above all in his being maintained by an aristocratic lady. He is supported by his elderly lover, Mme de S–, just as Rousseau was supported by his mistress Mme de Warens, and later by Mmes Dupin, d'Epinay, d'Houdetot and several others.

The opinions about Russia expressed in *Under Western Eyes* seem sometimes to echo Rousseau. Thus when the teacher of languages says that Russia has what she deserves, he could easily have been made to quote Rousseau's theoretical rule that 'The sovereign by the mere fact that it is, is always all that it ought to be.' More specifically, Rousseau maintained that Russia, with her natural historical tradition broken by Peter the Great, had lost her ability to develop normally,[14] an idea which is also reflected in the novel.

However, the main advantage of looking at *Under Western Eyes* from the angle of Conrad's relation to Rousseau is that it not only makes us realize to what extent this is a novel of ideas – in a manner similar to Thomas Mann's *The Magic Mountain* – but also puts us on the right track in looking for the historical origins of those ideas. Thus the declaration of Mr de P–, the Minister of State, that 'the thought of liberty has never existed in the Act of the Creator. From the multitude of men's counsel nothing could come but revolt and disorder; and revolt and disorder in a world created for obedience and stability is sin. It was not Reason but Authority which expressed the Divine Intention' echoes, surely not by accident, the views of Joseph de Maistre, one of the most outspoken and influential conservative critics of Rousseau and the Enlightenment.[15] De Maistre's voice can be heard as well in Razumov's dispute with Haldin, when he pits historical tradition against radical change, and in Razumov's five principles, which he puts down after Haldin's arrest:

> History not Theory.
> Patriotism not Internationalism.
> Evolution not Revolution.
> Direction not Destruction.
> Unity not Disruption.

Another conservative philosopher who was very influential in Russia – Hegel – is echoed by Razumov when he says that what was needed for 'the travail of maturing destiny' of Russia was 'not the conflicting aspirations of a people, but a will strong and one . . . not the babble of many voices, but a man – strong and one!' 'The logic of history made him unavoidable.'¹⁶

Neither are the narrator's critical comments on Russia, her people, and her system of government, invented *ad hoc*; they reflect opinions voiced by several Polish writers (notably Mickiewicz, whom Conrad quotes twice), by many Russian dissenters (particularly Pyotr Chaadaev) and by the Marquis de Custine, author of the famous *La Russie en 1839*.¹⁷ By replaying arguments of the debate, which lasted in Russia throughout the nineteenth century, between the apologists of the Holy and autocratic Russia and the liberal-minded 'occidentalists', Conrad gives *Under Western Eyes* its solid factual foundations.

We find in this novel the conservative position presented more fully than the revolutionary programme, which is derided but remains only vaguely defined. There can be no doubt that Conrad condemns both alternatives. Generally speaking, the negative side of his political views is more easily discernible than the positive: we come to know pretty well what he is against; what he is for we find only adumbrated in his work. It seems that his ideal (and unattained) society would be one that was deeply rooted in national history, that observed basic liberties stemming from the recognition of man's dignity, and that was organically integrated and structuralized by a hierarchy of obligations.

This implicit vision does not differ from the idea of desirable society found in the writings of his father. The last should make us pause before calling Conrad a conservative. To what extent is this designation, so commonly applied to Conrad, adequate? 'Conservative' is, of course, a vague term which can be applied to many kinds of political, moral and cultural opinions and attitudes. As Conrad was neither a professional politician nor a publicist, the most sensible approach seems to be one of analysing his 'style of thought', as understood by Karl Mannheim. In his classic essay on 'Conservative Thought' Mannheim characterizes the conservative style of thought, as opposed to that of the eighteenth-century Enlightenment, liberal-progressive, 'natural law' philosophers. He shows that it stresses the importance of the following ideas:

1 History, life, the nation as opposed to reason;
2 The irrationality of reality;

3 The individuality of phenomena rather than their universal validity;
4 Society as an organism;
5 Social wholes which are not sums of their parts; 'belonging' to such wholes;
6 A dynamic conception of reason.[18]

Now with the possible exception of the sixth point Conrad's thought runs along the same conceptual lines. Moreover, his notion of man is qualitative, as opposed to the characteristically quantitative idea of man used by most radicals, and he stresses the superiority of experience over all theories. (Here again *Under Western Eyes* provides an excellent example: Razumov – a 'man of the mind', as his name suggests in Russian – had it all thought out, but his theories collapse in the face of reality, both psychological and moral.)

However, there are also evident in Conrad's work four factors which do not agree with the conservative style of thought. Firstly, political issues are for him essentially moral issues; in this, as in several other respects, he stands at the opposite pole to Carlyle. Conservatives would, typically, separate the two spheres. Secondly, he rejects the supremacy of the state, the government, all established official institutions, even the law, over traditional values and over individuals and their spiritual claims. Thirdly, the postulate of equality as a component of liberty, which evoked the strongest protests from conservatives, is evidently acceptable to him. And, fourthly, his attitude to property is as scornful as any revolutionary's.

Passing from the general categories of a style of thought to the concrete presentations of social reality in Conrad's work, we face the same puzzling dilemma: the author of *Nostromo* and *The Secret Agent* can hardly be described as a conservative; but how else can we define his political attitude? Not only in the two novels mentioned, but also in, for instance, *The Mirror of the Sea* and 'Autocracy and War' we discern an awareness of widespread injustice and corruption, a strong disapproval of the *status quo*, and an acute consciousness of the need for fundamental social and political change. This 'conservative' was an outspoken critic of contemporary bourgeois society and of a system which gives the first place and free play to 'material interests'. It is remarkable that his criticism reminds us rather of those romantic and 'feudal' critics of the capitalist money-grubbers and exploiters who were so vocal at the beginning of the nineteenth century, than of contemporary radical attacks on the prevailing social and economic stratifications. But, unlike those conservative critics of industrialism and capitalism, Conrad was no apologist for the *ancien régime*. How can we explain this dilemma? And how can we account for the fact that when Conrad postulates change, evolution, reform, he does not start from the present, but from some point in the past, before the plague of material interests has spread, and before other pernicious forces of today had begun their work of corruption?

The answer, I believe, is to be found in Conrad's personal political background. It is a peculiar characteristic of nineteenth-century Polish political thought that its dominant trends are at the same time traditionalist and progressive.[19] All Polish patriotic thinkers had to be traditionalist, or even conservative, because they wanted to restore their partitioned country. The restoration of national independence was the principal idea, the first point on the agenda, of everybody who did not acquiesce in Poland's annihilation. To accept the present as the basis for change would have meant to resign from the national dream, to renounce the dignity and the glories of the past. This conservative impulse was strengthened by a constant need to preserve the remnants of the old order in the form of the language, tradition and customs. But, despite all that, Poles would take their position in the vanguard of international radical democratic movements throughout the nineteenth century, fighting on innumerable barricades, and supporting or even leading revolutionary movements in Italy, Hungary and France – including the ill-starred Paris Commune, in which the commander of the armed forces was Jarosław Dąbrowski, an old companion of Conrad's father and uncle in their underground activity. One of the causes of this radicalism was that the main oppressor of Poland, the Tsarist Russia, was also the most autocratic and reactionary country of Europe.

The long and winding path we have taken since our initial comparison of Conrad and Rousseau has not been chosen at random, but was determined by the implications of the concepts we have analysed. We have not fully explored the similarities and the contrasts between the two men; one more, at least, deserves to be mentioned. Both Rousseau and Conrad were members of a new class: the intelligentsia. Both lived outside the main socio-economic strata of their societies, both had to earn money by writing (Rousseau had also his ladies . . .), both felt broader intellectual and political responsibilities, and both were critical of the societies in which they lived. Both were, for many years, footloose wanderers, and both were expatriates; but although Conrad spent his almost entire life without any concrete communal bonds, he was not, like Rousseau, spiritually rootless. Although he did not envisage any social groups in which he could put his trust (*The Nigger of the 'Narcissus'* shows that he did not idealize his seamen), he never broke his mental bond with the human community. In his traditionalism and his heroic clinging to an *ideal* fellowship, *ideal* institutions and *imagined* tradition, he seems to have been a characteristically Polish intellectual.

The difficulty in defining his politics reflects his own dilemma. Conrad passionately rejected autocracy and authoritarianism, as contrary to what he valued most in man. But he had strong objections to democracy which, he thought, 'had elected to pin its faith to the supremacy of material interests'.[20] The bulwarks of liberty seemed to him to be at the same time the strongholds of materialism and social atomization. To a European intellectual of the last quarter of the twentieth century this dilemma looks disturbingly familiar.

12

Conrad and the idea of honour

It is evident that the idea of honour was very important for Conrad as a person and stands at the heart of ethical problems that he raised in his books. Some of his contemporaries, such as Wells, noted this fact with an ironical shrug; others, such as Cunninghame Graham, with admiration. But even though the fact itself has been registered by many critics, the function and implications of the idea as present in Conrad's work remain by and large unanalysed. When Conrad deals with honour in its simple form, as in 'The Duel', *Chance*, or *The Rescue*, there is little chance for misinterpretation. But whenever the problems raised become more intricate and a deeper comprehension of the whole ethos of which honour forms the centre is required, confusion arises, for instance in interpretations of the final part of *Lord Jim*, or of the predicament of Nostromo.

Many critics simply fail to identify the moral and literary tradition to which Conrad belongs, and persist in interpreting him in the terms of, and as within, the conventions of middle-class nineteenth-century prose. And if one does not know the history and logic of the concept of honour, one certainly cannot appreciate what was new in Conrad's handling of it. Some of his greatest admirers, like Faulkner or Camus, seem to have seen it quite well, but we are unable to comprehend their links with Conrad as long as we do not place the connection in a historical perspective. Therefore, if we wish to understand more clearly what Conrad as a moral writer was about, we have first to ask what were the origins and the history of the idea of honour, and what are the ramifications and implications of this concept. Unfortunately, this is not a subject much written about. Apart from C. B. Watson's excellent book *Shakespeare and the Renaissance Concept of Honor* (where, however, only the intellectual, and not the literary, tradition is presented),[1] most other studies are fragmentary and limited in scope.

We have to look into the history of 'honour' because it is neither a simple, psychologically definable ideal (like truthfulness or mercy), nor, in spite of some appearances, a formal concept – like the categorical imperative, which it resembles in its absolute stringency. The categorical imperative says only that one must not advocate any moral rules which one is unwilling to regard as universally binding; the content of these rules, however, remains open. The ideal of honour, on the contrary, requires not simply that one remain faithful to one's principles and defend them in spite of any odds, but also determines, to a large extent, the kind of principles one ought to stick to. Thus, for instance, when in Conrad's *Under Western Eyes* the General, to whom Razumov denounces Victor Haldin, talks of himself as a defendant of 'fidelity' and 'honour',[2] the reader is supposed to feel no doubt that the scene is ironical and that the General has no right to his claim of representing these values.

Perhaps the most striking thing about honour is that it is a 'Janus concept': it has to have its public face (reputation) and private face (consciousness). This characteristic and essential duality has been present in the ideal since its very beginnings, which go back at least to Homeric Greece. Honour consisted then of rewards and reputation on the one hand, and of a consciousness of accomplishment and dignity on the other – or, to put it differently, of external marks of honour and a feeling of inherent worth. Of course, the external aspect was the earlier one. As Conrad wrote: 'We are children of the earth. It may be that the noblest tradition is but the offspring of material conditions, of the hard necessities besetting men's precarious lives. But once it has been born it becomes a spirit.'[3] What began as a matter of material prizes and acquired authority developed quickly into an answer to the perennial question: what makes life worth living? As early as in the *Iliad* we see Achilles asking himself: is it preferable to live a long, safe and obscure life, or to meet an early death adorned with honour and glory? As we know, he chose the latter.

The answer to this question, offered by the ideal of honour, has been repeatedly stated. Its essence is best visible in the paradoxical formula that to give your life a meaning you must act as if your life by itself had no value.

Honour is, therefore, basically a secular ideal. Glory, its crown, results in secular immortality. As Balzac said, 'La gloire est le soleil des morts.' 'Glory is the sun of the dead.'[4]

The idea of honour has been bound up with a specific concept of man and his nature. Man is seen as an individual person, not as a particle in a crowd (and, by the same token, society is not a simple sum of its members). He possesses a free will and can use it. But he is not 'naturally' good: there are higher and lower elements in him, and he has to be carefully educated. This idea of man is in some respects similar to the Christian one: personalism and man's inborn defectiveness, obligation to fight his lower inclinations – all that made possible a coexistence (by no means peaceful) of the chivalric ethos and Christianity.

Jean-Jacques Rousseau eloquently proclaims almost the very opposite of this idea of man. He insists on the natural goodness of man, goodness marred by civilization and restraints. He stresses the importance of emotions and intentions, rejects discipline, and suggests that the uniqueness of the individual makes general rules of conduct absurdly cruel. Rousseau calls the following principle his 'great moral lesson': 'to avoid those situations in life which bring our duties into conflict with our interests'.[5] But for Rousseau our interests – and feelings, instincts, passions, propensities – were inherently good; duties were not. The great patron of the Declaration of the Rights of Man postulated, in the words of Anatole France, 'an excessive and unfair separation between man and the gorilla',[6] idealizing the former. In spite of appearances, the ethics of honour and the chivalric code make more modest claims concerning human nature.

For the concept of man implied by the idea of honour, Pindar's formula 'become what you are' is superbly characteristic. Rousseau, while liberating man from external constraints, makes him a prisoner of his own character. The Pindarian tradition, on the contrary, while subjecting man to external obligations, restraints and rules, makes him internally free: he can shape, mould and model himself; he is an object of his will and aspirations.

Within the ethics of honour, a morally relevant act is taken to have, in principle, irreversible consequences. Originally, it was understood to influence, literally, the very essence of a man. A man who lost his honour would become qualitatively different – as if another person, or, rather, depersonalized. Later this magical conception was toned down, but the basic idea that moral implications of behaviour are qualitative, not quantitative, and that once an act is committed there is no way to erase it, remained among the fundamental differences between this ethic and, for instance, utilitarianism with its quantitative and cumulative approach. Here we see another analogy with Christian morality and its doctrine of mortal sin.

Irreparable, or reparable only through special, great acts of regaining honour lost (and not only by acts of repentance or material retribution), are the misdeeds of the heroes of medieval romances, of Shakespeare, Mickiewicz and Conrad. And when André Malraux, in his preface to Faulkner's *Sanctuary*, identified 'his only true subject' as *l'irrémédiable*, he put his finger on the very spot where, in Faulkner's work, the traditions of honour and of Christianity converge.[7]

The ideal of honour did not originate and exist in isolation: it formed the central part of a whole ethos. For lack of a better name we may call it the 'chivalric ethos', although it is much older than medieval chivalry, has survived it, and did not stop developing long after the last knights disappeared from courts and battlefields. It has been a matter of pride, within this ethos, to be judged by severe standards. Legendary and half-legendary heroes were set as examples to follow. Since reputation was a component of honour, the opinion of one's equals was of a paramount importance. What distinguished this reverence of public opinion from crude opportunism was the fact that both the individual and his community were supposed to adhere to identical ideals and neither of them established rules at will. The community was an arbiter, not a lawmaker. Therefore, a man could claim that his arbiters were wrong. Thus, for instance, Achilles' wrath was not, as it may seem today, an expression of his egocentric pride, but of a consciousness of injustice.[8]

The direct opposite of honour is shame, and the fear of shame was considered praiseworthy. Ajax invokes his comrades-in-arms: 'My friends, be men and think of your honour. Fear nothing in the field but dishonour in each other's eyes. When soldiers fear disgrace, then more are saved than killed.'[9] Aristotle maintained that courage instigated by shame was more valuable than courage elicited by fear of punishment.[10]

Courage is, in fact, a necessary concomitant of honour. And not only military courage. If a steady link between self-esteem and public esteem is essential for honour, then only a man who is ready to stand up and fight against any infringement of his reputation can be honourable. Other implications of the ideal are perhaps less obvious but no less important. The immediate consequences of an act are irrelevant for evaluating it as honourable or dishonourable. Whether the hero won or lost, whether he gained wealth or ruined his family, whether he saved his life or died, whether his glorious death was of any help to the cause he defended – nothing of that really counts. What matters is fidelity to a principle. (However, fidelity to principles can be defended also on practical grounds, by pointing at their far-reaching consequences.) This impracticality of honour is most obvious in the disregard of material advantages. 'For if, Socrates, there be one point in which the man who thirsts for honour differs from him who thirsts for gain, it is, I think, in willingness to toil, face danger, and abstain from shameful gains – for the sake of honour only and fair fame.'[11]

Honour is, as I have said, theoretically and basically a conservative ideal, but with a paradoxical rider. Although since the earliest times honour has been considered a monopoly of the well-born and privileged, this ideal has also been, for well over two thousand years, used as a weapon against inequality grounded in differences of birth and class. The more forcibly it was argued that honour and virtue were the basic characteristics of the nobility and that the nobles morally deserved to be nobles, the easier it was to turn the tables and ask the question: why should good men of humble birth or profession be considered 'lower' and unworthy of honour? Thus the argument that the well-born are at the top because they are better would repeatedly turn out to be a double-edged one: by establishing honour and virtue as the criteria of nobility it made, by definition, all virtuous and honourable men equal to the nobles. Furthermore, the ideal of honour gave birth to, and then fostered the idea of, human dignity; but once this idea had taken shape, it became impossible to keep it within socially closed confines.

Seen from this angle, the Renaissance was perhaps the most important period in the development of the concept of honour. In spite of the proliferation of statements about a gulf separating the aristocratic and the lower classes, the stress on virtue as the basis of nobility and on honour as a mark of virtue prepared the theoretical ground for a social emancipation of the ideal. (The intellectuals were the first to profit from this process.) Robert Ashley, in the best-known English Renaissance definition of honour, does not mention social origin at all:

> *Honour* therefore ys a certaine testemonie of vertue shining of yt self, geven of some man by the iudgement of good men: For when any one ys of such and so apparant vertue that he turneth others into admiracion and love of him, yf as the shadow followeth the body so prayse and reverence followeth him, then he ys called honourable, and the same which is geven unto him as an approbacion of his vertue is termed Honour.[12]

At the same time, the ideal of honour, within the medieval chivalric code at least overtly 'Christianized', revealed more fully its secular essence and loosened its links with religious beliefs. Reformation and Counter-Reformation theologians were quick to assail the vogue of honour.[13] However, more momentous was the spread of the bourgeois ethics of capitalism, based on work, usefulness and profit. It brought along more palpably attractive possibilities of vertical social change and drove the ethos centred around honour into a valiant retreat.

The next stage of development came with the French Revolution and the Napoleonic Wars. Suddenly, every Frenchman became officially capable of honour; military glory, previously exclusive to the nobility, became attainable to all *citoyens*. Then the Romantic vogue of chivalry spread across Europe at the same time as did new liberal and democratic tendencies, and an Italian *carbonaro* felt that he could vie in his thirst for honour with any *marchese*.

Let us now focus on Conrad's home country, which occupies in the history of the idea of honour a rather special position. It was unusual for two main reasons. (1) The nobility–gentry class (within which there was no legal stratification) was in Poland exceptionally numerous and formed some 10–12 per cent of the population.[14] Thus a large section of the population, proportionately larger than the enfranchised electorate in England until 1867, consisted of fully privileged men, adhering, at least in principle, to the characteristic values of the nobility. (2) After the partition of Poland between Russia, Prussia and Austria at the end of the eighteenth century, there was a long line of insurrections and wars of national liberation (1794, 1806, 1830, 1846, 1863). For several generations, military virtues remained in the forefront of national values; all Poles were assumed to be under an obligation to fight or work for national independence; by and large, the classes which were becoming emancipated joined in and combined their struggle for social equality with the struggle for national identity; individual honour was generally identified with fulfilment of patriotic duties.[15]

This was the tradition to which Konrad Korzeniowski was born as a Pole. But as a writer, Joseph Conrad belonged also to another tradition – an ancient tradition of literature steeped in the idea of honour. The *Iliad* and the *Chanson de Roland* belong to it, and it boasts of such names as Calderón and Cervantes, Shakespeare and Torquato Tasso, Stendhal, Adam Mickiewicz and Alfred de Vigny. To conceive of this tradition as one simply extolling the glories of honourable and heroic deeds is as naive as to suppose that most dramas and novels concerned with the power of love culminate in scenes of happy matrimony. Rather, it probes the implications of the ideal, it explores both its splendours and its dangers and excesses, pitfalls and perversions. The writers saturated with chivalric ethos seem to describe and analyse most frequently either the duality of honour and the resulting conflicts between its private and public side, or the tragic practical consequences of a strict adherence to the ideal.

It is perhaps not the impracticality of honour that makes it and its literary presentations frequently so difficult to comprehend for the modern public. More often, the confusion stems from the failure of contemporary readers to realize that – for all its fascination with the *beau geste*, flourish and glory – this is not a cheerfully optimistic tradition. The view of life historically and philosophically associated with the idea of honour does not entail a belief in a universal and just order of things. On the contrary, it is essentially a tragic outlook[16] – if only because it makes all value of a man's existence reside in his actions and the resulting reputation and consciousness, but at the same time commands man to throw away, at any moment of challenge or test, 'the dearest thing he ow'd / As 'twere a careless trifle.'[17] The more a man achieves, the greater he succeeds in becoming, the more we lose by his death; but to shun death means to destroy one's greatness.

Turning now directly to Conrad, we may ask two kinds of question: what was his personal attitude towards the ideal of honour? And what role does this ideal play in his works? Of course, I can only sample the issue involved and try to give fragmentary answers.

For Conrad, whose father was, in the long line of his ancestors, the first to be employed (as administrator of a country estate), the choice of occupation was, even if unconsciously, a matter of special concern. Whatever a nobleman would do was supposed to be meaningful not primarily in the sense of being profitable; and his accomplishments could not be judged by the simple standard of material rewards. Therefore, the decision to become a sailor and live a life filled with risks and exacting duties, subject to a paramilitary code of behaviour, was in a sense quite consistent with Conrad's background.*

It is worth noticing here that Conrad does not idealize work; just the contrary, he presents it as a hard necessity, even a curse. What he does idealize is duty. This is the standpoint from which he looks with such a scorching disdain at all these Donkins, Ossipons and Verlocs who manage to wheedle out a living without honest work.

Conrad was strongly opposed to the typically middle-class and capitalistic tendency to regard success as the measure of worth. To separate the value of one's achievements and activities from one's profits and rewards was for him a problem of immediate personal concern. Writing his famous Preface to *The Nigger of the 'Narcissus'* he penned a few sentences which he then grudgingly deleted upon the advice of his friend Edward Garnett:

> For in art alone of all the enterprises of men there is meaning in endeavour disassociated from success, and merit – if any merit there be – is not wholly centred in achievement but may be faintly discerned in the aim.
>
> For, art is long and life is short, and ideals are practically unreachable except by the very great who can command the sanction of recognized success. To others the consciousness of a worthy aim is everything; it is conscience, dignity, truth, honour – the reward and the peace.[18]

Garnett mistakenly took these statements to be self-defensive, an apology for lack of success, while in fact they expressed a positive programme of a non-pragmatic approach. In a letter to Arthur Quiller-

---

* At the same time, though, Conrad took pride in his mercantile success as captain of the *Otago* and in his financial enterprises; a behaviour typical for a nobleman who dabbles in trade and wishes everybody to know that, although it is only his hobby, he is doing it like an expert. It was also characteristic that Conrad's financial ventures, which would invariably start in a most promising way, almost invariably ended in disaster.

Couch, sent in response to his appreciation of the *Nigger*, Conrad wrote that a 'solitary writer', such as himself, when working, 'thinks only of a small knot of men – three or four perhaps – the only ones who matter'.[19] These 'select few', mentioned in several other letters, formed the group of the arbiters of his achievement – of his literary 'honour'. But they did not form a coterie. Conrad's contempt for the 'mass public' was simply a result of his exasperation at being financially dependent on its favour. But it never marred his 'subtle but invincible conviction of solidarity' with 'all humanity', about which he wrote in the quoted Preface. He never addressed himself to a caste; he toiled for a few friends – and at the same time for all men.[20]

Now let me give but two examples of the use to which we can put the concept of honour in analysing Conrad's novels. *Lord Jim*, of course, comes first to one's mind. In assessing Jim's behaviour, many critics consider primarily the practical consequences of his actions. They point at, e.g., the disastrous results of Jim's decision to let Gentleman Brown leave unharmed, and deem it to be not only a fatal error but also a sign of weakness. But are we supposed to judge the hero simply by the practical outcome of his moral decisions? If we go back to Jim's original crime, his desertion of the *Patna*, we notice that the evaluation of Jim's act does not at all hinge on its consequences. Had Jim stayed on board, it would not have made the slightest difference to the situation of the boat and her passengers. His remaining on the *Patna* would not have saved a single life if the steamer went down. But still we, like the court, condemn him for his escape.

At the end of the novel, after Brown kills Dain Waris, Jim decides to go and face Doramin as a matter of principle. But his decision could also be based on practical considerations: the only alternative open to him was to fight – and kill more innocent people. Here the principle of honour, of taking full responsibility for one's word, coincides with simple concern for preserving human lives.

It is often maintained that Brown appealed to Jim's weakest and most shameful side, to a common bond between two fallen men. This is a misunderstanding, based on a failure to grasp what is the moral structure of the story, and on taking Brown's own point of view too seriously. (Perhaps Conrad exaggerated here in his attempt to make the reader get at the truth by her- or himself; we learn of many things Jim did not know about and naively wish that he avoided the trap.) In fact, Brown appeals to what is best in Jim, to this trait which constitutes the difference between him and an average autocrat: to the principle of fairness, implied by honour. Anyway – and this is a point most critics seem to have missed – it is not Brown, but Cornelius, spared by Jim's humanitarian pity, who causes the catastrophe.

Seen in the terms of honour, the basic conflicts in *Lord Jim* are between motives, principles and consequences of action. In *Nostromo* we see another characteristic tension: between the public and the private side of honour. When the action begins, there exists a correspondence between Nostromo's reputation and his consciousness of his own worth. Then there develops a dialectical interplay of these two factors, and Nostromo passes through a phase of false fear of losing his 'image' to the state of guilt-ridden and dishonourable fame. His vice is vanity: excessive deference to public acclaim. Seen in this light, his melodramatic death appears strikingly apt: he dies as a result of an error of the same kind within which he lived, of mistaking external marks for the whole truth.

Apart from using honour as his pivotal moral concept and presenting its various aspects and entanglements, Conrad pioneered in his fiction the shedding of the social class ramifications of this ideal. Most of his heroes are neither noblemen nor soldiers. With him, honour has finally lost its status of a privilege and has become a right, if not a duty.

What I have said above represents only a bare outline of the theme indicated by the title. To discuss it in any detail would require considerably more space – in fact, a whole book. This applies particularly to the more recent developments.

The legacy of Conrad the moralist seems to have been picked up, in their different ways, by writers such as Camus, Faulkner, Hemingway, Malraux, Saint-Exupéry. Each of these names raises its specific problems. For instance, in Hemingway's work we would have to penetrate through the thick plumage of pose and swagger to the hard body of ethical stance. One of the many books on Malraux bears the title *The Honor of Being a Man*;[21] but perhaps Malraux's concept of man belongs rather to the tradition of Nietzsche, a tradition which, in its radical individualism and total disregard for society and its inherited values, stands in sharp opposition to the ethos of honour. Faulkner's *Absalom, Absalom!* has been called 'a puritan tragedy'. But is not the Sutpen family saga also a tale of the myth of chivalry enacted, a drama of honour real and apparent; in a word, a tragedy of a search for honour? And was not Faulkner's morbid fascination with puritanism at least partly due to the paradoxical affinities between the puritan ethos and the concept of man inherent in the ethics of honour? The work of Saint-Exupéry – particularly his ideas of human solidarity and of the 'solitude fraternelle', his stress on action and responsibility – resembles Conrad most obviously. But strangely little has been written about this resemblance; and we would have to ask, for instance, to what extent Saint-Exupéry's religious beliefs constitute a difference between him and the sceptic Conrad. Camus said once that 'honour, like pity, is an irrational virtue that carries on after justice and reason have become powerless'.[22] But what is the role of the idea of honour in Camus' own work? I think it is certainly present in *The Plague* – but to go beyond this bland statement would take another paper.

However, in order not to end this chapter with a string of question marks and topics for future study, I shall give an example, symbolic in its conciseness, of the continuity of the tradition I have briefly described.

In the last paragraph of his Nobel Prize address, Faulkner tried to sum up his message. Ian Watt, in one of the best pieces ever written on Conrad, has pointed out that the crucial passage in the first part of this paragraph, the passage expressing Faulkner's belief that man will endure and prevail, closely echoes a fragment in Conrad's essay on Henry James.[23] Faulkner's passage echoes it not only in its images, but in the very cadence of its phrases. And in the other part of this last paragraph, Faulkner formulates his answer to the question of the purpose of a writer's work: 'The poet's, the writer's, duty is ... to help man endure by lifting his heart, by reminding him of the courage and honor and hope and pride and compassion and pity and sacrifice which have been the glory of his past.'[24]

In another place, Faulkner describes his quest for that answer, the quest which lasted 'until suddenly one day I saw that that half-forgotten Pole had had the answer all the time. To uplift man's heart ...'[25] That half-forgotten Pole (for several generations the most popular novelist in

Poland) was Henryk Sienkiewicz,* whom Faulkner had read as a young man. He goes on to explain this answer:

> This does not mean that we are trying to change man, improve him, though this is the hope – maybe even the intention – of many of us. On the contrary, in the last analysis this hope and desire to uplift man's heart is completely selfish, completely personal. He would lift up man's heart for his own benefit because in that way he can say No to death.

Saying 'No' to death is, in fact, what the ethic of honour is fundamentally about.

Thus we have here, within the space of a few sentences, a linking together of Polish literature – of all modern literatures probably the one most obsessed by the idea of honour – with the work of the greatest of contemporary American writers. It shows that the tradition to which Conrad belonged, and which he greatly enriched, is very much alive and transcends national boundaries.

* (1846–1916), Nobel Prize 1905.

13
Joseph Conrad: a European writer

As the twentieth century draws to its close, Conrad's position in the front rank of its literature seems to have become (after several up and down fluctuations) unquestionable. Also, it is now generally agreed that he was an exceptional writer. Various arguments for his eminence and reasons for his exceptionality have been given (also in the present volume), and they are – and will continue to be – much discussed. Here I wish to look at an aspect of his work which until now has not attracted much attention: his Europeanism. What follows is, however, only a tentative outline of a study, which I hope will be written some day.

Joseph Conrad was a European writer in several senses of this expression, in several aspects. Let us begin by listing the most important.

1. As a writer he blended (successfully) elements of three cultures: Polish, French and English. What were these elements? What did he absorb from these cultures and make use of? In brief:

From Poland: honour, fidelity and duty as essential moral values; a Romantic literary tradition – with its striking imagery and characteristic problems of moral responsibility and of the individual and his relations with society; the idea of nation as a spiritual unity; the importance of friendship. And thus, generally: elements of the imagery and basic ethical concepts and problems.

From France: his interest in the mechanisms of great historical events – the French Revolution, the Napoleonic era; Rousseau as an ideological enemy, in his concepts of man and of society; Flaubert's vision of the novel as art; from Anatole France the expanse of his intellectual interests and his philosophical scepticism; from Anatole Leroy-Beaulieu the idea of the link between democracy and the role of money; a fascination with anarchism. To sum up: many philosophical and political concepts and problems, elements of historical consciousness, and the artistic criteria which Conrad adopted as his own. The late Yves Hervouet has shown the extent of Conrad's borrowings from French literature, but not of his connections with French culture.

From England: the sea and the seamen; works of Shakespeare as a mine of literary motifs; Dickens with his incomparably rich picture of English society; London as the archetype of the modern city and the hub of the empire; contemporary social and political problems; an interest in the role of finance. Thus: the sea, problems of contemporary society; and of course the English language as the blending machine.

2. In about half of Conrad's works action takes place in Europe, often in several European countries in the same novel or story.

In France: *The Sisters* (part), 'The Idiots', *The Mirror of the Sea* (part), 'The Duel', 'An Anarchist', *A Personal Record* (part), *The Arrow of Gold*, *The Rover*. If, pedantically, we count the number of pages, we shall end by discovering that there are more pages with action in France than in England!

In England itself: *The Nigger of the 'Narcissus'* (part), 'The Return', *Lord Jim* (two fragments), 'Youth' (part), 'Amy Foster', 'To-morrow', 'The Informer', 'The Brute', *The Mirror of the Sea* (partly), *The Secret Agent*, *A Personal Record* (part), *Chance*, 'The Black Mate'.

In Italy: *Nostromo* (small fragments), 'Il Conde', *Suspense* (most).

In Poland: *A Personal Record* (part), 'Prince Roman'.

In Switzerland: *A Personal Record* (a fragment), *Under Western Eyes* (most).

In Belgium: 'Heart of Darkness' (part).

In Russia: *The Sisters* (a fragment), *Under Western Eyes* (part), 'The Warrior's Soul'.

In Spain: 'The Inn of Two Witches'.

There are also snippets of action in Scandinavia, the Netherlands, Germany, and the Ukraine.

In the other half of Conrad's work the action takes place outside Europe, in the Far East, in Africa and in Latin America – but generally speaking with Europe as a point of reference. This does not imply that Europe is being idealized but that usually, as in 'Heart of Darkness', *Lord Jim, Nostromo*, 'The Planter of Malata' or *Victory*, ideas and problems essentially European are pivotal. Conrad was a 'Eurosceptic' in assessing Europe's role overseas. He stressed the hypocrisy and rapaciousness of colonialists, and the inadequacy of the white 'civilization' when faced with a completely different culture. In other words, he critically evaluated Europe from an external perspective, observing its political influence and watching the behaviour of Europeans in 'exotic' countries.

3. We notice in Conrad's fiction and his essays the presence of most of the major European cultures: not only Polish, French and English, but also Italian, Spanish and Russian; and even German – although Conrad was consistently anti-German, or rather, anti-Prussian, in his political statements. But in *Lord Jim* we find a motto from Novalis and one of the central, and most attractive, figures of this novel is Stein, a German veteran of the 1848 Revolution and representative of European Romantic idealism. There is also, in one of the key scenes of the novel, a quotation (in the original) from Goethe's *Torquato Tasso*.

Conrad's Polish cultural background included his knowledge of the ancient classics. Although nobody, as far as I know, has investigated Conrad's Greek and Latin references, there is no doubt that he was well acquainted with Homer and Virgil and felt at ease with Latin expressions and allusions. In 'Heart of Darkness', next to Virgilian and Dantesque motifs, we can hear in the description of Kurtz's last days an echo of a legend of the death of Alexander the Great, the first self-proclaimed superman of Europe.* If we hear it, we recognize better how deeply rooted in European mythology Conrad's tale is.

Conrad felt at home in several European national civilizations and raised in his work issues both characteristic of and relevant to them. I shall give, briefly, just a few examples.

* According to some legends, Alexander demanded to be paid the homage due to a god, and killed Callisthenes, who refused to do so. When he fell ill with malaria, he had himself carried on a litter to attend sacrifices. His soldiers thronged to look at him and pay him tribute. The night before he died, he crawled out on all fours from his palace to drown himself in the Euphrates, hoping that his body would be lost and his people would believe that he had disappeared like an immortal. But his wife traced him and brought him back to die in bed.[1]

In 'An Outpost of Progress' and 'Heart of Darkness' he analysed the consequences produced by the application of the idea of 'white man's civilizing mission' in the Belgian Congo. In 'The Duel' Conrad has managed not only – in his own words – 'to realize the spirit of the Napoleonic Era',[2] but also to present a captivating (and amusing) picture of latent class antagonisms within the Emperor's army. In *The Secret Agent* we see London as a modern metropolis, 'a monstrous town' and 'a cruel devourer of the world's light',[3] a site of depersonalized mass society and of loneliness; and also as the playing-field of international plots and subversion. *Under Western Eyes* is a novel which juxtaposes the hopeless Russian struggle between traditional autocracy and revolutionary liberty with the solid and peaceful but barren Swiss democracy. *Chance* shows London as a centre of financial power and speculation and illustrates the topical issue of women's suffrage. In *The Rover* Conrad describes the horrors of the Great Revolution – and the exhilaration of the new French patriotism. In the unfinished *Suspense* we are shown the impact of the Napoleonic myth on political and social developments in Italy.

Conrad also uses his knowledge of various cultural traditions and conceptual frameworks in another way: to look at the described events from different angles. His European multiculturalism was ineluctably linked to his condition as an exile and with what Anne Luyat-Moore aptly calls 'la nécessaire étrangeté';[4] it made him particularly sensitive to cultural differences. The clash, or contrast, of cultures is a recurrent motif in his fiction: from *Almayer's Folly* and *An Outcast of the Islands* to *Suspense*. For us, of special interest here are the distinctions and divergences between European national spirits, as shown in *The Sisters, A Personal Record, Under Western Eyes*, or *The Rover*. Less obvious instances are even more revealing. Thus in *Lord Jim*, after Marlow confesses his inability to understand and evaluate the working of Jim's mind, two representatives of different national cultures are called upon to pronounce their judgements: the French navy lieutenant, entitled by his origin and profession to pronounce on matters of the code, and Stein, a German romantic and thus a specialist both in abstract philosophy and in matters of imagination. Together with the empiricist Marlow they lift Jim's case onto a high plateau of universal human condition.[5]

4. In his work Conrad tackled ideas, problems and movements which were important for the whole of Europe – and particularly for Europe.

Again, just a few examples: Rousseau's concepts of man and society and of their interrelations; Rousseau's vision of individual responsibility, with the paramount importance given to intentions; the Great French Revolution and its heritage; the problem of national self-determination; modern democracy and universal suffrage; autocracy versus revolution; colonialism; imperialism; the working class and trade unionism; democracy and the rule of money; the theory and practice of anarchism; political provocation and international terrorism; the abuse of power and twisting the law in the defence of the existing social and political order. We may agree or disagree with Conrad's perceptions and opinions, but it is unquestionable that he faced in his work the essential issues of the last 150 years of European history.

5. It has barely been noticed that Conrad held an idea of Europe as a potential *political* entity based, implicitly, on shared elements of civilization and culture.[6] (In the name of such an idea he even suggested, in 1912, a joint European protectorate for independent Constantinople.[7]) In 'Autocracy and War' he wrote about 'the solidarity of Europeanism, which must be the next step towards the advent of Concord and Justice', that remains 'the only possible goal of our progress'.[8]

Conrad's idea of Europe, in which there will be 'no frontiers' (p. 103), can be traced back to the mid-nineteenth-century contemporaries and comrades-in-arms of Stein (the butterfly collector of *Lord Jim*), leaders of the Young Europe movement, in the first place to Giuseppe Mazzini – about whom he most probably heard from his father. (Russia, as a tyranny, had no place in such a Europe, to be sure: no right to be 'an arbiter of Europe', as she had been after 1815.)

His was, to use contemporary terminology, a vision of the 'Europe des patries' – the idea ascribed, erroneously, to Charles de Gaulle.* While arguing for the necessity of a European 'concord', Conrad also considered 'the national spirit' to be the most reliable element in international politics. He realized that the coexistence of so many nations and cultures results in immense difficulties. He spoke about 'the insufficiency of

---

* Conrad, by the way, shared with de Gaulle a highly suspicious, if not hostile, attitude towards the USA, as a capitalist empire without its own deeper spiritual tradition; this attitude mellowed only towards the end of his life.

Europe' (p. 85), in the sense of its inability, at the end of the eighteenth century, to cope with the challenges of the day. And, writing in 1905, he was exceptionally well aware that the present trend of events was contrary to his vision of European 'solidarity': Europe had been diverted from that goal by the imperialistic ambitions of competing military powers, in the first place of Prussia. '*Il n'y a plus d'Europe* – there is only an armed and trading continent, the home of slowly maturing economical contests for life and death and of loudly proclaimed world-wide ambitions' (p. 112). In other words, he saw with an unusual clarity what was the alternative to European unity, which will have to 'be built on less perishable foundations than those of material interests' (p. 107).

He realized as well that noble principles do not constitute a satisfactory ground for international co-operation. He saw that 'no single Western nation as yet will brook the restraint of abstract ideas as against the fascination of a material advantage' (p. 111). This sentence, old-fashioned as it sounds, expresses a most topical truth and sounds like a present-day exhortation to establish supra-national institutions.

6. And, finally, the sixth aspect. Conrad wrote four political novels which were European in their thematic scope; three contemporary, one historical: *The Inheritors* (together with F. M. Ford, 1901) – about the decline of idealistic liberalism and the inexorable rise of aggressive imperialism; *The Secret Agent* (1908) – about order and anarchy, democracy and subversion, security and law, England and Russia; *Under Western Eyes* (1911) – about Russia, Switzerland and Western Europe in general, despotism and revolution, historical heritage and theoretical doctrines, the future of the Russian Empire and the spiritual deficiencies of democracy (in his review of 1911 Richard Curle called it 'a novel of Europe'[9]); and the unfinished *Suspense* – about Napoleon's influence on Italy and Central Europe. Conrad himself called this last 'the great Mediterranean novel';[10] reviewers immediately noticed its grand thematic scope.[11]

To sum up: we may thus call Joseph Conrad a 'European writer' in at least six senses: 1. a writer of three different European cultural spheres, spanning East–Central and Western Europe; 2. the author of books with action taking place in many European countries; 3. a writer versed in several major European literatures; 4. a writer grappling with the most important issues of European history of the past 150 years; 5. a thinker using the concept of a European political solidarity; 6. the author of novels on 'European' themes.

The above list is not intended to be taken as complete. Professor Przemysław Mroczkowski, in his paper 'Conrad the European', justifies the title by pointing at the presence in Conrad's work of motifs which he considers typical of the European cultural tradition;[12] his pioneering essay is at the same time both more ambitious and narrower in scope than the present chapter.

I have so far argued that Conrad may be considered a European writer on the grounds of what he himself thought and wrote. However, we may put forward the same claim on the basis of his reception by readers. In several European countries Joseph Conrad has been accepted as 'one of us', as part of a shared cultural heritage – not simply as a foreign writer. We observe this kind of reception in Poland,[13] France[14] and Italy,[15] – not by chance the three countries where collected editions of Conrad's works preceded the Anglo-American one . . . In Poland Conrad was initially criticized (as by Eliza Orzeszkowa) for writing in a foreign language; but he was early recognized as an 'author-compatriot'. And although Stefan Żeromski, who was the first to use this formula, maintained with a blithe magnanimity that 'the purely artistic accomplishment of Conrad is not connected with Polish literature with even a single thread',[16] the readers felt otherwise, and scholars have shown that there are many such 'threads', visible and hidden, in Conrad's work.[17] During the Second World War Conrad became a moral authority for the young members of the Polish Underground.

The French easily recognize the presence of their literature in Conrad's theory and practice. They like to quote Jorge Luis Borges who, unaware of the overlapping of Polish- and French-language influence on Conrad's prose, claimed that it sounded 'rather French' to him. The enthusiastic interest with which a new series of translations, by Odette Lamolle, was greeted in 1996 offers yet another example. The Italians find in Conrad a way of looking at the recent history of Europe and Latin America which is familiar to them, with which they can identify. It would be interesting to compare the image of Conrad in these and other countries.

On the other hand, in Britain, Conrad was often seen as a foreigner, an *international* force. F. M. Ford (another outsider, son of a German immigrant) claimed in his reminiscences that Conrad did not feel mentally at home in England; Ford himself thought of him as an Elizabethan – because of Conrad's Polishness.[18] Evidently, Ford considered the Elizabethans non-insular. H. G. Wells, hearing about the plans for a collaboration between Conrad and Ford, warned that Ford might destroy Conrad's 'delicate oriental [!] style'.[19] Kipling thought that Conrad's prose read 'like a perfect translation of an excellent foreign writer'. One of Conrad's closest British friends, Edward Garnett, wrote that he 'had [the continental] tradition in his blood and his nerves in a way no Englishman has'.[20] Another close friend, John Galsworthy, mentioning the faults of Conrad's English style, thought that he looked at his British heroes from the outside, 'objectively and without confusion'.[21]

An anonymous reviewer of *Suspense*, summing up Conrad's achievement, wrote tersely: 'indeed, he does not lie in any English tradition at all, nor has he in the least influenced English thought or English writers as other lesser artists have done'.[22]

Thus we have here a sort of a negative argument for Conrad's European quality: the English, whose language he had adopted, did not claim him as fully their own.

Conrad's European multiculturalism is unquestionable and undoubtedly may be considered an enriching factor which opens fresh perspectives, attracting readers on the one hand by a surprising familiarity and possibility of identification, on the other by a fascination with not-too-distant exoticness. It propounds, however, some general methodological questions. How should we interpret particular elements of his works, when doubt arises as to the cultural sphere in which they belong?

Even on the level of language we cannot always be sure. Conrad made mistakes – no doubt unintentional – in all the languages he used in his writings: in English as well as in numerous expressions and words in French, Italian, German, Spanish and Dutch. It seems obvious that these words and expressions ought to be understood on the basis of their correct forms, although we may wonder whether Conrad himself was not confused as to what the correct forms were. Thus when we read in *Nostromo* about Leonarda, Mrs Gould's 'own camerista', we may look in vain for this word in Italian and Spanish dictionaries, but we shall guess that Leonarda is a chambermaid.²³ Three pages later we find the Spanish word 'chulo' (pimp) used instead of 'chola', Indian. Sometimes, however, the given English sentence is made comprehensible only by reference to the French sense of a word used in it. In *Nostromo* and twice in *Under Western Eyes* we have the word 'deception' used in the sense of 'disillusionment';²⁴ Sylvère Monod quotes (from 'A Smile of Fortune') the example of the phrase 'nothing but to look at', a literal transposition of the French 'rien qu'à les voir', 'enough to have just a look';²⁵ etc.

Conrad's Polonisms (occasionally indistinguishable from Gallicisms, as in 'to make a few steps') sometimes present a puzzle. Should we treat them as lapses in correct English, or as innovative enrichments? The looseness of his syntax seems to be due to the unconscious pressure of Polish which, as a heavily inflected language, allows for many liberties in word order and phrasing not normally permitted in English. The construction of twin prepositions, strange in English but often used by Conrad, like 'from-under', may be another and minor example: 'a fixed from-under stare which made you think of a charging bull'.²⁶ This is, of course, a direct translation of the Polish *spod*.

The problem becomes even more complicated in the case of allusions, or assumed allusions. My favourite example is the fragment of *The Mirror of the Sea*, in the essay 'The Nursery of the Craft', opening with the words 'Happy he who, like Ulysses, has made an adventurous voyage.' It is clearly based on the beginning of Joachim Du Bellay's famous sonnet: 'Heureux qui, comme Ulysse, a fait un beau voyage.'²⁷ A French reader will presumably notice the allusion and understand the implicit irony of the fragment – because in Du Bellay's poem the full happiness of Ulysses consists in returning home after all his wanderings. But what about non-French readers? Would we say that they would be 'right' to interpret the fragment as the straightforward praise of adventurous travels?

Another example of cross-cultural ambiguities: I believe that in *Lord Jim* the hero's relation to his 'home', to which he feels he cannot return, becomes both clearer and more significant if we interpret it within the conceptual framework of Polish traditions. For a Polish expatriate his home country, his *ojczyzna*, his *patria* (English does not even possess the word for this concept; in Polish we do not have an exact equivalent of 'home'), is the locus of his obligations and of his ethical ideals.* In the case of an Englishman, for whom living and working overseas did not present any moral problems, Jim's obsessive insistence on the break of all links (even with his father), the whole psychological tension connected with the issue of a possible return, the very elevation of 'home' to the status of a quasi-mystical supreme moral authority, would seem to me excessive and contrived.[28]

Questions concerning Conrad's multiculturalism require further study. They can be restated in a more general form: do we have, or can we develop, multicultural or cross-cultural frameworks of interpretation? And equivalent criteria of judgement? Conrad himself seems to have realized the possibility of such questions. For example, in the 'Author's Note' to *Lord Jim* he implied that the essential subject of his novel, 'the acute consciousness of lost honour', should be perfectly understandable at least to the 'Latin temperament'.[29] By 1917, when the Note was written, it had become evident that *Lord Jim* might cause difficulties to the English critics when they attempted to interpret the novel within their own contemporary cultural framework.

However, the theoretical and practical complexities of interpretation, while presenting us scholars with a challenge and perhaps a headache, seem to be a boon to Conrad's readers. This, again, is another question demanding a further study: how is Conrad's popularity enhanced by the fact that he exploited the entire European culture as raw material and that the artistic conventions he used span various literatures? His books are seen by readers in many European languages as at

---

* In Polish, *ojczyzna* has been a term carrying an unusual emotional weight – and not only since the partition of Poland at the end of the eighteenth century, but much earlier. Jan Kochanowski (1530–86) wrote in a poem that 'if the way to heaven is open to any – it is open to those who serve *ojczyzna*'. Therefore I think that in Conrad's mind even a subliminal association of 'home' with *ojczyzna* would result in loading the concept both emotionally and morally. When he writes about a special devotion to one's *patria*, he uses either the Latin word (*A Personal Record*, p. 35), or the expression 'native country' ('Prince Roman', *Tales of Hearsay*, p. 51).

the same time national (or multinational) and not alien; as written in English, suffused with Polish and French elements, and essentially European.

Therefore, today, if the European Union were to award literary prizes, Joseph Conrad would be a perfect candidate.

14

Joseph Conrad after a century

On 28 February 1889 Konrad Korzeniowski (not yet 'Joseph Conrad', but a British subject with a name which kept presenting difficulties, rarely surmountable, to many scribes in various maritime offices), Ordinary Master of the British Merchant Marine, was master of a small – 346 tons – iron barque, *Otago*, moored at Port Minlacowie in Spencer Bay, Southern Australia. A few weeks before, he had returned from a long voyage to the island of Mauritius, where he had flirted – in French, his second language – with a local girl whom he proposed to marry. In another month or so, upon arrival at Port Adelaide, he would resign his first (and, as it turned out, only) command and return to Europe.

At that time he was not yet writing anything apart from long letters in Polish to his uncle and former guardian, a landowner in the Ukraine. He would start writing fiction about six months later, during a prolonged stay in London in the autumn of 1889. He left the sea permanently in 1894 and made his literary début a year later.

These few biographical facts show immediately that he was a highly unusual person. Immediately, but far from fully. Outstanding artists tend to have untypical lives; but Conrad-Korzeniowski was untypical to the extreme. Brought up in Polish culture, with his father a poet and a politically active patriot, as a teenager he left his home country for France. French literature and French intellectual tradition were the second element which shaped his mentality and artistic attitude. And then he became a professional seaman, serving mainly in sailing-ships – which meant physical effort and hardships on a scale now difficult to imagine. As a child he experienced the barbaric oppression of Russian autocracy, the imprisonment of his father, forced exile to northern Russia, the early deaths of both his parents. As an adolescent in Marseilles he basked in the exciting charms of the Mediterranean. And later he experienced for many years the loneliness of an émigré and the solitude of a brooding introvert who led the hectic life of a sailor surrounded by men very different from himself.

When Joseph Conrad began to write, it was in his third language, one which he had started to learn at the age of twenty and about his difficulties with which he would complain for many years. He was to write all his works in that language, to which he introduced new imagery and novel cadences, for readers to whom only one element of his own heritage and experiences was familiar: the sea. Everything else he wanted to write about was, to his English contemporaries, alien and exotic: from the struggle between autocracy and freedom to the idea of the novel as a form of art. In the idiom of Anglo-Saxons, permeated with utilitarian, Protestant, commonsensical and middle-class notions, he would concern himself with issues characteristic of Central European and Latin civilizations, of the traditions of the chivalric ethos and Catholicism.

Conrad's artistic programme, which he formulated early in his career in the celebrated – but initially suppressed at the request of his publishers – Preface to *The Nigger of the 'Narcissus'*, was also unusual, particularly in England. It was, in brief, a highly original amalgam of Flaubertian realism and modern symbolism; of the novel as a work of art and as a communal deed; of the artist's work as an act of individual creative effort and as an assertion of human solidarity. Conrad was conscious of being original, of going it alone; and that was why he protested against all attempts at using established labels to describe and classify his works.

Although he treated the writer's craft with utmost seriousness, and although he devoted much study to his masters, especially Flaubert and Maupassant, Conrad was never a writer of and for an élite. At the time when withdrawing into High Art's ivory tower was becoming increasingly common among the more ambitious writers he, not lowering his exacting standards, wrote for all.

Present-day literary scholars and critics have a tendency to consider works of literature as books about other books, poems about other poems, novels about other novels. This attitude, which tends to entrap the art of fiction in a vicious circle of self-reflection, may be defensible with regard to much of contemporary high-brow production. It misses the mark if applied to the tales and novels of Joseph Conrad. To understand him we have to read his texts as referring not to other texts, but to external, misleadingly called 'objective', reality. This is not to say that we have to regard, for instance, 'Heart of Darkness' as reportage from the Belgian Congo, but we have to realize that the problems tackled in this long short story are problems which existed in real life, not just on the pages of books.

A hundred years separate us from the world Joseph Conrad knew and wrote about. Although he is now acclaimed as the first twentieth-century writer, he set in it, in its early years, the action of only two of his novels – *Under Western Eyes* and *Chance* – and a few stories. The favoured time for the location of his plots was the 1880s and 1890s: as in *Almayer's Folly*, *The Nigger of the 'Narcissus'*, 'Youth', 'Heart of Darkness', *Lord Jim*, 'Typhoon', *Nostromo*, *The Secret Agent*, *The Shadow Line* and most of his shorter pieces.

Still, as we approach the beginning of the twenty-first century, Conrad's reputation as one of the greatest modern novelists looks securely established.

What did he write about? What did he notice in the world, long gone now, and *how* did he see it?

He saw it as a world in a state of multifaceted crisis; of change which did not translate into progress, as many of his contemporaries tended to believe; of overt and violent clashes between forces and tendencies none of which deserved full support; of a less tangible but ubiquitous struggle between what he called 'les valeurs idéales', idealistic values, and the prevailing materialism.

The world of Conrad's experience encompassed almost the entire earth as known to man a century ago: from London, the commercial capital of the globe, to the jungles of the Congo; from what is today Indonesia to Latin America; from northern Russia to southern Italy; from the Australian bush to the streets of Geneva. He did not know, nor write about, North America – but he did not leave it unnoticed either, as is shown in his novel *Nostromo*, with its criticism of the role played by US capital in Latin America.

He also knew and sailed many seas – and all the oceans. In his rendering of the life of seamen he concentrated not on adventure, but on moral and philosophical questions, posed (or illustrated) by their existence and their work. He returned, insistently, obsessively, to the problem of the relation between man's work and its rewards, between man's worth and his social and economic status. The glaring discrepancy between the hard toil of seamen who risked their lives almost daily, and their meagre pay, was for him a model of the human condition in general, with its contrast between leading a moral life and being successful. Behind the question of social and economic injustice, which he neither glossed over nor waxed sentimental about, he saw a more essential issue: the need for a hierarchy of values founded on something other than financial gain and social position.

In the far-away, exotic lands of Africa and Asia, at that time mostly European colonies, Conrad saw a progressive destruction of indigenous cultures, sometimes barbaric but usually much more sophisticated than the colonizers wanted to admit: destruction undertaken in the name of Western civilization, which was a slogan frequently covering nothing else than greed, corruption, and wanton disregard for humanity. But in his 'Heart of Darkness' he showed something else: the ideology of a superior race put to the service of a dark, savage urge for power and domination. He gave, in the figure of the talented, idealistic and murderous Kurtz, a portrait of a proto-Nazi, of a totalitarian fanatic.

When we read Conrad's description of forced labour at the Company's station and the grove of death there, we cannot but feel that he discerned in the depths of the Belgian Congo a prototype of the twentieth-century Soviet and Nazi labour camps.

> A slight clinking behind me made me turn my head. Six black men advanced in a file, toiling up the path. They walked erect and slow, balancing small baskets full of earth on their heads ... I could see every rib, the joints of their limbs were like knots in a rope; each had an iron collar on his neck, and all were connected together with a chain whose bights swung between them, rhythmically clinking ... All their meagre breasts panted together, the violently dilated nostrils quivered, the eyes stared stonily uphill. They passed me within six inches, without a glance, with that complete, deathlike indifference ...

And then the grove of death, like a snapshot from Kolyma or Auschwitz:

> Black shapes crouched, lay, sat between the trees leaning against the trunks, clinging to the earth, half coming out, half effaced within the dim light, in all the attitudes of pain, abandonment, and despair... I saw a face near my hand. The black bones reclined at full length with one shoulder against the tree and slowly the eyelids rose and the sunken eyes looked up at me, enormous and vacant.[1]

Latin America, where the action of *Nostromo* takes place, Conrad perceived as caught in a vicious tangle of internal conflicts between indolent, aristocratic liberals and destitute, volatile masses – and the intrusion of external, imperialist, domineering foreign capital. He recognized there as well the paradoxes of foreign assistance, which starts as a benevolent, idealistic action, and ends up becoming a tool of sordid local interests.

Tsarist Russia was for Conrad a 'prison of the nations'; an oppressive autocracy within which internal contradictions had reached a point of no return, of no possible resolution. Repeating the image which the Polish poet Adam Mickiewicz had taken from the Russian thinker Pyotr Chaadaev, Conrad compared Russia to 'a monstrous blank page awaiting the record of an inconceivable history'.[2] It was in his eyes an immense country where a death-like peace of passive and ignorant submission of the masses was to be broken by the convulsive violence of a nihilistic rebellion. Its 'inconceivable history' was to be written by an unavoidable, bloody explosion. Conrad understood that Russian freedom-thirsty radicals would, to quote the motto of his *Under Western Eyes*, 'take liberty from any hand as a hungry man would snatch a piece of bread'. But he saw in the Russia of his time, as in the France of one hundred years earlier, also a conflict between the stultifying force of ossified tradition and nihilism, which results from rejection of the whole historical heritage.

Conrad's dissatisfaction with all contemporary socio-economic systems and political programmes had at least three sources. Personal experience and the mordant wit of Anatole France had taught him to look with suspicion at all established political institutions. Secondly, he refused to accept the prevailing utilitarianism as the only and unquestioned system of values. And perhaps most important was his contempt for the rule of 'material interests'.[3] We hear about them in one of the culminating scenes of *Nostromo*, when Dr Monygham says: 'There is no peace and no rest in the development of material interests. They have their law, and their justice. But it is founded on expediency, and is inhuman; it is without rectitude, without the continuity and the force that can be found only in a moral principle.'4 Their rule results in the calculation of the value of every human act or person in the terms of financial worth or gain.

But Conrad's disapproval of the present was not linked to an idealized vision of a better past or a glorious future. He did not *reject* the present; he only regarded it coolly, with his deeply rooted scepticism about human nature, which he did not consider naturally good. However, even when criticizing most severely, he was never petulant. While castigating self-satisfaction, he was also against despair. The universe we live within may be devoid of any inherent ethical idea; it is full of 'cruel and absurd contradictions', but it is a 'spectacle for awe, love, adoration, or hate... but... never for despair!' Our 'appointed task on this earth' is mainly a task for our conscience.5 Without illusions about human nature, Conrad believed in man's indomitable spirit.

Art was one of its manifestations. 'For in art alone of all the enterprises of men there is a meaning in endeavour disassociated from success[,] and merit – if any merit there be – is not wholly centred in achievement but may be faintly discerned in the aim.'6

I have mentioned Joseph Conrad's artistic programme, as expounded in his Preface to *The Nigger of the 'Narcissus'*. Let us now have a closer look at it. This programme implies a renunciation of the fantastic and fanciful, of fable-making and inventing non-existent worlds. It postulates concentration on the real, essential and true. It defines art, in the celebrated formula, as 'a single-minded attempt to render the highest kind of justice to the visible universe, by bringing to light the truth'.7 Conrad declares himself here as a representationalist, a writer who wants to describe what there is. 'Inspiration comes from the earth, which has a past, a history, a future, not from the cold and immutable heaven.'8 A novelist's imagination is for him essentially a re-imagination, a reconstruction. The processes of learning about facts, of gaining knowledge about an event or a person, of searching for the truth, are a most frequent motif in Conrad's works. He traces, and reproduces with a highly inventive skill, the sinuous and bumpy ways of our understanding. *Lord Jim* can be read also as a textbook in the psychology of knowledge.

In his admirable study *Conrad in the Nineteenth Century* Ian Watt analyses Conrad's device of 'delayed decoding'. When applying this device, Conrad first presents a sense impression but withholds 'naming it or explaining its meaning until later; as readers we witness every step by which the gap between the individual perception and its cause is belatedly closed within the consciousness of the protagonist'.⁹ But that was only one of Conrad's means of reconstructing the process of 'cognition', and at the same time forcing the reader to participate in that process.

Another celebrated formula in the Preface to *The Nigger of the 'Narcissus'* signals another original component of Conrad's artistic programme: 'My task which I am trying to achieve is, by the power of the written word to make you hear, to make you feel – it is, before all, to make you *see*!' Thus Conrad's conscious aim is to make the reader share in the reconstructing and re-imagining. And he goes about his task by forcing the reader to assume an active role as well: by engaging her or him directly, by making her or him a partner in the enterprise of art.

An early and exceptionally perceptive critic of *Lord Jim* wrote:

> we note an incessant regard for the reader: the author does not improvise, 'singing for himself' – but acts consciously as a strategist of impressions, a Machiavelli always remembering about our own point of view and about the state of our attention; a clever and inventive Amphitryon of a feast of intellect, a magician who dazzles the spectator with the swift gyrations of an object, the same but constantly changing its visual shape; a master of the punch line.¹⁰

Conrad's cognitive interests, and his direct engagement of the reader as a co-reconstructor, co-creator of the work of literature, was closely linked to his other and equally modern obsession: his concern with the difficulties of human communication. He was acutely conscious of the essential impossibility of communicating to others one's deepest thoughts and emotions: 'It is impossible to convey the life-sensation of any given epoch of one's existence – that which makes its truth, its meaning.' And again: 'There are no words for the things I wanted to say.'¹¹

Written language, the novelist's basic means of expression, is essentially a passive rendering of an action.¹² Conrad, however, wanted to render justice to reality which is not only always changing but which has many not mutually translatable aspects. That was one of the reasons he favoured, in his prose, the spoken word of an imaginary, personal narrator. Such a narrator, be it Charlie Marlow or some other teller of a story (or a story within the story), approaches us, the readers, more dynamically than does an impersonally narrated text. At the same time he also forces us to adopt an active attitude to work out, from a juxtaposition of differing points of view, our own perception of the story's plot and its protagonists.

These artistic concerns – with cognition, with communication, with engaging the reader – were for Joseph Conrad essentially philosophical concerns. The means he applied to reconstruct the process of understanding, to communicate the results of that process, to make us see, were ultimately and most fundamentally the devices to break through our isolation and speak 'to the subtle but invincible conviction of solidarity that knits together the loneliness of innumerable hearts: to the solidarity in dreams, in joy, in sorrow, in aspirations, in illusions, in hope, in fear, which binds men to each other, which binds together all humanity'.[13]

Loneliness was for Conrad an inherent element of the human condition: 'We live, as we dream, alone.'[14] But it was a fact against which, he believed, we have to struggle incessantly – because we are fully human only as members of a community. Indeed, the aim of art, and the supreme goal of his own writing, was for Conrad to 'awaken in the hearts of the beholders that feeling of unavoidable solidarity; of the solidarity in mysterious origin, in toil, in joy, in hope, in uncertain fate – which binds men to each other'.[15]

Human solidarity was thus for Conrad not just a postulated and distant ideal, but something we can consciously affirm and which gives meaning to our existence. 'Haven't we, together and upon the immortal sea, wrung out a meaning from our sinful lives?' – says the narrator of *The Nigger* in the closing words of the novel. Mrs Emilia Gould, the moral heroine of *Nostromo*, expresses her vision of human community in a different but equally memorable way: 'It had come into her mind that for life to be large and full, it must contain the care of the past and of the future in every passing moment of the present. Our daily work must be done to the glory of the dead, and for the good of those who come after.'[16]

All great art may be said to entail a search for a meaning of life. Such a search, passionate and probing, is present in all the major works of Conrad. It assumes many forms. It opens both starkly secular and transcendental perspectives. Although Conrad was not a religious writer, and although he mistrusted metaphysical speculations, he evidently believed that the experience of humanity cannot be contained within the framework of physics and biology, that our consciousness transcends our bodily existence. 'The horror! The horror!', the now notorious cry of the dying Kurtz in 'Heart of Darkness', expresses both the shock of his moral discovery and the crushing awareness of his own finiteness; and we can guess that the content of that moral discovery has been conditioned by the awareness that he has to look at his life from the outside.

The eponymous hero of *Lord Jim* illustrates with his life and death the validity of the old paradoxical principle: to give one's life a value one has to treat life itself as lacking in value. Perhaps he knew the words of Shakespeare:

> Mine honour keeps the weather of my fate.
> Life every man holds dear, but the dear man
> Holds honour much more precious-dear than life.[17]

The ideal of honour, as pursued by Jim, is essentially a secular ideal. But as it leads to heroic sacrifice and readiness for death, it produces an other-worldly glow of immortality through glory.

Conrad's Jim is also that rarity in modern literature: a tragic hero in the strictest, classic sense of the term, fully corresponding to Friedrich Schiller's formula about tragic fate which elevates man at the moment of crushing him. This adds to the exceptionality of *Lord Jim* as a novel – and makes it harder to accept. The contemporary mind bears with tragedy, but only in theatre. In real life apparently there is, or ought to be, always some way out, some 'solution'.

Razumov, the main protagonist of Conrad's *Under Western Eyes*, lacks Jim's moral dimensions. The conflict he lives through, and which destroys him, is of a more sordid if also – even in our time – more common type. It is a conflict between the force of political realities and exigencies, dressed up as a law of historical necessity, and the demands of ethics founded on compassion and fidelity.

It was Joseph Conrad's unique combination of unflinching soberness of mind with an ability to look beyond the boundaries of the tangible, the physical, the empirically present, which produced in Bertrand Russell, not an easily impressionable man, a powerful response. They met in 1912 and became good friends, to the point of Russell giving his son the name Conrad. In his *Portraits from Memory* Russell gave one of the most penetrating characterisations of Conrad as a person and an artist:

> At our very first meeting, we talked with continually increasing intimacy. We seemed to sink through layer after layer of what was superficial, till gradually both reached the central fire. It was an experience unlike any other that I have known. We looked into each other's eyes, half appalled and half intoxicated to find ourselves together in such a region.'

Russell felt that Conrad 'thought of civilized and morally tolerable human life as a dangerous walk on a thin crust of barely cooled lava which at any moment might break and let the unwary sink into fiery depths'.

Presenting Conrad's ethics, Russell writes:

> Conrad's point of view was far from modern. In the modern world there are two philosophies: the one, which stems from Rousseau, and sweeps aside all discipline as unnecessary; the other, which finds its fullest expression in totalitarianism, which thinks of discipline as essentially imposed from without. Conrad adhered to the older tradition, that discipline should come from within.[18]

Contrasting Conrad with Rousseau is an excellent point. Conrad indeed rejected scornfully Rousseau's optimistic belief in the innate goodness of human nature. To the famous opening sentence of *The Social Contract*, 'L'homme est né libre' (Man is born free), he answered, also in French, in the words of one of the characters in *Lord Jim*, a lieutenant of the French Navy: 'Man is born a coward (*L'homme est né poltron*). It is a difficulty – *parbleu*! ... But habit – habit – necessity – do you see? – the eye of others – *voilà*. One puts up with it.'[19]

Betrand Russell ends his reminiscence by saying that Conrad's 'intense and passionate nobility shines in my memory like a star seen from the bottom of a well' – but adds that 'Conrad, I suppose, is in process of being forgotten.'

This was written in 1953, when Conrad's critical reputation in England was indeed at its lowest ebb; a state from which it would soon rebound, partly under the influence of Americans, such as Robert Penn Warren and Morton Dauwen Zabel.

And Conrad has never ceased to be a popular writer. The only one, and perhaps the last, of the great and most innovative novelists who is read not only by specialists, connoisseurs, the high-brow crowd, and by students who are not given a choice, but by men and women of all walks of life. What is his secret?

I have been trying to accumulate the elements of an answer which cannot be a simple one. Of the factors mentioned thus far three seem to play the most prominent role. The first is Conrad's mastery in making use, in English, of the resources of his non-English cultural traditions. The second is his artistic inventiveness, not limited to the confines of a single artistic movement. And the third is Conrad's endeavour to make the reader his partner. Psychologically, the last factor is perhaps of greatest consequence, as the 'partnership' is not coupled with condescension on the part of the writer and requires the reader to make an effort to keep up, an exhilarating and rewarding effort. Conrad's invitation to the reader to become his accomplice in the re-creation of a work of art and in asserting human solidarity makes the reader also an associate in the writer's lasting presence, lifts the reader up in the consciousness of sharing in an important experience, gives all readers a boost to their spirits and self-esteem.

Historically, however, the first two factors may turn out to be no less important. For all his uniqueness, Conrad was not an eccentric. His life put at his disposal different strains of the same broadly understood Western civilization. He made these currents, akin but distinct, converge. Polish Romanticism, with its idea of a work of art as a moral deed and its obsession with the problems of honour and responsibility; and Gustave Flaubert's realism, with its combination of disillusionment and passion, are just two examples of literary traditions absorbed and made use of by Conrad. It is impossible to understand fully the cultural dictionary of his work – the ideas he expressed and analysed, the artistic means he employed – without some knowledge of his Polish, French and British heritage. But it seems to be possible to enjoy reading him and to be moved by him without any special preparatory training; because all the above is not yet the whole answer to the question about Conrad's lasting importance and popularity. While writing about the world now a century old, Conrad saw in it elements which are still with us today – more so than any other writer of his time. On the pages of his books that world of a hundred years ago looks strikingly, disturbingly familiar.

In Latin America counter-revolutions follow revolutions, and populist leaders keep turning into dictators, with oil and cocaine having taken over the role of silver as the coveted source of wealth. On the streets of our cities – in Europe, in North America – Verlocs, secret agents, sneak to explode bombs at the behest of foreign embassies. The Razumovs of today, having nowhere to go, keep entering into pacts with totalitarian authorities, persuading themselves that they do it for the sake of their country. Political police organize conspiracies to demonstrate that they are needed and to have their budget increased. And we keep asking ourselves whether 'For the autocracy of the Holy Russia the only conceivable self-reform is – suicide.'[20]

But that is not yet the whole answer either. The most enduring problems posed by Conrad's works are those of moral values and individual moral responsibility. The Jims and Steins of today continue asking themselves 'how to be', how to live so as to preserve human dignity and self-respect in a universe which is at best indifferent to man's ethics. We all have to struggle with what Conrad called 'the most obstinate ghost of man's creation... the doubt of the sovereign power enthroned in a fixed standard of conduct'.[21]

And thus, more than a century since his maturity and sixty-five years after his death, Joseph Conrad remains, in his own favoured phrase, 'one of us'. He saw, a hundred years ago, the shape of things lasting, and of things to come. He identified problems and perils which are still with us today. We need him.

15
Joseph Conrad in his historical perspective

Joseph Conrad was born in 1857; his first novel was published in 1895; and he died in 1924. The lapse of time since then constitutes, I suppose, a distance sufficient to see him in a historical perspective. It allows us to ask, without an excessive fear of of having our picture blurred by the closeness of the object, what is Conrad's place in the history of literature.

This issue, as I see it, involves three groups of questions: what were the traditions, intellectual and artistic, which nursed Conrad's creative talent? What was the position of his work within contemporary spiritual and literary trends and movements? And, thirdly, who were his followers and what sort of inheritance has he left to them? Of course, within the scope of a short chapter one can hope only to open a few vistas on the problem, announced boldly in its title.

Luckily for us historians of literature, most writers, including those of the first rank, fit more or less neatly into some general pattern of artistic and intellectual life of their time. Even when 'exceptional', 'outstanding' and 'breaking new ground' they allow themselves to be arranged in groups and sequences. They loyally contribute to the 'temper of the era', allowing us to draw dividing lines between periods and to talk about typicality and representativeness. Occasionally, however, we encounter figures so peculiar, so aberrant, that it is virtually impossible to fit them into the general formula of their time. Conrad seems to be a good candidate for the first place among these freaks.

He published his most important books between the years 1897 and 1911. It was the time when, on the Continent, Maurice Maeterlinck and August Strindberg, Gabriele D'Annunzio and Anatole France, Paul

Bourget and Anton Chekhov, and also Leonid Andreiev, Bjørnstjerne Bjørnson, Hermann Sudermann, Henryk Sienkiewicz and Gerhart Hauptmann reached the peak of their fame. Maxim Gorki, Thomas Mann and André Gide were just beginning their great careers. European intellectuals idolized Friedrich Nietzsche and Henri Bergson. In Britain Bennett, Galsworthy, Hardy, James, Kipling, Wells and Wilde were recognized as the leading writers.

With the sole exception of Henry James, another expatriate and spiritual solitary, there is not another name on this list which we could link with Conrad's to form a distinct 'micro- group'. Therefore it should not be surprising that the early critics of Conrad had great difficulties in classifying him and were almost compelled to resort to patently superficial formulas, as, for example, 'Kipling of the Malay Archipelago' or 'writer of the sea and adventure'. Evidently he was not an epigone; but he does not fit easily among his contemporaries either. Even Conrad himself, surely feeling not a little lost and lonely, tended towards the end of his life to succumb to the temptation of easy self-labelling and described himself, against the evidence of his best work, as a promoter of simple and unquestioned ideals.

Conrad's exceptionality as a writer was, of course, connected with the peculiarity of his biography. He was fluent in three languages, but wrote all his books in the language he learned last, at the age of twenty. Born into a Polish gentry family in the Ukraine, at the age of four he had to accompany his parents to exile in Russia. Early orphaned, he never regularly attended any school; still, he managed to educate himself to an impressive level, especially in history. He left Poland at the age of seventeen, and for the next twenty years led the life of a sailor, beginning as a simple seaman and reaching the rank of captain. He started to write his first book when he was already thirty-two, and published it six years later. When his sea years were over, he settled in England; but even at the height of his creative power he would confess to a friend: 'English is still for me a foreign language whose handling demands a fearful effort.'[1]

As Jocelyn Baines, Albert J. Guerard and many other scholars have pointed out, Conrad's immediate literary predecessors were French; he was a diligent (and self-avowed) disciple of Flaubert and Maupassant. From Flaubert he took the idea of the novel as a laboriously shaped work of art; from Maupassant the impressionistic elements of his literary manifesto in the famous Preface to *The Nigger of the 'Narcissus'*. Certain elements of his narrative method are also best explained by reference to Flaubert's programme of restrained, objective realism. The writer, advised Flaubert, should be like God: present everywhere, nowhere visible.

However, we find in Conrad's work elements which cannot be explained by reference either to his French masters, or to his English contemporaries. For clues, we have to look to Conrad's biography, which reveals that there were in his attitude and background some factors conflicting with Flaubert's model of fiction.

Firstly, and this is perhaps the most important factor of all, the influence of the French realists clashed with the tradition of the Polish Romantics. Secondly, Conrad, a philosophical agnostic, was also sceptical as to the possibilities of a full understanding of the motives of human actions; the monadic separateness of every individual and the inscrutability of forces governing our behaviour formed according to him an obstacle not to be overcome by any amount of intellectual analysis. And, thirdly, writing was for him evidently a compensative action: to create meant to make up for the shortcomings, psychological as well as external, of real life.

The two latter factors are usually, although in various ways, taken into account by English and American critics; the first one tends to elude or baffle some of them. In fact, traces of Polish inheritance are not difficult to identify.[2] The evidence consists of numerous motives, scenes, even particular sentences borrowed from Polish Romantic poetry. It is also easy to recognize in many of Conrad's heroes a family likeness to the typical hero of Polish Romantic literature: a lonely uprooted individual, endowed with an outstanding awareness of his moral obligations, very self-conscious but not self-centred.

Of the same origin, and of infinitely greater consequence, is the notion, underlying Conrad's whole work, of the writer's role as analyst of basic moral issues – stated in terms not only psychological, but primarily socio-political. In spite of all the ostentatious individualism of 'typically Polish' behaviour, Polish literature has been traditionally a literature of communal feelings, of solidarity. Archetypal in this literature are the concepts of man as a member of his social group and of his nation, and conscience as a reflexion of communal responsibility. 'Movement from alienation towards commitment', which Ian Watt discerns in Conrad's work in his admirable essay,³ is also something characteristic of Polish literature, from the sixteenth century onwards. Therefore, to take issue with Watt's essay, Conrad's national background not only enforced his alienation, but was at the same time giving him an original impulse to battle against it.

All three factors, national, philosophical and psychological, worked in the direction of anything but dispassionate objectivism and traditional, direct kind of realism. Consequently, Conrad's novels and short stories have, as a rule, some distinct moral focus, and it is impossible to overlook their ideological involvement. Furthermore, his heroes are not studies in character, not unrepeatable individuals, but types – he conceives them not as psychologically unique personalities, but as symptomatic cases.⁴ Although his protagonists, such as Kurtz in 'Heart of Darkness', Jim in *Lord Jim*, Captain McWhirr in 'Typhoon', Emilia and Charles Gould in *Nostromo*, Razumov in *Under Western Eyes*, are all distinctly defined, the stress in their presentation is put on the fact that they face model ethical and philosophical problems. Such a 'typological' approach has behind it an old and distinguished tradition, but evidently runs counter to the trends prevailing in the European prose of the last hundred and fifty years.

To what extent Conrad was conscious of those diverse components and influences is a question of interest mainly to a psychological biographer. We do not need, however, any psychological hypotheses to see that these elements had to be somehow adapted to blend into an artistically congruous whole; and it is not biography but structural analysis which suggests that this is precisely the function of Conrad's two most characteristic devices: the narrator within the story and the time shifts. The consequence of the application of these devices is a sort of 'sceptical realism'. The convention of the omniscient narrator is abandoned (why it does not happen in all Conrad's books – is another matter); what is being told is not too far removed from the possible experience of a living person. What is understood and explained is also carefully limited and distilled; in the place of the author's direct comments, or his *porte-parole*'s pronouncements, we are faced with a subtle interplay of points of view, varying scopes of knowledge and insight, flashes of moral revelation. The time shifts create an illusion of a gradual getting at the truth about facts and about the character of the heroes. Both devices focus our attention on problems rather than personalities, and they also make it possible to achieve the impression of a tragic necessity so important in Conrad's work and so difficult to attain in realistic novels, which at any moment present us with innumerable possibilities of a further development of action.

This is perhaps how we can describe, in most general terms, the peculiar artistic result of the merger of Conrad's manifold cultural traditions. His unusual, polycentric background and aesthetic taste made him an exceptional, even unique writer. Still, we cannot say that he was not a man of his time.

By the time of Conrad's début as a writer the growth of industrial society, the progress of science and the crisis of religious beliefs resulted in a widespread breakdown of established moral codes. Most contemporary writers were conscious of this process – but nobody more deeply than the desperately probing Dostoevsky, who summed up the age's predicament in a cry, which was supposed to open anew the road to Christianity: 'if God does not exist, everything is permissible'. Conrad, who hated Dostoevsky and rejected his positive programme, was nevertheless very close to him in his intensity of being aware of the crisis in Western ethics.

The reaction of unrest and alarm was by no means universal in literature. Naturalistic novelists were ready to supplant, without qualms, the old moral dogmas with the newly discovered laws of biology. Popularized Nietzsche and fashionable Wilde were understood as champions of the idea that the rules of the moral game can and should be changed at will: a strong, independent, self-sufficient man's will. And many a writer of the *fin de siècle* was inclined to the escapist gesture of turning his back on the whole hideous and nasty world.

Conrad belonged to none of these groups. He was, like Turgenev and James, conscious that the traditions of enlightened generations were falling apart. Like Flaubert, Maupassant, France and Ibsen, he was shocked by the hypocrisy of the contemporary bourgeois morality. Like Hardy, he was dismayed by the moral plight of man, left defenceless at the mercy of heredity and natural forces. But, unlike Wells, he did not believe in the almost automatically beneficent influence of scientific progress.

Despite being, thus, by no means exceptional in his awareness of the general crisis of morals, he was probably unique in his response. It would be rash and presumptuous to attempt to describe this response in any simple terms, or to extract from Conrad's books some straightforward recipe or programme. But we can perhaps analyse his attitude by distinguishing its three aspects, corresponding to three possible levels of understanding and appreciation of his work.

First, we have the most accessible level of the famous 'few very simple ideas': fidelity, honour, friendship, obeying the sailor's code, etc. To many unwary readers, and even to many a critic, unreserved trust in these plain rules is *the* Conrad message. But if we remain on this level of interpretation, then our understanding of even a comparatively simple story like 'Typhoon' will be primitive, and the more complex ones, like 'Heart of Darkness' or *Nostromo*, will appear confusing and even incomprehensible.

The second aspect or level consists in pitiless confrontation of the 'simple ideas' with their actual working in life. This confrontation is conducted on two planes – individual and general – and in both cases the outcome is highly disconcerting. Although the 'simple ideas' or principles are supposed to provide ethically dependable guidelines for individual behaviour, the individual's ability to grasp them, to stick to them and to preserve their purity and humane meaning turns out to be rather doubtful. This is why whenever Conrad uses the expression 'true to himself', he does so ironically; and to the notion of 'being sure of himself', he retorts: 'it is the last thing man should be sure about'.[5] Moreover, there exists an eternally gaping chasm between man's intentions and the results of his actions. As the examples of Kurtz and Charles Gould show, even the most idealistic intentions can become corrupt, if they are not constantly controlled by reference to the practical results of the ensuing actions.

This highly dispiriting picture is also frequently taken to represent *the* Conrad view of man's situation in the world. With regard to some of his works, such as 'Heart of Darkness', such a critical conclusion seems to be justified. Conrad, an explorer of the 'extreme situations',[6] had no illusions about man's natural virtues or the world's moral order. However, there is also the third aspect, or level of understanding. The acceptance of the 'simple principles' does not imply a belief in their 'objective' truth or ontological necessity; man is not 'naturally' good; history does not follow a rational and just course; contemporary society is materialistic and debased; and, whatever men do, the surrounding universe is equally indifferent to their heroic efforts and to their failures. But still, Conrad seems to maintain that the code of honour and fidelity, 'of the few very simple ideas ... as old as the hills', is the best we can hope for. It does not guarantee anything: neither success nor sympathy, nor righteousness – but it is the only code worthy of the ancient dignity of mankind's traditions. In other words, these human values are not natural laws but only postulates difficult to implement and impossible to justify pragmatically, perhaps even illusory – but still worth our stubborn, if stumbling, adherence.

At this point it is perhaps fitting to say a few words about the problem of Conrad's 'pessimism'. That he was a pessimist, most of his critics readily pronounce. But pessimism is not a simple notion. An average pessimist seems to be a person who thinks, or says, something to the effect: 'the world could have been good, it can be good – but it won't be'. Now Conrad is plainly not this kind of pessimist, since he suggests rather that the world has never been good, it cannot be good, but there is some possibility of our diminishing the amount of evil.⁷

The idea of an autonomous morality, man-created, secular and related to social life, is not a new one; among Conrad's contemporaries we find it, for instance, in Jean-Marie Guyau. It is rather unlikely that Conrad knew his work. But whatever theoretical predecessors he might have had, Conrad is indisputably one of the leading pioneers of moral thinking in fiction. To a large extent it is to him that we owe today the vision of man as facing the indifferent or even hostile universe with his own code of behaviour, his own concept of moral order.

However, the content of the code, the body of values, was not of Conrad's own making. It represented a continuation of an ancient tradition philosophically based on the notions of loyalty, honour and mutual responsibility; socially it has been linked to the nobility and the military. In literature it is the tradition of the *Iliad* and *Chanson de Roland*, Calderón, Corneille's *Le Cid*, Walter Scott and Alfred de Vigny's *Servitude et grandeur militaires*. This is also a literature of extreme situations, of violent conflicts and decisive choices, of physical defeats from which man's dignity has to be rescued. There is no easy consolation to be found there, but only an enthusiasm of the in-spite-of-everything type. The foundations of the moral code, embodied in this tradition, are both anti-pragmatic and secular (in spite of religious affiliations, as in the medieval code of chivalry).[8]

But Conrad was not a simple inheritor of the 'chivalric' tradition. He introduced a major novelty: most of his heroes are neither noblemen nor soldiers. The moral code remained basically the same, but its social ramifications disappeared. Preserving the principles while shedding their genetic and environmental basis has struck many critics as odd and anachronistic, but it turned out to be very fruitful, as the example of Conrad's literary followers will show.

The impression of Conrad's strangeness has been grounded, however, mainly in the contrast he presents with the background of most of the nineteenth-century European novel. He was, in his mature work, opposed to the whole middle-class spirit of modern fiction and far removed from both the literary heritage of Rousseau (whom he disliked) and Richardson, and the heritage of Balzac (whom he valued).[9] Peculiarities of individual psychology, extensive introspection, analysis of strange emotions and unusual human relationships, the liberation of man from the shackles of communal constraints concerned him as marginally as did the descriptions of social intercourse, revelations about the primacy of economic and political over moral motivations, or explorations of the possibly infinite number of marital geometrical figures.

To talk about 'influences' with regard to contemporary literature is rather risky and perhaps even trivial; it is safer and potentially more illuminating to talk in terms of shared affinities, of trends and common legacies. The most conspicuous part of Conrad's legacy in twentieth-century literature is perhaps the revival of the ethics of honour, with its peculiar problems: conflict of honour and emotional attachment, contrast between principles and success in life, fidelity and personal interest, etc. It was to him and, on a lower level of sophistication, to Henryk Sienkiewicz, a superb story-teller, that this revival has been due.[10]

Not that Conrad's 'formal' achievement has not been followed. F. Scott Fitzgerald was perhaps the most effusive in his confessions of how much he owed to Conrad in the shaping of his work, and the influence is most easily discernible in *The Great Gatsby*.[11] William Faulkner's type of narrative is also evidently a development of Conrad's – a development in two directions. On the one hand in, *The Sound and the Fury*, Faulkner contrasts personal points of view more sharply than Conrad ever did; on the other, the almost continuous and stylistically homogeneous yarn of *Absalom, Absalom!* goes even further than Conrad's *Chance* in its use of changes in the scope of its hero's consciousness. Also

> always Faulkner's style resembles Conrad's in its rhythms as well as in its dependence on sonorous Latinism, on abstractions paired in paradoxical phrases, on word-motifs, and on 'negative ultimates' – negative words of ultimate degree. Finally, the function of Faulkner's style is the same as that of Conrad's, to draw the reader into the compelling trance of the language.[12]

But even in the case of Faulkner the real affinity consists in something else: in the tensely dramatic concept of life, in the insistence on moral involvement, and in the basically analogous hierarchy of values stressing honour, loyalty, endurance and friendship. Hemingway's vision and values, although differently expressed and clothed, belong to the same sphere; and his fundamental moral problem of an autonomously defined code of behaviour is a continuation of Conrad's quest. His heroes, enveloped in their painful consciousness of *nada*, the metaphysical void within which we are condemned to act, embrace principles which are neither egocentric nor utilitarian.

In the writings of Antoine de Saint-Exupéry, who crossed as many skies as Conrad had seas, we find not only techniques deliberately paralleling Conrad's, but also a generally similar attitude, which finds its most memorable expression in the words of Guillaumet, the crashed pilot who saves himself, in an incredible effort, because he remembers his comrades' trust in him: 'Ce que j'ai fait, je te le jure, jamais aucune bête ne l'aurait fait!' (I swear that what I have done no animal would ever have done).[13] And Camus' idea that man's only salvation in the face of the besieging evil is a desperate solidarity and preservation of honour also recalls Conrad's message about man's tragic and heroic dignity.[14]

Conrad's political novels, *Nostromo*, *The Secret Agent*, *Under Western Eyes*, rather neglected during his lifetime, have attracted more and more attention in recent years. Although it would be difficult and risky to talk about their direct influence, they present an approach to political problems which has become quite common in contemporary literature.

A part of Conrad's legacy as a political novelist consists simply of the themes he raised, some of them for the first time: the themes of ineffectual liberalism, of destructive revolutions which appeal to the best and bring out the worst in men, of 'material interests' which corrupt both their exploited victims and their supposed beneficiaries, of political provocation and terroristic idealism, of the state demanding a total loyalty and still distrusting those who are loyal not because of a feeling of absolute dependence but from personal conviction. In the middle of the twentieth century they would become only too frequently not literary motifs, but elements of everybody's life; and Europeans, particularly Central and Eastern Europeans, have been compelled to experience them on a painfully grand scale.

Political problems were for Conrad moral problems, fundamentally. 'The French Revolution [he wrote] was [initially] not a political movement at all, but a great outburst of morality.'[15] This way of looking at a political conflict as a massive outburst of moral indignation or depravity was characteristic of many conservative thinkers. It was, however, usually coupled with a certain degree of either benevolent *naïveté*, social ignorance or selfishness. Conrad, unfair as he sometimes was to the anarchists, showed an acute awareness of the existing social conflicts and their sources, and did not have many illusions about the convergence of interests of the haves and the have-nots. For him moral evaluation was not a screen to hide real social and political issues.

His mistrust of purely political terms of reference was undoubtedly determined by the fact that he looked at all abstract political programmes as at a many-headed body of false promises. Political theory of the bourgeois world deceptively suggested that all was well and shall be better. Political theories intending to change this world seemed to endanger the national spirit (which he cherished) and threaten to upset this precarious structure we call human civilization, a structure delicately balanced on the surface of a vulcanic swamp.

This is why he seems to be the only major European writer of his time whose outlook did not have to change as a result of World War I and perhaps the only one who would not have been surprised by the emergence of the modern totalitarian state.

On the larger plane of the general development of fiction, Conrad has bolstered anti-psychologic and anti-naturalistic trends – at a time when naturalism and psychology in the novel rule supreme.

Paradoxically, this avowed individualist and agnostic left a heritage of social and metaphysical concerns. He was, as Robert Penn Warren wrote in one of the best appreciations of Conrad's work, a 'philosophical novelist':[16] not in the sense of discussing philosophical ideas (as do Anatole France, H. G. Wells or Thomas Mann) – although occasionally he does that as well (as in *Nostromo*, *The Secret Agent*, or *Under Western Eyes*) – but mainly in the sense of enacting ideas, of presenting their implications and consequences (as in the three mentioned novels, in 'Heart of Darkness', *Lord Jim*, *Victory*, or *The Shadow Line*.

Concentration on types and problems rather than on exceptions and psychological subtleties is also a part of his legacy. Whenever we encounter a contemporary novel which deals with moral issues not by way of emphasizing the biological and psychological uniqueness of every person, but by way of looking for the core of common human condition, we may suppose that it runs parallel, or even belongs, to the Conrad tradition.

Focusing on general problems and typical situations is in Conrad's work one of the means to overcome the oppressive consciousness of man's loneliness. He was intensely aware of the all-pervading problem of uprootedness and isolation; more so than any of his contemporaries or any writer since, with the possible exception of Kafka. 'We live, as we dream – alone.'[17] Solitude was for Conrad an element of the human condition that is inescapable but against which we should fight relentlessly (here he differed from the fatalistic Kafka). In view of our present preoccupation with alienation and with the individual's loneliness within mass society, and in the face of a universe expanding in all directions, Conrad seems to be a prophet. But not a despairing prophet of helplessness in the face of unavoidable doom.

16

Fidelity and art: Joseph Conrad's cultural heritage and literary programme

1

I am sure all Conrad readers remember well his words from 'A Familiar Preface' to *A Personal Record*: 'Those who read me know my conviction that the world, the temporal world, rests on a few very simple ideas; so simple that they must be as old as the hills. It rests notably, among others, on the idea of Fidelity.'[1]

That the concept of fidelity occupies a central position within the framework of Conrad's ethical concerns seems quite evident. Ian Watt is, I believe, right in claiming that 'fidelity is the supreme value in Conrad's ethics'.[2] I propose here to take a closer look at the origins, contents and implications of this concept. I shall also try to demonstrate that there exists a strong conceptual link between Conrad's moral and artistic ideas, and that it is the idea of fidelity which has furnished this link.

2

The concept of fidelity is, in European tradition, most closely associated with the ethics of medieval chivalry. In fact, it belongs to a tradition which goes back thousands of years. Fidelity to a person, or fidelity to an object or idea, is perhaps the most ancient non-pragmatic rule in human relations. (By non-pragmatic I mean: not following from practical considerations of gain, success, satisfaction of wishes or needs, etc.[3]) Gilgamesh is faithful to Enkindu, Achilles faithful both to the memory of Patroclus and to his obligations to the status of a hero, Hector faithful to his duty in defending Troy, Roland faithful to Charlemagne and to his honour... The line is very long. It is the line of conservative ethics, of moral values and ideals, based on past experience, on tradition – not on abstract reasoning or visions of a better future.

Among the virtues of chivalry fidelity stood out as the main one. In fact, it forms the indispensable backbone of every morality based on a *code*, on inflexible principles, and not on the possible or expected results of our actions.

In the code of chivalry 'fidelity' (or 'loyalty') meant a mutual obligation of the lord and his knightly vassals. While a knight was duty-bound to stand by his lord in battle, and to support him with his counsel and vote in the time of peace, his feudal lord, his *seigneur*, was by the same token obliged to provide for him in need and, in the case of his death, to look after his widow and orphans.[4] Chivalric fidelity was thus not a psychological, but a moral relation. It implied deference to the rules, recognized by both parties. It was a bond, resulting in the growth of mutually reflected prestige. To be faithful was to be honourable; and equally honourable was to be an object of fidelity. Charlemagne and France basked in the glory of Roland; and Roland was elevated by serving Charlemagne and France.

3

The problem of the function of fidelity in Joseph Conrad's system of values I am going to approach first from the direction of his personal and cultural heritage. However, when analysing the elements of that heritage I shall not do it with the view of demonstrating the *influence* of Apollo Korzeniowski on his son's beliefs or of Polish Romanticism on Conrad's idea of art. Influence is always hypothetical: we have to assume that X has read or heard something which made him, consciously or not, reshape his own beliefs or style or interests. I want to base my contentions on safer ground and am going to present my case in the terms not of influence, but of affinity, similarity and continuation.

Therefore I shall, by and large, skirt the issue of the *causes* of this continuation. I want to behave like a lexicographer, who identifies and analyses the meanings of particular expressions, but for whom the accidental mechanisms of semantic change are of only a marginal concern.[5]

However, after this general disclaimer, I do have to delve, if only briefly, into matters biographical. This seems to be the simplest and most natural way to display the ideas and attitudes which were continued by Conrad.

We do not know, nor shall we ever know, the precise details of Apollo Korzeniowski's role as the chief organizer of what in 1863 became the clandestine Polish 'National Government'.[6] He and his fellow-conspirators managed to cover their tracks quite well; and the destruction of Polish archives in two world wars did the rest. But we know enough to realize that the Russian authorities were right in assuming that for a few years (and thus since the birth of his only son) Korzeniowski's literary activities were mainly a cover for political ones.

After his imprisonment, trial and exile, and thus during the last illness-ridden years of his life, Apollo Korzeniowski turned to writing as the only form of both earning money and discharging what he saw as his national obligations. In the acute awareness of his public duties he was, again, outstanding but at the same time typical of his milieu and his generation.

'But, my Dearest, I am a Monk and indeed among other monks only a simple *frater* [brother] in the Polish Order. I have closed all my thinking within a narrow cell of patriotism; and nothing else moves me than what leads myself and mine towards the desired goal', wrote Apollo Korzeniowski to his friend Buszczyński in May 1868.[7] Quoting Giosué Carducci, he confessed: 'I am now writing only because I cannot act.'[8] He believed that there are circumstances in which 'the questions of art must give way to those of life' – national and social life in the first place. Ruefully, he admitted that such an attitude resulted in 'sins against the indifferent heavens of Aesthetics'.[9] In other words, he thought that the demands of art – a fidelity to art – could collide with the demands of 'life', with the fidelity to national and social obligations of the artist. And he was certain that the latter demands were more important, that the second kind of fidelity was paramount.

The young Konrad must have known if not the content then at least the sentiment of Apollo Korzeniowski's talks and writings. We know that the son occasionally wrote letters for his father, when Apollo, ill with tuberculosis, felt too weak. Moreover, whatever Joseph Conrad read as a boy in Poland (and we know that he read a lot, and there are many echoes of that reading in his work) was undoubtedly filtered through his daily intercourse with his father. Polish Romantic poetry and patriotic literature were read and revered in the schools in Cracow and Lwów which Konrad Korzeniowski attended.

After the partition of Poland at the end of the eighteenth century Polish literature became the repository of national existence. This is why the principle of regarding national obligations as morally binding, of elevating national fidelity to the position of the writer's supreme duty, was generally accepted in Polish post-partition literature. The paradigm of this attitude we find in Adam Mickiewicz's drama *Dziady* (The Forefathers' Eve, 1832), one of the most influential works in Polish literature. The main hero, Gustaw, undergoes a symbolic transformation: from a self-centred poet of love and folkloristic fantasy he changes into a poet of patriotic struggle, a conscious representative of the oppressed nation. He rejects subjectivity to become a spokesman both to and for his 'millions'. He breaks out of his isolation to affirm solidarity with his compatriots. By this act he becomes the archetype of and a model for all Polish Romantic writers. And at the moment of his transformation Gustaw assumes a new name – 'Konrad'. It is to him that Konrad Korzeniowski, Joseph Conrad, owed both his given name and his English pen-name.

4

Fidelity implies perseverance. Tadeusz Bobrowski, the young Conrad's guardian, repeatedly exhorted his ward, prone both to instability and to pessimism, to follow the maxim of a 'devotion to duty interpreted more widely or narrowly, according to the circumstances and time' – 'usque ad finem [till the very end]'.[10] We should realize that Bobrowski is here – as were many so called 'positivists' in Polish late nineteenth-century literature – a faithful follower of the Polish Romantics. It was, in fact always the case: whenever a Polish nineteenth-century writer or thinker wished to advocate something other than resignation from striving for national independence and something more than a concentration on 'material interests', he had to resort to the Romantic formulas and principles. And it is superbly significant, and characteristic, that we find the maxim 'usque ad finem' repeated in *Lord Jim* by no one else but Stein, a Romantic German, a veteran of the 1848 Revolution of the 'Spring of the

Nations'. His is also an invocation to fidelity: 'To follow the dream, and again to follow the dream – and so – *ewig – usque ad finem.*'[11]

The reason why Bobrowski, when exhorting his nephew to perseverance, had to use a Romantic formula was not only that the Romantic message of the great poet–prophets, Mickiewicz and Juliusz Słowacki, was so powerful. Simply, no other arguments for Polish national fidelity were available. Conrad wrote to Edward Garnett in 1907: 'You forget that we have been used to go to battle without illusions. It's you Britishers that "go in to win" only. We have been "going in" these last hundred years repeatedly, to be knocked on the head only – as was visible to any calm intellect.'[12] The difference between the appeaser Tadeusz Bobrowski and the rebel Apollo Korzeniowski consisted here in the fact that the former advocated a passive, and the latter an active resistance.

To sum up and amplify this part of my argument: the idea of fidelity was crucial to Polish nineteenth-century public morality and was strongly present in Polish literature of that time. It was in the first place a fidelity to the cause of national independence. It imposed on Polish writers an obligation to serve – by means of communicating to their readers the message, the essential truth, that they must not capitulate and accept the fact of Poland's demise. By the fact of his service, by doing his duty, a Polish writer would confirm his solidarity with the partitioned nation and would overcome the bondage of isolation, typical for every artist bound to live within the confines of his sensibility.

5

Conrad's declaration about fidelity, quoted at the beginning of this chapter, is phrased in words which indicate that he assumed his readers had by then noticed the role of fidelity in his works: 'Those who read me know my conviction . . .' This is important, as it implies that Conrad regarded the idea of fidelity as characteristic for his work, as recurrent and evident in the fabric of his novels and tales.

The context of the declaration seems to make its meaning definite – and narrower. Conrad follows his statement about the role of fidelity with a sally against the 'revolutionary spirit', which he deems fashionable at his time. 'The revolutionary spirit is mighty convenient in this, that it frees one from all scruples as regards ideas. Its hard, absolute optimism is repulsive to my mind by the menace of fanaticism and intolerance it contains.' These words, written in 1911, today sound painfully prophetic. But of course Conrad does not have in mind only specific revolutions, but all arbitrariness, all voluntarism in the treatment of human past – personal and communal – and its heritage. And he does not simply profess his personal allegiance to the ethical principle of fidelity. He also suggests that this idea has been essential in the age-long experience of mankind.

Thus his statement about fidelity plays a double role: of a moral postulate and of a descriptive thesis. Fidelity is for Conrad both a fact and a norm.

To appreciate that we have to have a look, if only glancingly, at the ways the problems of fidelity – or faithfulness, which is a synonymous concept – versus temptation and betrayal are treated in Conrad's works. We find these issues at the heart of many, if not most, of his novels and tales. I am going to mention only the more obvious examples.

In *An Outcast of the Islands* (1896) we have a fairly straightforward story of Lingard's trust and Willems' faithlessness.

'Youth' (1898) may be seen as a tale of fidelity to a ship, and even more to a foolhardy maritime endeavour: 'the test, the trial of life'.

In 'Heart of Darkness' (1899) the idea of fidelity presents a tangle. Marlow tries to be faithful both to his code and to Kurtz. It is remarkable that on the plane of practical action these two obligations do not conflict with each other: when he takes the raving superman Kurtz on board the river-boat and tends him in his cabin, Marlow follows his own principles, not Kurtz's. He shows his loyalty to Kurtz, bearding the manager and the other 'pilgrims', who in comparison to Kurtz are to him simply despicable. Kurtz broke moral laws; they would brush them away as something irrelevant.

Marlow says that he never betrayed Kurtz, that he was loyal to him (as a person), because he saw Kurtz's soul 'at least, struggling blindly with itself' and he heard the dying Kurtz pronounce the words of self-condemnation: 'The horror! The horror!' – the words suggestive of the flames and sulphur of Dante's *Inferno*; the words in which he recognized a moral 'victory' of the depraved and tragic hero.

When later facing Kurtz's Intended, Marlow notes that 'She had a mature capacity for fidelity.' In lying to her about Kurtz's last words (he says, 'The last word he pronounced was – your name'). Marlow pays homage to that fidelity. He feels obliged by her trust in himself. Also, he recognizes the inherent value of that fidelity to the memory and to the cherished (if utterly mistaken) image of her beloved – and lies, because hurting her and offending her loyalty would produce only pain and damage.

Conscious that his decision to have lied resulted from an inescapable conflict of values, Marlow muses: 'Would they [the heavens] have fallen, I wonder, if I had rendered Kurtz that justice which was his due?' 'Render justice' is here the phrase to remember.

In 'The End of the Tether' (1902) we encounter a tragic but simple conflict of two fidelities, two loyalties: Captain Whalley's fidelity to his daughter and to his employers.

In *Lord Jim* (1900) the motif of fidelity reverberates throughout the novel. I shall refer to just three instances: Stein invokes the maxim *usque ad finem*; Jim assures Marlow, when he visits him in Patusan, that he will 'be faithful'; after Jim's death Jewel accuses him – in spite of Stein's protestations – of 'falsity'.[13]

In *Nostromo* (1904) the hero's nickname, 'captain Fidanza', signals his trustworthiness and fidelity. However, as Jacques Berthoud points out, Nostromo 'can think of his deeds only in their immediate relation to himself'; he is faithful – but in fact only to himself, or, rather, to his own reputation.[14]

The fidelity to his own image makes Nostromo both incorruptible, and faithless to those by whom he felt he was being used. When we realize that, we also become aware that 'Fidanza' ('trust' or 'confidence' in Italian) is in fact an unintentionally ironical nickname. It is a function of Nostromo's being regarded as 'our man', which is his name's etymology ('nostro uomo'). Captain Mitchell and the others, who have so dubbed him, thought they could trust Nostromo, because they had made him theirs. And in the event Nostromo betrays them to recover his full autonomy, to remain his own man. Thus we see in this novel an illustration of something which can be called the dialectics of fidelity: a man can be faithful to something or somebody only at the expense of his own egotism. Fidelity, in other words, demands self-denial.

The Secret Agent (1907) presents a morbid tangle of loyalties: genuine and sham; true, apparent and purchased.

'Prince Roman' (1910), on the contrary, shows fidelity in its starkest, most heroic form. It contains also the fullest characterization of an archetypal object of fidelity: Poland, the hero's (and the author's) home country: 'That country which demands to be loved as no other country has ever been loved, with the mournful affection one bears to the unforgotten dead and with the unextinguishable fire of a hopeless passion which only a living, breathing, warm ideal can kindle in our breasts for our pride, for our weariness, for our exultation, for our undoing.'[15]

In *Under Western Eyes* (1911) the problems and implications of fidelity are again, as in *Lord Jim*, at the very centre of the story. Student Haldin, a revolutionary, has 'confidence' in his colleague Razumov, the main hero of the novel. But Razumov betrays him to the police and Haldin is executed. Later Razumov, sent to Geneva with a mission to penetrate the circles of Russian political émigrés, meets there Haldin's sister Natalia. Natalia's confidence in him throws Razumov into psychological and moral turmoil which leads him to an open admission of his treachery. In his diary Razumov confesses that Natalia (who 'has the most trustful eyes of any human being that ever walked this earth') was 'appointed to undo the evil by making me betray myself back into truth and peace'.[16] Fidelity is in *Under Western Eyes* shown consistently as the opposite of cynicism. But it is also something more. One of the pivotal statements of the novel is the following: 'A man's real life is that accorded to him in the thoughts of other men by reason of respect or natural love.'[17] In other words, a man's personal identity depends on the confidence other people put in him, on the loving trust with which others endow him. Razumov comes to realize that. He says: 'In giving Victor Haldin up, it was myself, after all, whom I have betrayed most basely.'[18] A breach of faith, a failing of trust, the absence of fidelity, undermine the hero's consciousness of his own identity. He may have been 'faithful to himself', but his idea of his own personality becomes fatally blurred.

Victory (1915) is, of course, also a novel about fidelity: Lena's fidelity to Heyst, which is countered by his fatal misconceptions of her personality and of their relationship.

The narrator's 'commitment' in *The Shadow Line* (1917), which – to follow Ian Watt's terminology – is the opposite to 'alienation',[19] may be also defined as a choice of fidelity: a choice the implications of which are not immediately realized; only gradually the hero become conscious of the extent of his obligations and of the need – and possibility – to 'entertain seemingly impossible ideals'.[20]

In *The Rescue* (1920) the issue of fidelity is presented with an operatic flourish. Lingard is faithful to Hassan and Immada, but his fidelity is tested and momentarily compromised by his infatuation with Mrs Travers; the old Jörgenson, however, blows himself up, remaining grimly faithful till his death.

And finally in *The Rover* (1923), his last completed work, Conrad takes up once more the theme of fidelity to one's home country. Peyrol returns to France and dies for France, although he thoroughly detests the concurrent revolution, because of the wanton cruelty of its terror and because of the mendacity it breeds. Thus the novel may be taken as a fictional rendering of the contrast between fidelity and the 'revolutionary spirit', against which Conrad had sallied in his declaration, quoted at the beginning of this chapter.

6

This galloping review allows us further to develop our analysis of the concept of fidelity as present in Conrad's work.

To begin with, fidelity precludes egocentricity. A faithful person puts the object of fidelity first, his ego second. It also precludes all voluntarism and arbitrariness (which last Conrad identified with 'revolutionary spirit'). Fidelity imposes limitations upon our potential choices. As Conrad said in one of his most striking and characteristic statements: 'Faithfulness is a great restraint, the strongest bond laid upon the self-will of men and ships on this globe of land and sea.'[21]

Further, fidelity implies respect for facts. Gentlemen don't dispute the facts, runs the old saw; and aptly, as gentlemen were expected to be faithful. In other words, fidelity opposes subjectivism: objective reality must not be twisted, has to be given its due.

Thus fidelity entails *external* obligations. Conrad's moral message is sometimes taken as being that one should remain 'faithful' or 'true to oneself'. Very misleadingly. The concept of 'being faithful to oneself' appears, as far as I have noticed, only twice in Conrad's works, and both times in an ironical context. Once in his early short story about marital infidelity, 'The Return' (1897), where we find the following dialogue:

'I tried to be faithful to myself – Alvan – and . . . and honest to you . . .'
'If you had tried to be faithful to me it would have been more to the purpose,' he interrupted, angrily.[22]

The second time we encounter the concept of 'fidelity to oneself' is in *Nostromo*. Dr Monygham tries to persuade Nostromo to undertake a very dangerous mission of carrying across the country swept by civil war an urgent message asking for help for the city of Sulaco and the silver mine of San Tomé. He pleads: 'I say you must be true to yourself, Capataz.' Nostromo retorts: 'True to myself... how do you know that I would not be true to myself if I told you to go to the devil with your propositions?'[23] Thus fidelity is shown to mean being true not to oneself, but to a principle.

7

There exists a tradition in Conrad scholarship of discussing the issue of fidelity in his works in terms primarily biographical. Conrad is thought to have been exceptionally sensitive to the problems of faithfulness because of his private experiences, his own struggles with conflicting loyalties. And indeed in *A Personal Record* Conrad writes, referring openly to himself: 'The fidelity to a special tradition may last through the events of an unrelated existence, following faithfully, too, the traced way of an inescapable impulse. It would take too long to explain the intimate alliance of contradictions in human nature which makes love itself wear at times the desperate shape of betrayal. And perhaps there is no possible explanation.' He has bolstered this argument with an earlier warning: 'No charge of faithlessness ought to be lightly uttered.'[24]

The context of these sentences indicates that Conrad was afraid that such a 'charge of faithlessness' could be levelled against himself on account of his emigration from Poland. He claims that, in spite of all appearances, he has remained faithful to the country of his ancestors. (I have characterized elsewhere his 'hopeless fidelity' and its implications.[25]) The problem with his claim is that it is based not on evidence but on a declaration; and thus the said 'fidelity' may be only mental, not behavioural. Jacques Berthoud, in his perceptive analysis of *A Personal Record*, writes that Conrad was very early exposed 'to the contradictions latent in the ideal of fidelity' and 'forced to learn that fidelity to one principle may mean infidelity to another'.[26] I think 'fidelity' is here understood in a broader and more abstract sense than that in which it is taken by Conrad. The choice of one principle of action necessarily involves rejecting innumerable other principles: fidelity is not exceptional in this respect. But the objects of 'fidelity' in the historically warranted sense which Conrad uses cannot be chosen at will; a choice of fidelities is in itself a slippery and suspicious business. One may be, as Konrad Korzeniowski was, born into an obligation of fidelity – and this is precisely what Conrad has in mind in *A Personal Record*.

However, Conrad's statements about fidelity have obviously a general, not only a personal import. Therefore I think it would be wrong to interpret them solely in terms of their specific biographical reference. A conceptual analysis may expose coherences invisible on the behavioural level; and only then may it offer the key to the understanding of Conrad's claim that deep inside he has remained faithful. Fidelity, he says, may take strange shapes...

8

I have said that the essence of fidelity lies in remaining loyal to something outside oneself and that fidelity precludes arbitrariness and implies respect for facts. In his celebrated Preface to *The Nigger of the 'Narcissus'* Conrad wrote: 'And art itself can be defined as a single-minded attempt to render the highest kind of justice to the visible universe, by bringing to light the truth, manifold and one, underlying its every aspect.'[27] After twelve years he continued this line of thought in *A Personal Record*:

> And the unwearied self-forgetful attention to every phase of the living universe reflected in our consciousness, may be our appointed task on this earth. A task in which fate has perhaps engaged nothing of us except our conscience [!], gifted with a voice in order to bear true testimony to the visible wonder, the haunting terror, the infinite passion and the illimitable serenity; to the supreme law and the abiding mystery of the sublime spectacle.[28]

This was Conrad's declared aim, his artistic programme. It does not mean that he has always realized it; but it means that it was as much a part of his professed ideology as his statements about fidelity.

The phrase 'render[ing] the highest kind of justice' is the key one: it joins together moral and artistic criteria, justice and veracity. This alloy of the ethical and the artistic norms is confirmed in the latter of the two quoted fragments by an appeal to 'conscience'.

In his Preface to *The Nigger* Conrad sets before the artist a double objective: to render justice to the visible universe by bringing to light the truth – and to communicate this truth to the readers: 'by the power of the written word to make you hear, to make you feel . . . before all, to make you *see*!' Bringing to light the truth is conceived as a *moral* act, since it consists in rendering *justice*, in giving what is rightly due. It is an act of loyalty to the facts. It combines the postulate of realism with the postulate of faithfulness, the objectives of the French realists with the Romantic idea of a work of art as a Deed.

Conrad uses the phrase 'a book is a deed' in the least known and the most polemical of his programmatic statements: in the essay 'A Glance at Two Books' written in 1904 but published only posthumously. There he takes an unusual public sweep at the 'national English novelist', who 'seldom regards his work – the exercise of his Art – as an achievement of active life by which he will produce certain definite effects upon the emotions of his readers . . . It never occurs to him that a book is a deed, that the writing of it is an enterprise as much as the conquest of a colony.'[29] Doubtless, such an elevation of the novelist's work to the level of creation – which echoes at the same time the Romantic belief in the power of Art and Flaubert's priestlike devotion to the selfless toil of a writer – endows literary effort with a moral significance. '. . . in art of all the works of men there is meaning in endeavour disassociated from success . . . the consciousness of worthy aim is everything; it is dignity, truth, honour – the reward and the peace', wrote Conrad in a fragment of the Preface to *The Nigger*, which he later unfortunately discarded on the advice of Edward Garnett.[30]

9

The second task of the artist, that of communicating the truth which has been '[brought] to light', strengthens the moral aspect of his work, because it is both based on and aiming at a confirmation of human solidarity 'which binds together all humanity – the dead to the living and the living to the unborn'.[31] As John Batchelor notes, the sense of solidarity is for Conrad the test of the truth communicated by a work of art.[32] Artistic communication, that 'making you see', or 'stimulating vision in the reader',[33] can therefore be seen as an act of faith in the possibility of mutual understanding. The artist, who 'descends into himself', into this solitude which – as Conrad reminds us repeatedly – is our metaphysical human condition, is still endowed with 'the invincible conviction of solidarity that binds together the loneliness of innumerable hearts', which obliges him to make his 'appeal'. This conviction turns him, in his solitary toil, into a representative of those for whom he writes.

(Here we notice most clearly a salient difference between Conrad and Flaubert, whom he considered his master. Flaubert, torn between his Romantic and realistic inclinations, between his furies and his *impassibilité*, between the veneration of Art and the cult of science, sought to escape from his inner conflicts without any thought about his readers, about his public role as a writer.)

The concept of solidarity is a close relative of the concept of fidelity. And although Conrad does not use the word 'fidelity' when he describes the work of the artist in his Preface to *The Nigger*, the idea itself seems to reverberate on its pages. We read about the demands of 'complete, unswerving devotion' and about 'the only justification for the worker in prose' which consists of 'the sincere endeavour to accomplish that creative task, to go as far on that road as his strength will carry him'. Four years later Conrad took up the same point in his letter to the *New York Times Saturday Review*, stressing the postulate of loyalty to the truth as perceived by the artist: 'Fiction ... demands from the writer a spirit of scrupulous abnegation ... It is only the writer's self-forgetful fidelity to his sensations that matters.'[34]

10

'Fidelity to his sensations' sounds to me as a formula of evasion, hiding shyly behind a fashionable and ostensibly bold subjectivist phrase the much more ambitious belief in the task of 'rendering justice' and reaching out to the 'loneliness of innumerable hearts'.

Thus Conrad's artistic manifesto was at the same time an ethical proclamation. Artistic fidelity, which for Conrad means loyalty to the truth, links up here with ethical fidelity, which consists in solidarity with other men.

Or, to put it differently, morality and art are joined together by the principle of fidelity: to truth, to duty, to human solidarity.

Joseph Conrad can be seen here as continuing the role of his namesake, Mickiewicz's Konrad – and as remaining faithful to the spiritual legacy of his father Apollo. To return once more to *A Personal Record*: 'No charge of faithlessness ought to be lightly uttered ... The inner voice may remain true enough in its secret counsel.'

NOTES

1 Introduction, or confession of a mastodon
1 W. Kayser, 'Literarische Wertung und Interpretation', in *Die Vortragsreise*, Bern 1958, pp. 39–57.
2 E. R. Curtius, 'Europäische Literatur', *Merkur* (1947), repr. in *Europäische Literatur und Lateinisches Mittelalter*, Bern 1954, p. 22.

2 Conrad's Polish background, or from biography to a study of culture
1 G. Morf, *The Polish Heritage of Joseph Conrad*, London [1930], pp. 149–66.
2 A. Mickiewicz, *Pan Tadeusz*, 1834, The Epilogue.
3 J. Słowacki, *Rozmowa z Matką Makryną Mieczysławską* [A conversation with Mother Makryna Mieczysławska], 1846.
4 I. Watt, *Conrad in the Nineteenth Century*, Berkeley and Los Angeles 1979, p. 81.

3 Joseph Conrad's parents
1 Fragments of Joseph Conrad biographies apart, the main source of information about Apollo Korzeniowski available in English remains Czesław Miłosz's essay 'Apollo N. Korzeniowski: Joseph Conrad's Father', transl. by Reuel K. Wilson, *Mosaic* 6/4 (1971/2). It contains some basic data and several interesting comments. However, Miłosz was handicapped by his limited access to documentary evidence: he did not even have access to all published works, and had none to unpublished manuscripts. Apparently to make up for these limitations Miłosz ascribed to Korzeniowski opinions and attitudes of the protagonists of his plays, which resulted in grotesque if colourful overstatements. Of the numerous published reminiscences of Apollo Korzeniowski's contemporaries Miłosz used only Buszczyński's, otherwise relying exclusively on Tadeusz Bobrowski's evidently biased memoirs. More balanced is a chapter in Andrzej Busza's 'Conrad's Polish Literary Background and Some Illustrations of the Influence of Polish Literature on his Work', *Antemurale* 10 (Rome and London 1966), pp. 118–39. In Polish, Roman Taborski's *Apollo Korzeniowski, ostatni dramatopisarz romantyczny* [Apollo Korzeniowski: the last Romantic playwright], Wrocław 1957,

contains a dependable, if incomplete, review of Korzeniowski's literary output; it is, however, outdated in its presentation of his political activities.

2 Stefan Buszczyński's claim that Teodor Korzeniowski's estate was confiscated in punishment for his participation in the insurrection cannot be confirmed. See the list of confiscated estates in Daniel Beauvois, *Le Noble, le serf, et le révisor*, Montreux 1985, pp. 280–1.

3 Undated letter (from Żytomierz, 1859) to Karol Szajnocha, *Korespondencja Karola Szajnochy*, ed. Henryk Barycz, Wrocław 1959, vol. II, p. 174.

4 Biblioteka Jagiellońska, Cracow, MS 6577; see Taborski, *Apollo Korzeniowski*, p. 38.

5 In fact, the idea was of French origin. See Andrzej Walicki, *Filozofia a mesjanizm*, Warsaw 1970, p. 23.

6 Biblioteka Jagiellońska, MS 6577. On the Skwira mutiny see Beauvois, *Le Noble*, pp. 68–70. In an appendix to his 'memoirs' 'Polska i Moskwa' (see n. 36) Korzeniowski retells the story of the mutiny, claiming that the peasants initially did not demand their freedom but asked their Polish landlords to lead them in their fight against the Russian authorities. Beauvois considers this version fully apocryphal, but Korzeniowski was not the only one to believe it as testifies, e.g., Teodor Tomasz Jeż's (a well-known writer and democratic, pro-Ukrainian émigré political activist) novel *Hryhor Serdeczny*, Lwów 1874. However, the essential point is that both in 1855 and 1864 Korzeniowski's anger was directed against the landowners, who had refused their peasants' appeal.

7 As argued by Taborski, *Apollo Korzeniowski*, p. 54.

8 Rafał Blüth, 'Dwie rodziny kresowe' [Two borderland families], *Ateneum* (Warsaw 1939), no.1, pp. 12–13.

9 Poem beginning: 'Kochanko moja–Niewiasto–Żono!' [My lover–lady–wife!], Biblioteka Jagiellońska, MS 6577.

10 Tadeusz Bobrowski, *Pamiętnik mojego życia*, ed. Stefan Kieniewicz, Warsaw 1979, vol. II, p. 30.

11 *CUFE*, p. 25.

12 Władysław Mickiewicz, *Pamiętniki* [Memoirs], Cracow 1927, vol. II, p. 37.

13 See Bernard C. Meyer, *Joseph Conrad: A Psychoanalytic Biography*, Princeton 1967, pp. 340–1.

14 They consist of two batches, both of 1861: letters sent by Ewa Korzeniowska to her husband in Warsaw, confiscated in October that year and kept in the archives of the Special Military Court there (see

CUFE, pp. 37–55), and her letters to Antoni Pietkiewicz, kept in the police archives in Kiev (see ibid., pp. 57–61).
15 See, e.g., Apollo Korzeniowski to Kazimierz Kaszewski, 22 November 1866, *CUFE*, p. 105.
16 Ewa Korzeniowska to Apollo Korzeniowski, ibid., pp. 39–55.
17 Taborski, *Apollo Korzeniowski*, p. 73.
18 Ibid., pp. 87, 92.
19 'Jeszcze dziennikarstwo i przemysł', *Gazeta Codzienna 1860*, no. 335. For a critical comment see Jerzy Jedlicki, *Jakiej cywilizacji Polacy potrzebują* [What kind of civilization Poles need], Warsaw 1988, pp. 133–5.
20 Biblioteka Jagiellońska, MS 6577.
21 See, e.g., Leon Syroczyński, *Z przed 50 lat. Wspomnienia b. studenta kijowskiego Uniwersytetu* [From 50 years ago. Memories of a former student of Kiev University], Lwów 1914, pp. 19, 30, 36.
22 *Obshchestvenno-politicheskie dvizhenie na Ukrainie v 1856–1862 gg*, Kiev 1963, pp. 134–6.
23 See his extensive commentary to his own (untitled) poem, dated 10 April 186[2] and thus written in prison, Biblioteka Jagiellońska, MS 6577, pp. 52–5.
24 Jerzy Szacki, *Ojczyzna naród rewolucja* [Home country, nation, revolution], Warsaw 1962; *Polska myśl filozoficzna i społeczna* [Polish philosophical and social thought], ed. Andrzej Walicki, Warsaw 1973, vol. I, 1831–63; Andrzej Walicki, *Philosophy and Romantic Nationalism: The Case of Poland*, Oxford 1982.
25 See Damian Kalbarczyk, ed., *Wskrzesić Polskę, zbawić świat. Antologia polskiej chrześcijańskiej myśli społeczno-radykalnej 1831–1864* [To resurrect Poland, to bring salvation to the world. An anthology of Polish Christian radical social thought], Warsaw 1981, p. 6.
26 Stefan Buszczyński, *Mało znany poeta, stanowisko jego przed ostatnim powstaniem, wygnanie i śmierć* [A little-known poet, his position before the last insurrection, exile and death], Cracow 1870, p. 34; Franciszka Ramotowska, *Narodziny tajemnego państwa polskiego 1859–1862* [The birth of the secret Polish state 1859–1862], Warsaw 1990, pp. 103–24.
27 Letter (in Polish) to Wincenty Lutosławski, 9 June 1897, *CL*, I, p. 358.
28 See Zdzisław Najder, 'Conrad's Warsaw', in *Conrad's Cities. Essays for Hans van Marle*, ed. Gene M. Moore, Amsterdam 1992, pp. 31–8.
29 Archiwum Główne Akt Dawnych [The Central Archive of Ancient Records], Warsaw, documents of the Special Military Commission, part II, no. 4091.

30 *Obshchestvenno-politicheskie dvizhenie na Ukrainie v 1856–1862 gg*, p. 257.
31 Ibid.
32 'Zza kraty' [From behind the bars], Biblioteka Jagiellońska, MS 6577, pp. 50–60.
33 Apollo Korzeniowski to Gabriela and Jan Zagórski, 27 June 1862, *CUFE*, pp. 67–9.
34 Michał Rolle, *In illo tempore...*, Brody-Lwów 1914, pp. 47–9; Longin Panteleev, *Vospominania* [Memoirs], St Petersburg 1903.
35 Apollo Korzeniowski to Gabriela and Jan Zagórski, 27 March 1863, *CUFE*, p. 89.
36 'Polska i Moskwa. Pamiętnik *** zaczęty 186...' [Poland and Muscovy. Memoirs of *** begun in 186...], *Ojczyzna* (Leipzig 1864), no. 34; fragments in *CUFE*, pp. 77–9.
37 'Polska i Moskwa', *Ojczyzna* (1864), no. 42.
38 *Akt pierwszy. Dramat w jednej odsłonie. (Nieoryginalnie wierszem napisany)* [Act one. A drama in one scene. (Unoriginally written in verse)], Lwów 1869. An earlier version: 'Bez ratunku, urywek dramatu nieoryginalnego' [No rescue, a fragment of an unoriginal drama], *Tygodnik Illustrowany* (Warsaw 1866), nos. 339, 340, 341.
39 Apollo Korzeniowski to Kazimierz Kaszewski, 31 January 1866: 'I am aware that this drama cannot be called original in the full meaning of this term. From where I have taken it: much from life, much from memory – kill me, but I do not know.... In this *perplexity* I must not in any case call it original, while I am unable to say what my model was' (Biblioteka Jagiellońska, MS 6794).
40 Biblioteka Jagiellońska, MS 3057. It is mentioned in Ewa Korzeniowska's letter to Apollo of 2 July 1861, see *CUFE*, p. 51.
41 *Roman Rogiński, powstaniec 1863 r. Zeznania i wspomnienia* [Roman Rogiński, an insurgent of 1863. Testimony and reminiscences], ed. Stefan Kieniewicz, Warsaw 1983.
42 Apollo Korzeniowski to Kazimierz Kaszewski, 20 June 1865, *CUFE*, pp. 94–5.
43 Frederick R. Karl, *Joseph Conrad: The Three Lives*, New York 1979, p. 69.
44 Apollo Korzeniowski to Kazimierz Kaszewski, 1 February 1866, *CUFE*, p. 103.
45 *Akt pierwszy*, p. VII.
46 'Studia nad dramatycznością w utworach Szekspira' [Studies on the dramatic element in Shakespeare's works], *Biblioteka Warszawska* (April 1868), p. 14.

47 In his memoirs; *CUFE*, p. 16.
48 *Obshchestvenno-politicheskoe dvizhenie na Ukraine v 1856–1862 gg*, p. 141.
49 *CUFE*, pp. 17–18. Addison Bross accepts this charge with good faith in his 'Apollo Korzeniowski's Mythic Vision', *The Conradian* 20 (1995), pp. 83–4. However, any change in landed property relationships could have been initiated legally either by landowners themselves – or by the Tsarist authorities. No other bodies had anything to say in Russia; Korzeniowski would certainly prefer the landowners to start the reform themselves, but had no doubt it was necessary. Bross accepts Bobrowski's verdict that 'his brother-in-law was not a democrat' and that he sympathized with landowners (p. 90) on the strength of one fragment of Korzeniowski's 'memoirs'; he seems to ignore all other evidence, from Korzeniowski's repeated criticism of landowners in his poems and plays to the testimony of his fellow-conspirators. The issue of national independence apart, the peasant question was the cornerstone of the 'Reds'' ideology, and it is hard to imagine Korzeniowski disagreeing on it with other leaders of the movement. Bobrowski, we have to remember, knew little about Korzeniowski's secret activities in the Ukraine, and nothing about his role in Warsaw. To be a 'democrat' meant at the time in Russian-occupied Poland to be against existing class privileges and to advocate some kind of an elective form of government; or, more concretely, to sympathize with the programme of the Polish Democratic Society, formed in Paris in 1832. Apollo Korzeniowski meets both these criteria.
50 Taborski, *Apollo Korzeniowski*, p. 74.
51 To Karol Szajnocha, undated [1859]. *Korespondencja Karola Szajnochy*, vol. II, p. 175.
52 Letter to Garnett of 20 January 1900, *CL*, II, pp. 245–7; to Waliszewski of 5 December 1903, *CL*, III, p. 88. *A Personal Record*, 'Author's Note' (written in 1919), pp. VIII–X; main text (written in 1909), pp. 24, 34, 72. 'Poland Revisited' and 'First News' are included in Conrad's *Notes on Life and Letters*.
53 See, e.g., *Honour and Shame: The Values of Mediterranean Society*, ed. J. G. Peristiany, London 1965, pp. 9–18, 79–138.

4 Joseph Conrad and Tadeusz Bobrowski
1 Letter of 5 December 1903, *CL*, III, p. 89.
2 *A Personal Record*, p. 31.
3 Yves Hervouet, *The French Face of Joseph Conrad*, Cambridge 1990.
4 Tadeusz Bobrowski, *Pamiętnik mojego życia. O sprawach i ludziach*

mego czasu [Memoirs of my life. About affairs and men of my time], 2nd edn, ed. by Stefan Kieniewicz, Warsaw 1979, vol. I, pp. 410.

5 Letter to Władysław Górski, 31 March 1880, Biblioteka Jagiellońska, Cracow, MS 6711.

6 The reception of Bobrowski's memoirs is discussed by their editor, Stefan Kieniewicz; vol. I, pp. 6–11.

7 In a few cases (II, pp. 108–9 and 215; II, pp. 238–40) the same persons are called alternately 'Ruthenian', 'Little Russian', and 'Russian'.

8 Ibid., I, p. 182; Conrad's copy, inscribed by his wife, now in the POSK Library, London.

9 Ibid., II, p. 463; Ewa's wedding; II, p. 225.

10 Ibid., I, p. 151.

11 Ibid., II, pp. 466–7 and G. Marachow, 'Stefan Bobrowski i tajna drukarnia w Kijowie' [S. Bobrowski and the clandestine printing press in Kiev], *Przegąd Historyczny* (1958), pp. 711–12.

12 Bobrowski, *Pamiętnik*, II, pp. 458–9; Conrad, *A Personal Record*, pp. 64–7.

13 Bobrowski, *Pamiętnik*, II, pp. 64–5 and Kieniewicz's commentary, II, p. 547.

14 Bobrowski, *Pamiętnik*, II, p. 464 (also in *CUFE*, p. 73); II, pp. 472–3. All reviewers of Bobrowski's memoirs have pointed out similar errors.

15 'Qui des deux doit périr, car il paraît que périr il faut, est-ce la Russie ou la Pologne?' Letter of 15 January 1831, in N. K. Shilder, *Imperator Nikolai Pervyi, ego zhizn i tsarstvovanyie* [The Emperor Nicholas the First, his life and rule], St Petersburg 1903, vol. II, p. 475.

16 Bobrowski, *Pamiętnik*, II, p. 442.

17 Ibid., II, p. 517.

18 Bobrowski to Conrad, 23 September 1881, *CPB*, p. 78.

19 Letter of 9 November 1891, *CPB*, pp. 154–5.

20 See Daniel Beauvois, *Le Noble, le serf, et le révisor*, Montreux 1985, pp. 71 and 197–8.

21 Bobrowski, *Pamiętnik*, II, pp. 441–2.

22 Ibid., II, p. 518, and *CUFE*, p. 75.

23 *Obshchestvenno-politicheskie dvizhenie na Ukrainie v 1856–1862 gg*, Kiev 1963, p. 258.

24 In 1858 he planned to publish, together with Apollo Korzeniowski, a weekly for the local farmers (see above, Chapter 3, n. 48); August Iwański reports that in 1861 he volunteered money for future insurgents, A. Iwański, *Pamiętniki*, Warsaw 1968, p. 154.

25 *CUFE*, pp. 10–11.

26 Quoted by E. Heleniusz [Eustachy Iwanowski], *Listki wichrem do*

Krakowa z Ukrainy przyniesione [Leaves brought by wind to Cracow from the Ukraine], Cracow 1901, vol. II, p. 185.
27 *CUFE*, p. 28.
28 Bobrowski, *Pamiętnik*, I, pp. 350, 392; II, p. 70. *CUFE*, pp. 29–30.
29 See Ugo Mursia, *The True 'Discoverer' of Joseph Conrad's Literary Talent*, Varese 1971.
30 Letter of 28 June 1881, *CPB*, p. 71.
31 All these letters have been published in *CPB*, pp. 33–172.
32 *Lord Jim*, pp. 214–15.
33 Conrad to Józef Korzeniowski, 14 February 1901, *CPB*, pp. 233–4.
34 See Ludwik Krzyżanowski, 'Joseph Conrad's "Prince Roman": Fact and Fiction', in *Joseph Conrad: Centennial Essays*, ed. L. Krzyżanowski, New York 1960, pp. 27–69.
35 Rafał Blüth, 'Dwie rodziny kresowe' [Two borderland families], *Ateneum* (Warsaw 1939), no. 1.
36 Zdzisław Najder, 'Conrad i Bobrowski', *Przegląd Humanistyczny* (1964), no. 5, pp. 19–23.
37 Quotations are from Bobrowski, *Pamiętnik*, and Conrad, *A Personal Record*. The quoted fragments of Bobrowski's memoirs are included in *CUFE*. Here the translation has been slightly altered in a few places to make the text follow the original even more closely.
38 Letter of 9 November 1891, *CPB*, pp. 153–5. See above, n. 19.
39 Bobrowski, *Pamiętnik*, II, p. 518, and *CUFE*, pp. 74–5; see n. 8 above.
40 Bobrowski to Conrad, 23 September 1881, *CPB*, pp. 79–80.
41 Letter to Marguerite Poradowska, 18 February 1894, *CL*, I, p. 148.

5 *The Sisters*: a grandiose failure

1 *CL*, I, p. 272.
2 Letter to John Quinn, 18 July 1914, *CL*, V, p. 255.
3 F. M. Ford, Introduction to *The Sisters*, New York 1928, pp. 8–9.
4 Jocelyn Baines, *Joseph Conrad*, London 1960, pp. 167–8.
5 Albert Guerard, *Conrad the Novelist*, Cambridge, Mass., 1958, p. 94.
6 Joseph Conrad, *Congo Diary and Other Uncollected Pieces*, ed. Z. Najder, Garden City, NY, 1978, p. 59. Further parenthetical references are to this edition.
7 Thomas Moser, *Joseph Conrad: Achievement and Decline*, Cambridge, Mass., 1957, p. 62.
8 First published in *Twóczość* (1964), no. 10; reprinted as an afterword to Conrad's *Siostry* (a Polish translation of *The Sisters*), Warsaw 1967; references to this last.
9 Wyka, 'An Island', p. 58; but the MS of *The Sisters* is clearly only a draft.

10 Ibid., p. 75.
11 Stephen's mother, Malanya, is from the Dnieper region; his father, Sydor, called him 'Kossak' (Conrad uses here a polonized form of the noun, instead of the usual English 'Cossack'). Stephen is thus at least half-Ukrainian, although he does not express a specific national consciousness.
12 Wyka, 'An Island', pp. 59–60.
13 *Congo Diary*..., p. 57; Wyka, 'An Island', pp. 61–2.
14 Lord (George Gordon) Byron, *Childe Harold's Pilgrimage*, Canto II, stanzas 25 and 26.
15 Ibid., Canto III, stanza 113.
16 In the partly autobiographical 'Youth' (1898), with its action in 1881–3, the narrator tells of purchasing the complete works of Byron.
17 Wyka, 'An Island', p. 66.
18 *Congo Diary*, p. 51 ('anything may be done – only cautiously!').
19 Ibid., p. 53 ('priest's eyes – that see everything – and a wolf's maw – that would swallow everything').
20 Conrad to Poradowska, 2 April 1895, *CL*, I, p. 201; he is referring to the first part of her novel 'Marylka', published 15 February 1895 in the *Revue des Deux Mondes*.
21 Letter of 11 June 1895, *CL*, I, p. 228.
22 See Z. Najder, *Joseph Conrad: A Chronicle*, Cambridge 1983, pp. 186–96.
23 On Conrad's reluctance to write about Polish topics see: *Letters from Joseph Conrad*, ed. Edward Garnett, London 1928, Garnett's Introduction, p. x; Witold Chwalewik, 'Józef Conrad w Kardyfie' [Joseph Conrad in Cardiff], *Ruch Literacki* (1932), no. 8; Jessie Conrad, *Joseph Conrad and His Circle*, London 1935, pp. 49–50; Z. Najder, *Joseph Conrad*, pp. 204–5.
24 Conrad wrote to his cousin Aniela Zagórska: 'I wanted a purely Slavonic name which could not be distorted... so I decided on Borys', 21 January 1898, *CL*, I, p. 24.
25 Letter to Edward Garnett, 7 July 1919, *Letters from Conrad*, pp. 287–8.
26 See Najder, *Joseph Conrad*, p. 147.
27 Valentine Marcadé, *Le Renouveau de l'art pictural russe*, Lausanne 1971, pp. 131–4.
28 Quoted in ibid., p. 134.

6 *Lord Jim*: a Romantic tragedy of honour

1 Douglas Hewitt, *Conrad: A Reassessment*, Cambridge 1952, pp. 38–9.
2 *Lord Jim*, p. 58. Further references are given in parentheses in the text.
3 Robert Haugh, 'The Structure of *Lord Jim*', *College English* (December 1951), pp. 137–41.

4 Kazimierz Wyka, 'Czas powieściowy' [Time in the novel], in *Inter Arma. Zbiór prac ofiarowanych K Nitschowi w 70 rocznicę vrodzin*. [A collection of papers offered to K. Nitschowi on his 70th anniversary], Cracow 1946, p. 122. This opinion is not quite true, as the whole narrative of *Tristram Shandy* is based on the same contrast; and it is worth remembering that Conrad knew Sterne and in *A Personal Record* followed the footsteps of his *Sentimental Journey*; but then, *Tristram Shandy* is not a novel but rather an anti-novel, perhaps the first and original one, preceding and surpassing various specimens of the twentieth-century *nouveau roman*.
5 Cf. *Lord Jim*, pp. 339, 361. John Batchelor, *Lord Jim*, London 1988, p. 143.
6 It is perhaps worth mentioning also that the allegorical interpretation of *Lord Jim*, with the *Patna* representing Poland and Jim standing for Conrad himself, usually credited to Gustav Morf's *The Polish Heritage of Joseph Conrad* (London 1930), had been proposed much earlier by a Polish poet and critic, Wiktor Gomulicki. He wrote:

> But perhaps all this is only – a symbol? This doomed ship . . . these travellers, overcome by sleep, their nerves exhausted by religious ecstasy . . . these selfish men, whom their own will to survive compels to flee the ship which has been entrusted to them . . . and above all this young man, fallen among those blackguards, essentially honest, whose heart will be torn till the end of his days by a Promethean vulture of remorse . . . this 'nobleman', who in a foreign land finds prosperity, love, and trust, but who still seeks his final deliverance in a voluntary death – does all this indeed mean only what it seems to the English reader?' ('Polak czy Anglik?' [Pole or Englishman?], *Życie i Sztuka* (1905), no. 1).

7 Richard Curle, *Joseph Conrad: A Study*, London 1914, p. 245.
8 Cf. Curtis Brown Watson, *Shakespeare and the Renaissance Concept of Honor*, Princeton 1960, *passim*.
9 *Macbeth*, I, iv, 7–11.
10 *Il duello*, Venice [1554], discussed in F. R. Bryson, *The Point of Honor in Sixteenth-Century Italy*, Chicago 1935, p. 11. See *Lord Jim*, pp. 202, 235.
11 Published 1834; available in several English translations.
12 Published in Paris in 1833, *Kordian* is the most important work in Polish literature concerning the 1830 insurrection.
13 *Lord Jim*, pp. 214–15; cf. also pp. 349–50: 'She [Jewel] had said he had been driven away from her by a dream . . . And yet is not mankind itself, pushing on its blind way, driven by a dream of its greatness and its power

upon the dark paths of excessive cruelty and of excessive devotion? And what is the pursuit of truth, after all?'
14 Modern Library edition, p. 387.
15 See below, Chapter 11.
16 Mickiewicz, 'Ode to Youth', 1820.
17 See *CPB*, pp. 4–5, and Andrzej Busza, 'Conrad's Polish Literary Background and Some Illustrations of the Influence of Polish Literature on his Work', *Antemurale* 10 (Rome and London 1966), p. 206.
18 See below, Chapter 12.

7 *The Mirror of the Sea*

1 First collected by G. Jean-Aubry in *Twenty Letters to Joseph Conrad*, London 1926, and republished in *A Portrait in Letters: Correspondence to and about Conrad*, eds. J. H. Stape and Owen Knowles, Amsterdam and Atlanta, Ga. 1996 (*The Conradian*, vol. 19).
2 Tadeusz Skutnik, 'O semantyce kompozycji *Zwierciadła morza*' [On the semantics of the composition of *The Mirror of the Sea*], in *O kompozycji tekstu Conradowskiego*, ed. A. Zgorzelski, Gdańsk 1978. Of particular interest are Skutnik's remarks on the title, mottoes and dedication.
3 Pierre Lefranc, 'Notice', in Conrad's *Oeuvres*, ed. Sylvère Monod, Paris 1985, vol. II: especially valuable in the analysis of nautical aspects and in tracing the autobiographical counterparts, or more often lack of them, of the events described by Conrad.
4 'Initiation', *The Mirror of the Sea*, p. 129.
5 See 'The Fine Art', *The Mirror*, pp. 23, 25. It is apparently from this fragment that Arnold Bennett received the idea that Conrad 'despised "Yachtsmen"'; but when he wrote to Conrad about that (22 November 1912, *A Portrait in Letters*, p. 87), the latter protested vigorously (25 November 1912, *CL*, V, p. 140).
6 'The Fine Art', *The Mirror*, p. 24.
7 *The Mirror*, pp. 136–7.
8 Ibid., p. 135. Still, in 'The Faithful River' Conrad gets carried away with his praise of the estuaries of rivers and not only says that 'Water is friendly to man', but claims that 'the ocean ... has ever been a friend to the enterprising nations of the earth' (ibid., p. 101).
9 See also below, Chapter 13.
10 'In Captivity', *The Mirror*, pp. 122–7. Further references to *The Mirror* in parentheses.
11 Letter of early February 1904, *CL*, III, pp. 113–14.
12 Characteristically, in his reminiscences Ford tended to exaggerate his

role in the writing of *The Mirror*; see Z. Najder, *Joseph Conrad: A Chronicle*, Cambridge 1983, p. 198.
13 3 May [1904], *CL*, III, p. 136.
14 Writing from Montpellier, *CL*, III, p. 318.
15 James to Conrad, 1 November 1906, *A Portrait in Letters*, pp. 57–8.

8 *A Personal Record*

1 *CL*, IV, p. 125.
2 Reprinted in *Conrad: The Critical Heritage*, ed. Norman Sherry, London 1973, pp. 210–12.
3 Letter of 21 August 1908, *CL*, III, pp. 107–8.
4 Letter of 3 November 1908, *CL*, III, p. 149.
5 See her 'The Emigration of Talent', *CUFE*, pp. 182–91.
6 Letter of [7] October 1908, *CL*, III, p. 138.
7 Ford to George T. Keating, n.d. [December 1936], *Letters of Ford Madox Ford*, ed. Richard M. Ludwig, Princeton 1965, pp. 267–8. Conrad to Ford, [29 September or 6 October 1908], *CL*, IV, p. 131; to Pinker, 30 September 1908 (about Miss Hallowes), *CL*, IV, p. 133; to Ford, 10 October 1908 (confirming that the second chapter was not dictated to him), *CL*, IV, p. 142; to Ford, [12 October 1908], *CL*, IV, p. 144; to Pinker, [21 or 28] October 1908 (about dictating chapter IV to Miss Hallowes), *CL*, IV, p. 146; to unknown recipient, 6 May 1909 (about a manuscript page of chapter VII), *CL*, IV, p. 231.
8 E.g., Conrad to Pinker, [7 December 1908], *CL*, IV, p. 158; to Galsworthy, 15 October 1911, *CL*, IV, p. 487.
9 Paul R. Reynolds to Pinker, 23 November 1908, NY Public Library.
10 Conrad to Galsworthy, 13 July 1909, *CL*, IV, p. 254; to Ford, 31 July 1909, *CL*, IV, p. 264; to Galsworthy, 27 November 1909, *CL*, IV, p. 292.
11 Conrad to Pinker, 15 April 1909, *CL*, IV, p. 216; to Galsworthy, 30 April 1909, *CL*, IV, pp. 224–5.
12 Conrad to Pinker, 25 November 1908, *CL*, IV, p. 153 (about a volume of 80,000 words); to same, 21 January 1909, *CL*, IV, p. 189 (about 'one or two vols.').
13 Conrad to Edward Verrall Lucas, 23 June 1909, *CL*, IV, p. 247 (about one or two volumes, 65,000 words each); to Henri-Durand Davray, 23 December 1909, *CL*, IV, p. 308 (about wanting to add 30,000 words, i.e. nearly to double the size).
14 Letter to Austin Harrison (at that time the new editor of the *English Review*), [15 February 1912], *CL*, V, pp. 20–1. In January 1913 Conrad informed Harrison that he was 'not in the mood to make a start'; *CL*, V, p. 161.

15 See, e.g., Eugene F. Saxton to Pinker, 26 February 1915, NY Public Library.
16 Conrad to E. L. Sanderson, 22 January 1912, *CL*, V, p. 8. Apparently Conrad had in mind Sidney Colvin; see n. 18 below.
17 See D. W. Jefferson, '*Tristram Shandy* and the Tradition of Learned Wit', *Essays in Criticism* 1 (1951).
18 To Sidney Colvin, 28 December 1908, *CL*, IV, p. 175.
19 See above, Chapter 4.
20 In 'The "Tremolino"', *The Mirror of the Sea*, p. 155.

9 Joseph Conrad's *The Secret Agent*, or the melodrama of reality
1 See Peter Brooks, 'The Melodramatic Imagination: The Example of Balzac and James', in *Romanticism: Vistas, Instances, Continuities*, eds. David Thorburn and Geoffrey Hartman, Ithaca, NY, 1973, pp. 198–220; Daniel Gerould, 'Russian Formalist Theories of Melodrama', *Journal of American Culture* (Spring 1978), pp. 152–68.
2 Letter of 7 October 1907, *CL*, III, p. 491. Conrad repeated the same formula in his letter to Marguerite Poradowska of 20 June 1912; *CL*, V, p. 75.
3 Cf. Irving Howe, *Politics and the Novel*, New York 1957, p. 97.
4 The numbers in parentheses refer to pages of *The Secret Agent*.
5 Robert D. Spector, 'Irony as Theme: Conrad's *The Secret Agent*', *Nineteenth-century Fiction* 13 (1958), pp. 69–71.
6 J. Hillis Miller, *Poets of Reality*, New York 1969, p. 39.
7 Conrad to Algernon Methuen, 7 November 1906, *CL*, III, p. 371.

10 Conrad, Russia and Dostoevsky
1 See Wiktor Borysow, *Joseph Conrad w Rosji. Recepcja twórczości Conrada w krytyce rosyjskiej* [Joseph Conrad in Russia. Reception of Conrad in Russian criticism], transl. from Russian by Wiera Bieńkowska, Warsaw 1987.
2 *Under Western Eyes*, p. 33. Further page references in parentheses.
3 See, e.g., Gustaw Herling-Grudziński, 'W oczach Conrada' [In Conrad's eyes], *Kultura* (Paris 1957), no. 10; Eloise Knapp Hay, *The Political Novels of Joseph Conrad*, Chicago 1963, pp. 287–8.
4 Wacław Lednicki, *Russia, Poland and the West*, New York 1954, pp. 33–9.
5 Pyotr Chaadaev, *The Major Works*, transl. and commentary by Raymond T. McNally, Notre Dame, Ind., 1969, pp. 27, 31–5.
6 Mikhail Lermontov, *Major Poetical Works*, ed. Anatoly Liberman, London and Canberra 1983, p. 250.

7 Alexander Herzen, *Du développement des idées révolutionnaires en Russie*, London 1853, pp. 99–100; *My Past and Thoughts*, transl. by Constance Garnett, London 1968, vol. III, p. 1350.
8 N. Chernyshevski, *Prologue* [1864]; Lenin, 'On the National Pride of Great Russians', first published in *Sotsyal-Demokrat*, 12 December 1914.
9 Letter of 13 October 1885, from Singapore; *CL*, I, p. 12.
10 Letter of 12 April [1898], *CL*, II, p. 54.
11 Letter of 25 October [1904], *CL*, III, pp. 173–5.
12 Letter of 25 January 1919, G. Jean-Aubry, *Joseph Conrad: Life and Letters*, London 1927, vol. II, p. 217.
13 To Galsworthy, 7 September 1909, *CL*, IV, p. 272.
14 Conrad to Christopher Sandeman, [30] November 1916, *CL*, V, p. 681.
15 Letter of [8 October 1907], *CL*, III, pp. 492–3.
16 To Robert Bontine Cunninghame Graham, 8 February 1898, *CL*, II, p. 158; to Sandeman, 31 August 1916, *CL*, V, p. 646; to Quinn, 2 March 1920, NY Public Library (fragment in Jean-Aubry, *Joseph Conrad*, II, p. 237, with a wrong date, 24 March).
17 *Notes on Life and Letters*, p. 95.
18 Astolphe de Custine, *La Russie en 1839*, Paris 1843; many editions; letter 36. Anatole Leroy-Beaulieu, *L'Empire des Tsars et les Russes*, Paris 1882, vol. II, pp. 196–7, 238.
19 To Ada Galsworthy, 2 November 1905, *CL*, III, p. 294.
20 To John Quinn, 6 February 1918, NY Public Library.
21 In his fine essay on 'Conrad and Russia' Edward Crankshaw praises Conrad for recognizing the 'Russian quality of nobility' and paying homage to it, in *Joseph Conrad: A Commemoration*, ed. Norman Sherry, London 1976, p. 97.
22 Letter of 22 February 1896; 7 December 1897, 'Turgenev', a Preface to Edward Garnett's study, in *Notes on Life and Letters*, p. 46.
23 To George Harvey (a publisher), 15 April 1904, *CL*, IV, p. 132.
24 To Garnett, 27 May [19]12, *CL*, V, p. 71; to Galsworthy, [2–3 September 1908], *CL*, IV, p. 116; to Garnett, 22 February 1914, *CL*, V, p. 358.
25 To Garnett, 27 May [19]12, *CL*, V, p. 70 and [2 May 1917], Yale (printed versions incomplete).
26 On Dostoevsky's anti-Polish bias see W. Lednicki, *Russia, Poland and the West*, pp. 262–91.
27 Ibid., pp. 291–5.
28 See Joseph Frank, 'The Lectures of Professor Pnin', in *Through the Russian Prism*, Princeton 1990, p. 51.
29 The thesis about Conrad's negative infatuation with Dostoevsky is

anything but new; it was first expressed by Richard Curle, *The Last Twelve Years of Joseph Conrad*, London 1928, pp. 28–9. Here I try to rationalize and amplify Curle's opinion.

30 *Through the Russian Prism*, p. 129.

31 Wit Tarnawski made a similar suggestion in his essay 'Dokoła Conrada' [Around Conrad], *Myśl Polska* (London 1948), no. 1, and was, I believe, the first to list the main analogies between the action in both novels. Andrzej Busza also thinks that 'Conrad meant his readers to make the connection' between his own text and Dostoevsky's writing and calls the relationship 'partly dialectical and partly parodic' ('Rhetoric and Ideology in *Under Western Eyes*', in *Joseph Conrad: A Commemoration*, ed. Norman Sherry, London 1976, p. 111).

32 See Yves Hervouet, *The French Face of Joseph Conrad*, Cambridge 1990, pp. 39–40, 107.

33 Cf. Jean Deurbergue in his Note in the Pléiade edition of Conrad's *Oeuvres*, Paris 1987, vol. III, p. 1355.

34 See Andrzej Busza, 'Rhetoric and Ideology', pp. 108–9.

35 Jacques Berthoud, *Joseph Conrad: The Major Phase*, Cambridge 1978, p. 164. Interestingly, we find an analogous idea in Chaadaev's second 'Philosophical Letter': 'In this indifference towards the good things of life, which some of us consider meritorious, there is something really cynical (*The Major Works*, p. 55).

36 Jocelyn Baines, *Joseph Conrad: A Critical Biography*, London 1960, pp. 369–70.

37 E.g., Baines, *Joseph Conrad*, pp. 370–2; Hay, *The Political Novels*, pp. 269, 279; Avrom Fleishman, *Conrad's Politics: Community and Anarchy in the Fiction of Joseph Conrad*, Baltimore 1967, pp. 219–20; Busza, 'Rhetoric and Ideology', pp. 111–13; Deurbergue in Conrad's *Oeuvres*, vol. III, pp. 1343–5, 1394.

38 Hay, *The Political Novels*, p. 279.

39 To Garnett, 20 October 1911, *CL*, IV, p. 490.

40 It is not, however, so hopelessly tangled as is sometimes assumed; see Boris Ford, Introduction to the Penguin Classics edn of *Under Western Eyes*, London 1985, pp. 24–6.

41 E. K. Hay, '*Under Western Eyes* and the Missing Center', in *Joseph Conrad's 'Under Western Eyes': Beginnings, Revisions, Final Forms*, ed. David R. Smith, Hamden, Conn., 1991. As if to illustrate my point about the requisite historical knowledge, Hay questions the possibility of Councillor Mikulin and Peter Ivanovitch 'exchanging confidences' and calls such an event an incredible case of 'candor' between two warring

camps (p. 140). Not candour but a conscious manipulation, a notorious game of the secret police.

42 I believe a Polish woman critic, Maria Komornicka, was the first to describe this feature of Conrad's technique in 1905 in her review of a translation of *Lord Jim*; *Chimera* (1905), pp. 333–4, reprinted in *Conrad w oczach krytyki światowej*, ed. Z. Najder, Warsaw 1974, pp. 737–40.

43 Anatole Leroy-Beaulieu, *La France, la Russie, et l'Europe*, Paris 1888, p. 94.

44 Herzen, *Du développement* (2nd edn, printed in London, 38 Regent Square, by the Polish Democratic Society Press; 1st edn 1851), pp. 121, 130, 131. It is not impossible that Conrad knew Herzen's writings, but he never even mentioned his name.

11 Conrad and Rousseau: concepts of man and society

1 A. Kettle, *An Introduction to the English Novel*, London 1953, vol. II, pp. 67–81; I. Howe, *Politics and the Novel*, New York 1957, pp. 76–113.
2 A. Fleishman, *Conrad's Politics: Community and Anarchy in the Fiction of Joseph Conrad*, Baltimore 1967. Fleishman compounds his difficulties by committing numerous factual errors in describing Conrad's Polish political background. And Rousseau was *not* a theorist of the organic state (see p. 231).
3 Conrad is linked to Carlyle by Fleishman, *Conrad's Politics*, pp. 62–4. One has to beware of such accidental analogies in analysing Conrad's philosophical views. For example, his affinity with Schopenhauer has been exaggerated: Conrad shared neither his ethics nor his epistemology, the two notable elements of Schopenhauer's thought.
4 *A Personal Record*, p. 97.
5 The Modern Library edition, New York; all further references are to this edition.
6 There are others in Conrad's work: in *Almayer's Folly*, *An Outcast of the Islands*, *Nostromo*, 'The Secret Sharer', also in *The Nature of a Crime* (written in collaboration with Ford Madox Ford) etc.
7 *Portraits from Memory*, London 1956, pp. 82, 84.
8 *The Social Contract*, transl. by Maurice Cranston, Harmondsworth 1968, p. 49. All further quotations in English are from this edition.
9 *Lord Jim*, p. 147.
10 See J. L. Talmon, *The Origins of Totalitarian Democracy*, London 1961, pp. 38–49.
11 Letter of 11 December 1885, from Calcutta, *CL*, I, pp. 15–17.
12 Alexis de Tocqueville, *De la démocratie en Amérique* . . ., IV, p. 6.

13 *The Secret Agent*, pp. 41–3; Conrad to R. B. Cunninghame Graham, 8 February 1899 (*CL*, II, pp. 158–9); see also Edward Crankshaw, 'Conrad and Russia', in *Joseph Conrad: A Commemoration*, ed. Norman Sherry, London 1976, p. 96.
14 *The Social Contract*, II, p. 8, pp. 89–90.
15 Particularly *Les Soirées de Saint-Pétersbourg* and *Etude sur la souveraineté*. De Maistre spent fourteen years (1803–17) in St Petersburg as ambassador of the King of Sardinia.
16 *Under Western Eyes*, pp. 8, 61, 66, 33, 35.
17 See above, Chapter 10.
18 K. Mannheim, *Essays in Sociology and Social Psychology*, London 1953, pp. 74–118.
19 See Jerzy Szacki, *Ojczyzna, naród, rewolucja* [Home country, nation, revolution], Warsaw 1962, pp. 13–14, 26–30.
20 'Autocracy and War', *Notes on Life and Letters*, p. 107.

12 Conrad and the idea of honour

1 Curtis Brown Watson, *Shakespeare and the Renaissance Concept of Honor*, Princeton 1960.
2 *Under Western Eyes*, p. 51.
3 *Notes on Life and Letters*, p. 183.
4 *La Recherche de l'absolu* [1834].
5 *The Confessions*, New York, The Modern Library, p. 56.
6 *The Opinions of Jérôme Coignard*, transl. by Mrs Wilfrid Jackson, New York 1930, p. 23.
7 André Malraux, Preface to *Sanctuaire*, transl. by R.-N. Raimbault and Henri Delgove, Paris 1933.
8 See Werner Jaeger, *Paideia: The Ideals of Greek Culture*, transl. by Gilbert Highet, New York 1945, vol. I, pp. 10–11.
9 Homer, *The Iliad*, transl. by E. V. Rieu, Harmondsworth 1966, p. 106.
10 *Nicomachean Ethics*, III, p. 8.
11 Xenophon, *Works*, transl. by H. G. Dakyns, London 1897, III, pt. 1, 262.
12 Robert Ashley, *Of Honour*, ed. Virgil B. Heltzel, San Marino, Calif., 1947, p. 34.
13 See Watson, *Shakespeare*, pp. 102–35.
14 Estimates vary from 8–10 per cent for the entire state to 15–25 per cent for ethnic Poland; see, e.g., Jarema Maciszewski, *Szlachta polska i jej państwo*, Warsaw 1969.
15 See *CPB*, pp. 2–3.

16 Watson, *Shakespeare*, p. 10.
17 Shakespeare, *Macbeth*, I, iv, 10–11.
18 MS of the Preface to *The Nigger*, Rosenbach Collection, Philadelphia. John Dozier Gordan, *Joseph Conrad: The Making of a Novelist*, Cambridge, Mass., 1940, p. 238.
19 See Ian Watt, 'Joseph Conrad: Alienation and Commitment', in *The English Mind: Studies in the English Moralists Presented to Basil Willey*, ed. H. S. Davies and G. Watson, Cambridge 1964, pp. 266–8.
20 Letter of 23 December 1897, *CL*, I, p. 430.
21 Edward Gannon, *The Honor of Being a Man: The World of André Malraux*, Chicago 1957.
22 Camus talking to J. Bloch-Michel, *The Reporter*, 28 November 1957.
23 Watt, 'Joseph Conrad', pp. 277–8.
24 William Faulkner, *Essays, Speeches, and Public Letters*, ed. J. B. Merriwether, New York 1965, p. 120.
25 Ibid., p. 181.

13 Joseph Conrad: a European writer

1 Curtius Rufus, *Historiae Alexandri Magni*, III, 32.4–7; see C. M. Bowra, *The Greek Experience*, New York 1957, p. 215.
2 Conrad to Algernon Methuen, 26 January 1908, *CL*, IV, p. 29.
3 'Author's Note' to *The Secret Agent*, p. XII.
4 Anne Luyat-Moore, 'L'Exil dans l'espace et le temps anglais', *Europe* (1992), nos. 758–9, p. 118.
5 Todd K. Bender ('Conrad's Lexicon', in *The Ugo Mursia Memorial Lectures*, ed. Mario Curreli, Milan 1988, p. 84) believes that the use of French expression signals that the French lieutenant is not as well qualified as Marlow to understand Jim. Such an attitude would result in disqualifying Stein as well; anyway, Marlow himself admires 'the discrimination' of the Frenchman (p. 145).
6 Only Avrom Fleishman devoted some attention to this problem, in *Conrad's Politics*, Baltimore 1967, p. 33.
7 Included in *Last Essays*, pp. 149–54.
8 *Notes on Life and Letters*, p. 97. Further page references in parentheses.
9 Norman Sherry, ed., *Conrad: The Critical Heritage*, London 1973, p. 229.
10 Conrad to Eric Pinker, 3 February 1924, Berg Collection, NY Public Library.
11 Sherry, *Conrad*, pp. 372–3, 375.
12 Przemysław Mroczkowski, 'Conrad the European', in *Studia*

Conradowskie, Katowice 1976, pp. 13–27. A shorter version appeared in *Joseph Conrad: Commemorative Essays*, eds. Adam Gillon and Ludwik Krzyżanowski, New York 1975.

13 The fullest presentation in Stefan Zabierowski, *Dziedzictwo Conrada w literaturze polskiej* [Conrad's heritage in Polish literature], Cracow 1992.

14 Walter C. Putnam III, 'Conrad Under French Eyes', *Conradiana* 21 (1989), no. 3, p. 173.

15 E.g., Jean-Baptiste Para, 'Conrad et quelques écrivains italiens', paper delivered in May 1994 in Valenciennes.

16 Stefan Żeromski, 'Autor–Rodak', *Naokoło Świata* (1925), no. 2; see also *CUFE*, pp. xix–xxi.

17 See *CPB*; Andrzej Busza, 'Conrad's Polish Literary Background and Some Illustrations of the Influence of Polish Literature on His Work', *Antemurale* 10 (Rome and London 1966).

18 F. M. Ford in the *English Review*, December 1911; see Sherry, *Conrad*, p. 240.

19 Alan Judd, *Ford Madox Ford*, London 1990, p. 70.

20 Garnett in the *Weekly Westminster*, 10 October 1925; see Sherry, *Conrad*, p. 369.

21 Galsworthy in the *Fortnightly Review*, 1 April 1908; see Sherry, *Conrad*, pp. 206–9.

22 *The Spectator*, 10 October 1925, reprinted in Sherry, *Conrad*, p. 373.

23 *Nostromo*, p. 68.

24 Ibid., p. 235; *Under Western Eyes*, pp. 102, 140; it certainly makes a difference whether Mme Haldin's generation was deceived (by whom?) or disappointed.

25 S. Monod, 'Editing Conrad . . . for Whom?', in *The Ugo Mursia Memorial Lectures*, ed. Mario Curreli, Milan 1988, p. 27; J. Conrad, *'Twixt Land and Sea*, p. 44.

26 *Lord Jim*, the opening sentence.

27 *The Mirror of the Sea*, p. 51; J. Du Bellay, *Les Regrets* [1558], sonnet 31.

28 *Lord Jim*, see esp. pp. 317–18, 334–5, 341.

29 *Lord Jim*, p. ix.

14 Joseph Conrad after a century

1 'Heart of Darkness', *Youth and Two Other Stories*, p. 66.

2 See above, Chapter 10.

3 I think that Conrad derived his concept of 'material interests' from Anatole Leroy-Beaulieu's article 'Le Règne de l'argent' in the *Revue des Deux Mondes* of 1894, particularly from its second part, 'Le

Mammonisme et la démocratie', vol. 122 (15 April 1894), pp. 721–41. Leroy-Beaulieu writes about 'les intérêts matériels'.
4 *Nostromo*, p. 511.
5 *A Personal Record*, p. 92.
6 From a fragment of Conrad's Preface to *The Nigger of the 'Narcissus'*, which he deleted following the advice of Edward Garnett. John Dozier Gordan, *Joseph Conrad: The Making of a Novelist*, Cambridge, Mass., 1940, p. 239.
7 *The Nigger of the 'Narcissus'*, p. XI.
8 *A Personal Record*, p. 95.
9 Ian Watt, *Conrad in the Nineteenth Century*, Berkeley and Los Angeles 1979, p. 175.
10 Maria Komornicka in *Chimera* (Warsaw 1905); reprinted in *Conrad w oczach krytyki światowej*, ed. Z. Najder, Warsaw 1974, pp. 739–40.
11 *Youth...*, p. 82; *Lord Jim*, p. 308.
12 See Edward W. Said, 'Conrad: The Presentation of a Narrative', in *Critical Essays on Joseph Conrad*, ed. Ted Billy, Boston 1987, pp. 28–46.
13 *The Nigger of the 'Narcissus'*, p. XII.
14 *Youth...*, p. 82.
15 *The Nigger of the 'Narcissus'*, p. XIV.
16 *Nostromo*, pp. 520–1.
17 *Troilus and Cressida*, v, iii, 26–8.
18 Bertrand Russell, *Portraits from Memory and Other Essays*, London 1956, pp. 81–5.
19 *Lord Jim*, pp. 146–7.
20 J. Conrad, 'Autocracy and War', *Notes on Life and Letters*, p. 101.
21 *Lord Jim*, p. 50.

15 Joseph Conrad in his historical perspective

1 Conrad to Marguerite Poradowska, 5 January 1907, *CL*, III, p. 401.
2 See my Introduction to *CPB*, pp. 15–17, 28–31, and Andrzej Busza, 'Conrad's Polish Literary Background and Some Illustrations of the Influence of Polish Literature on his Work', *Antemurale* 10 (Rome and London 1966). The risks involved in discussing Conrad's psychological make-up without a firsthand knowledge of his national background justify perhaps a moment of special attention. They may be illustrated by a fragment from Frederick Crews' 'The Power of Darkness', *Partisan Review*, 34 (Fall 1967), pp. 507–25. Analysing the autobiographical and subconscious content of 'Heart of Darkness', Professor Crews maintained that the hero, Kurtz, 'in many ways amounts to a vindictive

reconstruction of Conrad's father', Apollo Korzeniowski. He supported his assertion by pointing out that the names Kurtz and Korzeniowski 'are alike'. They may appear so only to a person unaware of the rules of Polish pronunciation: the only analogous sound in both names is 'k'. As a matter of fact, in the MS of 'Heart of Darkness' Kurtz still bears the name of the person on whom he was, physically at least, based: Klein. In the course of writing Conrad substituted the German 'short' for 'small'. However, even if the names had been really similar, Conrad might then have had in mind simply himself: legally he was a Korzeniowski till his death.

Furthermore, Crews argued that Conrad's father, like Kurtz, 'refused an offer of rescue' and in his youth 'experimented with dissipation'. There is no shred of evidence that it was ever so. And while it is indeed true that Apollo Korzeniowski had 'messianic political ambitions', if the word 'messianic' means anything, this term cannot be applied to Kurtz.

The real point here is that, pursuing on uncertain ground his thesis of Kurtz being for Conrad an effigy of his father, Crews missed a very interesting indication that Conrad had endowed Kurtz with at least one important autobiographical trait. In a letter sent in 1890 to the Congo, Tadeusz Bobrowski, Conrad's uncle and guardian, wrote to him: 'You are probably looking around at people and things as well as at the "civilizing" (confound it) affair in the machinery of which you are a cog' (*CPB*, pp.128–9). Every reader of 'Heart of Darkness' remembers well that the idea of a 'civilizing mission' was what originally obsessed Kurtz and made him go to Africa. This biographical detail enables us to see more clearly that 'Heart of Darkness' is primarily an ideological, not a psychological parable. (Frederick Crews has later become the leading critic of Freud's influence in the humanities; I think that Conrad would rejoice at the idea that perhaps Crews' experience in psychoanalysing him has turned the brilliant American scholar away from Freudian speculations.)

3 Ian Watt, 'Joseph Conrad: Alienation and Commitment', in *The English Mind: Studies in the English Moralists Presented to Basil Willey*, eds. H. S. Davies and G. Watson, Cambridge 1964, pp. 257–78.

4 Norman Douglas, who knew Conrad well, noted a little gruffly: 'I have heard the late Joseph Conrad called a great psychologist . . . Well, Conrad was first and foremost a Pole and like many Poles a politician and moralist *malgré lui*. These are his fundamentals. He was also a great writer with hardly an ounce of psychology in his composition' (*A Plea for Better Manners, a Selection*, ed. D. M. Low, London 1955, p. 308).

5 See below, Chapter 16. The warning: *Nostromo*, p. 310.
6 Cf. Johanna Burkhardt, *Das Erlebnis der Wirklichkeit und seine kunstlerische Gestaltung in Joseph Conrads Werken*, Marburg 1935.
7 Cf. Conrad in 'Books': 'To be hopeful in an artistic sense it is not necessary to think that the world is good. It is enough to believe that there is no impossibility of its being made so (*Notes on Life and Letters*, p. 9).
8 Jean Flori, *L'Idéologie du glaive. Préhistoire de la chevalerie*, Geneva 1983, pp. 167–73 and *passim*.
9 Perhaps the most perfect example of misunderstanding Conrad, which resulted from a thoroughly middle-class attitude of the author, can be found in H. G. Wells' remarks on Conrad in his *Experiment in Autobiography*, London 1934, p. 526. F. M. Ford (at that time still Hueffer), Conrad's literary partner and for many years a close friend, offered an intuitive explanation of his anachronism: 'I have thought very often that Conrad is an Elizabethan. That is possibly because he is a Pole – and the Poles have the virtues and the powers that served to make nations great in the sixteenth and seventeenth centuries. Roughly speaking, that was when Poland was a great Empire. They were romantic, they were heroic, they were aristocrats – they were all the impracticable things' ('Joseph Conrad', *English Review*, December 1911, p. 69). Conrad's admiration for Shakespeare, a writer thoroughly saturated with the ideas and problems of the chivalric code, had certainly a lot to do with his 'Elizabethan' outlook.
10 See Faulkner and Malcolm Cowley on Sienkiewicz, in *The Faulkner–Cowley File*, New York 1966, p. 115.
11 See Fitzgerald to H. L. Mencken in 1925 (*The Letters of F. Scott Fitzgerald*, ed. Andrew Turnbull, New York 1963), pp. 362, 363, 492, 510. Conrad's influence on Fitzgerald is discussed in detail by R. E. Long, '*The Great Gatsby* and the Tradition of Joseph Conrad', *Texas Studies in Literature and Language* 8 (Summer and Fall 1966), pp. 257–76, 407–22.
12 J. E. Tanner, 'The Twentieth Century Impressionistic Novel: Conrad and Faulkner', *Dissertation Abstracts* 25 (1964), p. 1927.
13 Antoine de Saint-Exupéry, *Terre des hommes* [1939], *Oeuvres*, Paris 1953, p. 161.
14 '... honour, like pity, is the irrational virtue that carries on after justice and reason have become powerless' (Camus talking to J. Bloch-Michel, *The Reporter*, 28 November 1957).
15 *A Personal Record*, p. 95.
16 In his Introduction to the Modern Library edition of *Nostromo*, 1951;

reprinted in *The Art of Joseph Conrad*, ed. Robert W. Stallman, East Lansing, Mich., 1960, p. 227.
17 'Heart of Darkness', *Youth and Two Other Stories*, p. 82.

16 Fidelity and art: Joseph Conrad's cultural heritage and literary programme

1 *A Personal Record*, p. xix.
2 Ian Watt, *Conrad in the Nineteenth Century*, Berkeley and Los Angeles 1979, p. 6.
3 See Zdzisław Najder, *Values and Evaluations*, Oxford 1975, p. 162; there I use a more technical classification into 'consequentialist' (= pragmatic) and 'non-consequentialist' (= based on a code) systems of value.
4 See, e.g., Aron Gurievich, *Katiegorii srednevekovoi kultury* [Categories of medieval culture], Moscow 1972, *passim*; Maurice Keen, *Chivalry*, New Haven 1984, pp. 2, 37 and *passim*; Georges Duby, *William Marshall*, New York 1985, p. 86; Friedhelm Guttandin, *Das paradoxe Schicksal der Ehre* [The paradoxical story of honour], Berlin 1993, pp. 77–9.
5 See above, Chapter 2.
6 Franciszka Ramotowska, *Narodziny tajemnego państwa polskiego: 1859–1862* [The birth of the secret Polish state], Warsaw 1990, pp. 102–10.
7 Undated letter, PAN Library, Cracow, MS 2064.
8 Apollo Korzeniowski, preface to his drama *Akt pierwszy*, Lwów 1869, p. VI.
9 In his essay on Shakespeare, 'Studia nad dramatycznością w utworach Szekspira' [Studies in the dramatic element in Shakespeare's plays], *Biblioteka Warszawska* (1868), vol. II. See *CUFE*, p. XIV.
10 Tadeusz Bobrowski to Konrad Korzeniowski, 9 November 1891, *CPB*, p. 155.
11 *Lord Jim*, pp. 214–15.
12 Conrad to Garnett [8 October 1907], *CL*, III, p. 492.
13 *Lord Jim*, pp. 215, 334, 350.
14 Jacques Berthoud, *Joseph Conrad: The Major Phase*, Cambridge 1978, pp. 113 and 120.
15 *Tales of Hearsay*, p. 51.
16 *Under Western Eyes*, pp. 19, 22, 358.
17 Ibid, p. 14.
18 Ibid, p. 361.
19 Ian Watt, 'Joseph Conrad: Alienation and Commitment', in *The English Mind: Studies in the English Moralists Presented to Basil Willey*, ed. H. S. Davies and G. Watson, Cambridge 1964, p. 264.

20 Edward Said, *Joseph Conrad and the Fiction of Autobiography*, Cambridge, Mass., 1966, p. 180.
21 'The Faithful River', *The Mirror of the Sea*, p. 111.
22 *Tales of Unrest*, p. 146.
23 *Nostromo*, p. 457.
24 *A Personal Record*, pp. 36, 35.
25 *CPB*, p. 26.
26 Berthoud, *Joseph Conrad: The Major Phase*, pp. 17–20.
27 *The Nigger of the 'Narcissus'*, ed. J. Berthoud, Oxford World Classics, 1984, p. xxxix.
28 *A Personal Record*, p. 92.
29 *Last Essays*, p. 132.
30 John Dozier Gordan, *Joseph Conrad: The Making of a Novelist*, Cambridge, Mass., 1940, p. 238. The MS is in the Rosenbach Collection, Philadelphia. The above is one of a number of possible final readings of the fragment in which several expressions have been left as alternatives.
31 Cf. Watt, *Conrad in the Nineteenth Century*, pp. 79–80.
32 John Batchelor, *The Life of Joseph Conrad*, Oxford 1994, p. 67.
33 Conrad to William Blackwell, [6 September 1897], *CL*, I, p. 381.
34 Dated 2 August 1901; *CL*, II, pp. 348–9.

INDEX

Alexander II of Russia, 54, 55
Alexander the Great, 167
Almayer's Folly, 12, 44, 58, 68, 168, 178
'Amy Foster', 166
'Anarchist, An', 142, 166
Andreiev, Leonid, 189
Annunzio, Gabriele d', 188
Aristotle, 89, 144, 156
Arrow of Gold, The, 58, 69, 70, 111, 166
Ashley, Robert, 158
Augustine, St, 2
'Autocracy and War', 123–5, 130, 132, 136, 138, 139, 150, 169

Baines, Jocelyn, 70, 133, 189
Bakunin, Mikhail, 133, 147
Balzac, Honoré de, 110, 155, 195
Batchelor, John, 210
Beardsley, Monroe C., 3
Beauvois, Daniel, 214
Bellay, Joachim Du, 98, 173
Bender, Todd K., 229
Bennett, Arnold, 95, 105, 189
Beowulf, 7
Bergson, Henri, 189
Bernatowicz, Konstanty, 63
Bernstein, Ludwik, 50
Berthoud, Jacques, 10, 133, 205, 208
Bible, 75, 84, 96
Bjørnson, Bjørnstjerne, 189
'Black Mate, The', 111, 166
Blake, William, 75
Blüth, Rafal, 59
Bobrowska, Józefa née Lubowidzka, 47, 57, 62
Bobrowska, Józefa Jr, 62
Bobrowska, Teofila née Pilchowska, 23, 45
Bobrowska, Teofila Jr, 46, 60, 62
Bobrowski, Józef, 22, 23, 45, 46, 61

Bobrowski, Kazimierz, 23, 46, 57, 62
Bobrowski, Mikolaj, 62, 63, 64, 107
Bobrowski, Stanisław, Conrad's uncle, 45, 46, 62
Bobrowski, Stanisław, son of Kazimierz, 51, 53
Bobrowski, Stefan, 23, 46, 50, 53, 55, 62, 105, 151
Bobrowski, Tadeusz, 9, 13, 14, 16, 23, 37, 42, 44–67, 104, 107, 127, 202–3, 213, 218, 232
Boethius, Anitius Manlius Severinus, 95
'Books', 233
Borges, Jorge Luis, 171
Bourget, Paul, 188–9
Brancusi, Constantin, 79
Brooke-Rose, Christine, 8
Bross, Addison, 217
'Brute, The', 166
Burke, Edmund, 140–1
Busza, Andrzej, 10, 213, 226
Buszczyński, Stefan, 23, 40, 41, 77, 201, 213, 214
Byron, George Gordon, 73–4, 86, 220

Calderón de la Barca, Pedro, 93, 159, 194
Callisthenes, 167
Camus, Albert, 5, 153, 162–3, 196, 233
Carducci, Giosué, 201
Carlyle, Thomas, 140
Carnot, Sadi, 135
Catherine the Great, 50
Cavour, Camillo Benso de, 2
Cervantes, Miguel de Saavedra, 159
Cézanne, Paul, 78
Chaadaev, Pyotr, 33, 120, 123, 149, 180, 226
Chagall, Marc, 79
Chance, 142, 153, 166, 168, 178, 196

Chanson de Roland, 93, 159, 194, 199
Chekhov, Anton, 189
Chernyshevski, Nikolai, 121
Chesson, Wilfred Hugh, 58
Chmielnicki, Bohdan, 11
Clifford, Sir Hugh, 122
Collini, Stefan, 8
'Conde, Il', 166
Conrad, Borys, 103, 220
Conrad, Jessie, 104, 218
Conrad, John, 103
Constantine, Grand Duke, 51
Corneille, Pierre, 194
Crankshaw, Edward, 10, 225
Crews, Frederick, 231–2
'Crime of Partition, The', 123
Cullen, Jonathan, 8
Curle, 170, 225–6
Curtius, Ernst Robert, 8
Custine, Astolphe de, 33, 123, 149

Dąbrowski, Marian, 151
Dante Alighieri, 3, 167, 204
Davies, Norman, 11
Delacampagne, Christian, 6
Dickens, Charles, 5, 6, 35, 75, 166
Dostoevsky, Fyodor, 106, 112, 119, 126–38, 192
Douglas, Norman, 232
Dreyfus, Alfred, 135
'Duel, The', 5, 153, 166, 168
Dupin, Mme, 148

Eco, Umberto, 6
Eliot, Thomas Stearns, 2
'End of the Tether, The', 205
English Review, 102, 103, 104, 122
Epinay, Mme d', 148
Estreicher, Leon, 50

'Falk', 142
Faulkner, William, 85, 153, 156, 162, 163, 195–6
Fielding, Henry, 114
'First News', 41
Fitzgerald, Francis Scott, 195
Flaubert, Gustave, 72, 75, 127, 134, 165, 177, 186, 189, 190, 192, 210, 211

Fleishman, Avrom, 140, 227
Ford, Ford Madox, 69, 70, 99, 102, 103, 104, 105, 122, 170, 172, 222–3, 233
Ford, Boris, 226
Fouché, Joseph, 5
France, Anatole, 7, 45, 155, 165, 180, 188, 192, 198
Frank, Joseph, 128

Gachet, Paul, 78
Galsworthy, John, 95, 172, 189
Gapon, Father, 133
Garnett, Constance, 126
Garnett, Edward, 39, 40, 41, 42, 58, 68, 69, 70, 103, 122, 126, 128, 160, 172, 210
Gaulle, Charles de, 169
Gide, André, 189
Gilgamesh, 199
'Glance at Two Books, A', 210
Goethe, Johann Wolfgang von, 75, 167
Gomulicki, Wiktor, 221
Gorki, Maxim, 189
Grabowski, Michal, 50
Graham, Robert Bontine Cunninghame, 111, 123, 153
Griboedov, Alexandr, 22
Guerard, Albert J., 70, 189
Guyau, Jean-Marie, 194

Hallowes, Lillian, 104
Hardy, Thomas, 2, 4, 91, 136, 189, 192
Harrison, Austin, 223
Haugh, Robert, 83
Hauptmann, Gerhard, 189
Hay, Eloise Knapp, 10, 134, 135, 226
'Heart of Darkness', 58, 59, 125, 136, 144, 166, 167, 168, 178, 179, 184, 191, 193, 198, 204, 231–2
Hegel, Friedrich, 52, 136, 145, 148
Hemingway, Ernest, 4, 162, 196
Hervouet, Ives, 45, 128, 166
Herzen, Alexandr, 121, 138, 227
Hewitt, Douglas, 81, 82
Homer, 75, 154, 156, 167, 194, 199
Houdetot, Mme d', 148
Howe, Irving, 112, 114, 140
Hugo, Victor, 20, 26, 31, 35

Ibsen, Henrik, 192
'Idiots, The', 166
Iliad, The, 8, 93, 159
'Informer, The', 166
Inheritors, The, 100, 170
'Inn of Two Witches, The', 166
Iwański, August, 48, 218

James, Henry, 72, 95, 100, 110, 163, 189, 192
Jaures, Jean, 147
Jawlensky, Alexei von, 79
Jefferson, Thomas, 146
Jeż, Teodor Tomasz, 48
Joël, Karl, 8

Kafka, Franz, 198
Kandinsky, Vassily, 79
'Karain', 12, 142
Karl, Frederick R., 35
Kaszewski, Kazimierz, 41
Katkov, Mikhail, 121
Kayser, Wolfgang, 8
Kettle, Arnold, 140
Kipling, Rudyard, 95, 172, 189
Kliszczewski, Spiridion, 122, 146
Kochanowski, Jan, 174
Komornicka, Maria, 227
Konarski, Szymon, 31
Kościuszko, Tadeusz, 11, 45
Korzeniowska, Emilia, 16
Korzeniowska, Ewa, 9, 14, 16, 18, 22–6, 29–35, 43, 46, 50, 56, 60, 61, 62, 64, 106, 107, 214–15
Korzeniowski, Apollo, 4, 6, 9, 11, 12, 14, 15, 16, 18–43, 49, 50, 53, 55, 61, 65, 106, 151, 201–2, 213–14, 216, 218, 232
Korzeniowski, Teodor, 214
Kraj, 36
Krasiński, Zygmunt, 20, 33
Kraszewski, Józef Ignacy, 53
Kropotkin, Pyotr, 133

'Lagoon, The', 12, 142
Lamolle, Odette, 171
Lefranc, Pierre, 222
Lermontov, Mikhail, 120–1
Leroy-Beaulieu, Anatole, 123, 165, 230

Lewis, Sinclair, 110
Liebknecht, Wilhelm, 147
Lloyd George, David, 122
Lord Jim, 11, 12, 59, 81–94, 127, 131, 135, 136, 142, 143, 153, 161, 166, 167, 168, 169, 173, 174, 178, 181, 184, 191, 198, 202, 205, 206, 221, 229
Lubowidzki, Stefan, 50
Lüders, Alexandr, 30
Luyat-Moore, Anne, 168
Lynd, Robert, 102, 103, 104

Maeterlinck, Maurice, 188
Maistre, Joseph de, 148, 228
Malczewski, Antoni, 75
Malraux, André, 156, 162
Mann, Thomas, 5, 148, 189, 198
Marcadé, Valentine, 79
Marmont, Viesse de, 62
Martin du Gard, Roger, 110
Marx, Karl, 33, 147
Maupassant, Guy de, 45, 70, 128, 177, 189, 192
Maurras, Charles, 135
Mazzini, Giuseppe, 135, 169
Miłosz, Czeslaw, 213
Mickiewicz, Adam, 13, 21, 23, 73, 74, 75, 86, 90, 120, 149, 156, 159, 180, 202, 203, 212
Mickiewicz, Władysław, 23
Miller, J. Hillis, 114
Mirror of the Sea, The, 95–101, 108, 126, 150, 166, 173, 207
Morf, Gustave, 11, 221
Moser, Thomas, 70, 71, 78, 142
Mroczkowski, Przemysław, 171
Muravëv, Mikhail, 121

Nabokov, Vladimir, 128
Najder, Zdzisław, 22, 234
Napoleon I, 62, 63, 123, 125, 168
Napoleon III, 54
New Yorker, The, 110
Nicholas, I, 51, 127
Nietzsche, Friedrich, 162, 189, 192
Nigger of the 'Narcissus', The, 69, 71, 128, 152, 160, 161, 166, 178, 183
Nostromo, 68, 78, 100, 101, 131, 134, 136,

144, 150, 153, 162, 166, 167, 173, 178, 180–1, 183, 191, 193, 196, 198, 205, 208
'Note on the Polish Problem, A', 123
Novalis, Friedrich von Hardenberg, 167

Orwell, George, 27
Orzeszkowa, Eliza, 12, 15, 51, 104, 171
Outcast of the Islands, An, 12, 68, 111, 168, 204
'Outpost of Progress, An', 168

Panofsky, Erwin, 3
Pascin, Jules, 79
Pasternak, Borys, 79
Pasternak, Leonid, 79
Personal Record, A, 39, 40, 41, 42, 44, 50, 59, 64, 102–9, 127, 141, 142, 166, 168, 174, 199, 203–4, 208–9, 212
Peter the Great, 123, 148
Petrarch, 3
Pietkiewicz, Antoni, 215
Pigna, Gianbattista, 85
Pilchowski, Adolf, 23, 45
Pilchowski, Piotr, 64
Pilchowski, Seweryn, 23, 45
Pindar, 155
Pinker, James B., 100, 102, 104
'Planter of Malata, The', 167
'Poland Revisited', 40
Popper, Karl, 135
Poradowska, Marguerite, 76
Preface to *The Nigger of the 'Narcissus'*, 17, 106, 160–1, 177, 181, 190, 209–11
'Prince Roman', 59, 166, 174, 206
Prus, Bolesław, 51

Quiller-Couch, Arthur, 160–1
Quine, Willard Van Orman, 6
Quinn, John, 123

Rescue, The, 12, 16, 68, 111, 153, 207
'Return, The', 69, 76, 166, 207–8
Revue des Deux Mondes, 29
Richardson, Samuel, 195
Rogiński, Roman, 34
Romance, 100
Rorty, Robert, 6–8

Rousseau, Jean-Jacques, 33, 87, 88, 89, 106, 131, 139–52, 155, 165, 169, 185, 195
Rover, The, 111, 166, 168, 207
Russell, Bertrand, 143, 185

Saint-Exupéry, Antoine de, 162, 163, 196
Sandeman, Christopher, 123
Schiller, Friedrich, 184
Schopenhauer, Arthur, 227
Scott, Walter, 194
Secret Agent, The, 4, 80, 101, 110–17, 132, 134, 147, 150, 160, 166, 168, 170, 178, 196, 198, 205
Shadow Line, The, 142, 178, 198, 206
Shakespeare, William, 7, 34, 36, 38, 40, 85, 154, 156, 159, 166, 184, 233
Shelley, Percy Bysshe, 7, 75
Shevchenko, Taras, 49
Sienkiewicz, Henryk, 51, 163–4, 189, 195
Sierakowski, Zygmunt, 46
Sisters, The, 68–80, 137, 166, 168, 220
Skutnik, Tadeusz, 222
Słowacki, Juliusz, 13, 87, 203, 221
Słowo, 26
'Smile of Fortune, A', 173
Smollett, Tobias George, 110
Socrates, 157
Soskice, David, 122
Soutine, Chaim, 79
Spasowicz, Włodzimierz, 127
Spector, Robert D., 113
Spontini, Gaspare, 133
Staniszewska, Katarzyna, 64, 107
Staniszewski, Leon, 64, 107
Stendhal (Henri Beyle), 129, 159
Sterne, Laurence, 75, 105, 221
Stirner, Max, 115
Strindberg, August, 188
Sudermann, Hermann, 189
Suspense, 68, 111, 166, 168, 170, 172

Taborski, Roman, 37, 213–14
Tarnawski, Wit, 72, 226
Tarski, Alfred, 8
Tasso, Torquato, 159
Times, The, 122
Tocqueville, Alexis de, 146
Tolstoy, Lev, 126, 127, 133

'To-morrow', 166
Trepov, Dmitry, 133
Turgenev, Ivan, 121, 126, 131, 134, 138, 192
'Typhoon', 111, 142, 178, 191, 193

Ujejski, Józef, 10
Umberto, I, 135
Under Western Eyes, 5, 46, 68, 80, 104, 119–21, 125, 128–38, 141, 142, 143, 146, 147, 148, 149, 154, 166, 168, 170, 173, 178, 180, 184, 191, 196, 198, 206, 230

Van Gogh, Vincent, 78
Vasilchikov, Illarion, 30
Victory, 111, 167, 198, 206
Vigny, Alfred de, 25, 159, 194
Virgil, 167
Vittorio Emanuele II, 2

Waliszewski, Kazimierz, 41, 44
Warens, Mme de, 148
'Warrior's Soul, The', 125, 166
Warren, Robert Penn, 10, 186, 198
Washington, George, 45
Watson, Curtis Brown, 154
Watt, Ian, 10, 17, 163, 182, 191, 199, 206
Wędrowiec, 58
Wells, Herbert George, 95, 103, 153, 172, 189, 192, 198, 233
Werfel, Franz, 85
Wilde, Oscar, 192
Wimsatt, William, C., 3
Wyka, Kazimierz, 71, 72, 74, 75

'Youth', 58, 166, 178, 204, 220

Zabel, Morton Dauwen, 95, 186
Żeromski, Stefan, 72, 171
Zola, Emile, 2, 75, 78, 91, 136